Imagic Moments

EST. 75 1938
YEARS
THE UNIVERSITY OF GEORGIA PRESS 2013

Imagic Moments

Indigenous North American Film

LEE SCHWENINGER

The University of Georgia Press *Athens and London*

© 2013 by the University of Georgia Press
Athens, Georgia 30602
www.ugapress.org
All rights reserved
Set in Sabon and Helvetica Neue by
  Graphic Composition, Inc., Bogart, GA.
Manufactured by Thomson-Shore
The paper in this book meets the guidelines for
permanence and durability of the Committee on
Production Guidelines for Book Longevity of the
Council on Library Resources.

Printed in the United States of America
17 16 15 14 13 P 5 4 3 2 1

Library of Congress Cataloging-in-Publication Data

Schweninger, Lee.
    Imagic moments : indigenous North American film / Lee Schweninger.
        pages cm
    Includes bibliographical references and index.
    Includes filmography.
    ISBN-13: 978-0-8203-4514-7 (hardcover : alk. paper)
    ISBN-10: 0-8203-4514-8 (hardcover : alk. paper)
    ISBN-13: 978-0-8203-4515-4 (pbk. : alk. paper)
    ISBN-10: 0-8203-4515-6 (pbk. : alk. paper)
    1. Indians in motion pictures. 2. Motion pictures—United States. 3. Motion
pictures—Canada. 4. Indians in the motion picture industry—United States.
5. Indians in the motion picture industry—Canada. I. Title.
    PN1995.9.I48S44 2013
    791.43'652997—dc23   2012042287

British Library Cataloging-in-Publication Data available

for my brothers
Loren and Mark

. . . Natives are the storiers of natural reason on this continent, and their stories are, as they have always been, the imagic moments of cultural conversions and native modernity.

—Gerald Vizenor, "Ontic Images," 161

The "imagic moment, or vision, is the story of the picture. . . . The imagic moment is the creation of an ontic sense of presence, another connection in a picture."

—Gerald Vizenor, "Ontic Images," 170

Contents

List of Illustrations

Acknowledgments

It is difficult to know where to begin in acknowledging and thanking the many, many people who have in some way or another, however wittingly or unwittingly, contributed to the completion of this book. And of course in attempting to acknowledge those individuals, one runs the risk of leaving someone out. But taking that risk and insisting that any mistakes or misguided arguments in this book are my responsibility exclusively, I dare to acknowledge the following people, whose help, support, advice, critique, and inspiration made this project possible.

Let me begin where American Indian film began for me: at a 1994 National Endowment for the Humanities Summer Seminar: "American Indian Written Literatures" in Chicago. I want to thank LaVonne Ruoff for making it all possible and Linda Vavra for facilitating. I also want to acknowledge the late Roseanne Hoefel for her insights and conversation. From that seminar too, I want to thank Simone Pellerine who has since hosted several symposia at Université Paul Valéry in Montpellier, France. She has several times brought together a group of scholars of American Indian literature, culture, and film, and thereby encouraged a wonderful venue for the sharing of ideas. Among those participating scholars, I especially want to acknowledge Chris LaLonde who has always both challenged and inspired me with his sharp mind and cutting insights. Lionel Larre has also been an inspiration, and I want to thank him too for hosting a conference at the Université Michel de Montaigne Bordeaux 3 where I was able to share some of the ideas that have found their way into this book.

I thank Peggy Parsons, Curator of Film, at the National Gallery of Art in Washington, D.C., who was generous with her time, responded helpfully to email queries, and made available screenings of several of the films I discuss. Melissa Bisagni, Film and Video Center Program Manager at the National

Museum of the American Indian, hosted a "Film Indians Now" series in 2008, and she makes Indigenous film available generally.

During the course of the research and writing for this book, I have had the great pleasure of meeting and/or corresponding with several of the people directly involved with the production of several of the films studied here. I thank Gerald Vizenor, author of the screenplay *Harold of Orange*, for his support and for a helpful critique of a conference paper, some ideas from which find their way into the book. I thank Thomas King, author of the novel and screenplay *Medicine River* for helping me procure an image from that film. I want to thank Shane Belcourt, director of *Tkaronto*, for his conversation and his on-going friendliness, helpfulness, and generosity. I had a delightful and informative conversation with actor Duane Murray, who plays Ray in *Tkaronto*, after a screening of that film. And I want to thank Valerie Red-Horse, co-director of and actor in *Naturally Native*, for her energetic responses to my queries to her. I also thank Barbara Allinson for her generous permissions of an image from *Medicine River*.

A special note of thanks goes to several people in the Media, Film, and Communication Department at University of Otago, Dunedin, New Zealand: Vijay Devadas, who helped with his technical and media expertise, and his support and encouragement; Kevin Fisher, who invited me to present a paper on this project as a part of the Media, Film, and Communication Research Seminar Series—2011; Brett Nicholls, who shared his insights and his sense of humor; and Erika Pearson, who provided technical assistance. I also want to thank Anne Begg for her provocative questions about and her heartening interest in this project. And finally in this context, I want to acknowledge the magnificent students in an Indigenous film seminar at Otago University, MFCO 318, students who taught me so much about how to see film.

I am indebted to Elise Marubbio for sharing her insights about the manuscript and for the excellent advice she offered and continues to offer. I also want to thank her for her hard work in organizing and hosting the Native American Film panels at the Southwest Texas Popular Culture Association and American Culture Association Conferences in Albuquerque, New Mexico, and San Antonio, Texas, panels which have provided a forum for a community of scholars and Indigenous filmmakers who are sharing their films and their ideas about film. I owe an enormous debt to the anonymous external readers of the manuscript; they offered insightful and extremely helpful suggestions; I thank them for what is so often a thankless but extremely important job. It has been a pleasure to work with Nancy Grayson, Executive Editor, and Beth Snead, Assistant Acquisitions Editor, at the University of Georgia Press. They have been absolutely delightful to work with, helpful, responsive, encouraging, and patient.

I wish to acknowledge Andreas Brockmann at the University of Leipzig, Germany, for inviting me to present a paper on American Indian film as a part of his Indianisches Echo seminar series and for his cogent feedback. I thank Anne Uhlig, with whom I had many conversations about Indigenous film in the early stages of this book. Her insistent questions and sometimes radical insights forced me to think and rethink many of the arguments as I articulated them to myself. Elizabeth Peterson, Humanities/Literature Librarian at the University of Oregon continues to be reliable and helpful with any number of the difficult research questions I confront her with. And I thank Jeremy Tirrell for his assistance with some of the images reproduced here.

I want to express my deep gratitude to Cara Cilano for her friendship, her unflagging support and encouragement, her expertise, her insights, her advice, and her critiques of my thinking and writing. She has been an inspiration and a help throughout all phases of the writing of this book.

And finally I acknowledge and dedicate the book to my brothers, Mark and Loren. Mark taught me so much in so many different ways over so many years, from how to ride a bicycle to how to think about and analyze music and film, and, perhaps most importantly, how to laugh at myself. Loren has offered steadfast encouragement, excellent advice, compassionate understanding and has been my inspiration both personally and professionally in ways he can never know. To them both I owe a debt I can never repay; I can merely acknowledge my gratitude.

Where to Concentrate

The Indian filmmakers, I would imagine, you know, we would
concentrate on life, life itself. —*Imagining Indians*

Imagic Moments

"Native ceremonies, and imagic moments," contends Anishinaabe writer
Gerald Vizenor, "create a sense of presence, and, at the same time, mask an
absence: the rites of presence are ecstatic unions of time and place, and the
absence, virtual masks of sorcery. Alas, the images of Indians are simulations" ("Interimage" 231). In another place, he writes that "clearly, natives
are the storiers of natural reason on this continent, and their stories are, as
they have always been, the imagic moments of cultural conversions and native modernity" ("Ontic" 161). I take the phrase "imagic moments" as the
title of this study in part because it so effectively allows for a crucial distinction: "images of Indians" are not the same as imagic moments. Images of
Indians, Vizenor argues, are the inherited representations that mainstream
culture offers back to mainstream culture: they are the images it offers to itself, that is. These (mis)representations can be seen to include depictions that
Hollywood produces or those that ethnographic photography submits, for
example. "The native persons in most portraits and photographs," writes
Vizenor, "became mere ethnographic simulations, silenced without names or
narratives; the pictures were the coincidence of discoveries in the course of
dominance" ("Interimage" 239).

Imagic moments, in stark contrast, as I understand Vizenor's concept and
use it here, are the Indigenous stories, whether verbal or visual, that Indigenous people offer of themselves. These stories, the Indigenous films themselves in my context, are "ecstatic unions of place and time"; they constitute
instances of self-representation and a form of visual sovereignty, and in every
single frame they insist on survival. Indigenous films create a sense of presence, and through their presence they refute Hollywood depictions, other
simulations or "images of Indians." They replace both mainstream (mis)rep-
resentations and the absence that results from such. They replace simulations
with what Vizenor calls *postindians*. Indigenous films provide a Native presence where before there was none.

Survivors. *The Dead Can't Dance*. Screen Capture. Harmy Films.

Self-Representation and a Cinema of Sovereignty

In his essay "Ontic Images," Vizenor writes that "natives must create their own stories; otherwise, the sources of their identities are not their own." They "create stories of survivance, a sense of presence and distinctive identities in the very midst of . . . many contradictions and contingencies" (162, 164). In these few sentences, it seems to me, Vizenor articulates a concise and fundamental explanation of one of the major achievements of American Indian film: it is a medium through which Indigenous North Americans create and tell their own stories and thereby not only confront and challenge a range of political and historical contradictions but at the same time establish and maintain a presence that includes and privileges self-representation and self-determination. In her book *Decolonizing Methodologies*, Māori scholar Linda Tuhiwai Smith makes an argument similar to Vizenor's: "Telling our [Indigenous] stories from the past, reclaiming the past, giving testimony to the injustices of the past are strategies which are commonly employed by indigenous peoples struggling for justice. . . . The need to tell our stories remains the powerful imperative of a powerful form of resistance" (34–35). Inspired by these understandings of Indigenous self-representation and resistance, this study looks in detail at a selection of mostly narrative fiction films from the United States and Canada that—when placed in historical and generic contexts and explored through detailed readings—participate in creating instances of Smith's forms of resistance as well as Vizenor's "stories of survivance." Indeed, the very existence of the films emphatically demonstrates Indigenous survival.

The significance of self-representation as a form of resistance and as fundamental to appreciating Indigenous North American film cannot be overstated. In another context Vizenor reiterates the dangers of not allowing Native American Indians to speak for themselves. He writes that "anterior simulations of the other are cited in the generative *interimages* of the 'discovered' *indian*, and without a substantive reference; one simulation becomes the specious evidence of another" ("Interimage" 229). The perpetuation and proliferation of these specious (mis)representations result in stereotypes and reductive renditions and misunderstandings. The simulation replaces the real and thereby becomes the real; hence the real real is lost. Several scholars of Indigenous literature and film make this assertion. In an essay on the importance of sovereignty, especially in the context of print and radio media, Shoshone-Bannok writer Mark Trahant declares emphatically the importance of Indigenous peoples' telling their own stories: "We need a new sovereignty movement—a sovereignty of storytelling" (30). Similarly, according to Elise Marubbio, "Native film is about employing and centering Native voices in the act of media self-determination and representation" ("Introduction" 3). In his study *Indigenous Aesthetics* (1998), Steven Leuthold maintains that "as a means of expressing identities, the aesthetic emerges as an important aspect of self-representation to the larger non-native public" (1). Kerstin Knopf argues that "as Indigenous people gradually take control over the image-making process in the domain of film- and videomaking, they cease to be studied and described as objects and become subjects who create self-controlled images of Indigenous cultures" in the introduction to her study of Indigenous films in North America, *Decolonizing the Lens of Power* (2008; xii–xiii). Writing about Zacharias Kunuk's 2001 film *Atanarjuat (The Fast Runner)* specifically, Michelle Raheja sees "a discussion of visual sovereignty as a way of reimagining Native-centered articulations of self-representation and autonomy that engage the powerful ideologies of mass media" (1163). Randolph Lewis uses the phrase "cinema of sovereignty" to suggest that Indigenous films are "the embodiment of an insider's perspective, one that is attuned to cultural subtleties in the process of imagemaking as well as in the final image itself" (180). Māori filmmaker Barry Barclay, in discussing Indigenous cinema, writes that he anticipates finding "examples at every turn of how the old principles have been reworked to give vitality and richness to the way we conceive, develop, manufacture and present our films" (11). Noting its inherent value, Sigurón Baldur Hafsteinsson and Marian Bredin point out that in its own right "Aboriginal media content can clearly be treated as a corpus of texts, interpreted using methods of discourse analysis or film criticism" (6). As this glance at the comments of several scholars of Indigenous film makes clear, self-representation can be seen as a valid form of resistance and as an aspect of a cinema of sovereignty in which the Indigenous peoples represented are the people who engage in the filming and who control the camera.

A cinema of sovereignty is one in which Native North American filmmakers, writers, and actors take control of telling their own stories. The mere existence of the films celebrates Indigenous worldviews and, to repeat Lewis's phrase, their "ways of knowing and remembering" (184). The films provide a Native presence where there was absence, and the films thereby challenge by positive example the myth of the vanishing Indian or the last of a race or tribe. In Vizenor's terms, "stories of a native presence are survivance" ("Ontic Images" 166). Indigenous film, by its very presence, constitutes a celebration of indigeneity and Indigenous survival.

In discussing the work of Abenaki Canadian Alanis Obomsawin, Randolph Lewis asserts that as a director of Indigenous documentaries, Obomsawin serves as a model Indigenous filmmaker in demonstrating a "profound respect for Native ways of knowing and remembering," in working "from a position of unqualified faith in the merits of indigenous worldviews," and in continually replacing "Native absence with an unexpected presence" (184, 185, 186). One can generalize from Lewis's specifics to suggest that in these ways Indigenous films do indeed celebrate indigeneity; and, in replacing an absence with Native presence, the films embody a form of sovereignty. "Native people have created hundreds of titles," Lewis notes. He argues that if "there is a general tendency in this incredible surge of indigenous media, it has been toward the reestablishment of representational sovereignty, by which [he means] the right, as well as the ability, for a group of people to depict themselves with their own ambitions at heart" (175). The films are by definition a celebration of sovereignty, when, as Lewis writes, "cultural insiders are the controlling intelligence behind the filmmaking process" (182).

Fourth Cinema and Indigenous Film

Barry Barclay articulates a similar idea of what constitutes Indigenous film and the role it plays. In an essay titled "Celebrating Fourth Cinema," he distinguishes what he calls "Fourth Cinema" from other cinemas: "First Cinema being American cinema; Second Cinema Art House cinema; and Third cinema the cinema of the so-called Third World" (7). He refers to film versions of *The Mutiny on the Bounty* to argue that First Cinema, or Hollywood cinema, is characterized in part by the practical reality that "the camera is owned and controlled by the people who own the ship." That is, he clarifies, "The First Cinema Camera sits firmly on the deck of the ship. It sits there by definition. The Camera Ashore, the Fourth Cinema Camera, is the one held by the people for whom 'ashore' is their ancestral home" (8). Kirsty Bennett explicates and elaborates on Barclay's definition, writing that Fourth Cinema "still exhibits the indigenous world insofar as it creates something the West can look at, namely the film itself; however it seeks to create a representation of indigeneity that is free from the debilitating gaze of the outsider" (19). This is not to say that Indigenous film cannot borrow from and share characteristics with other types of cinema. As Marubbio maintains, a Native American film "does not simply fit into or reject" these other cinemas, "rather it is the referencing, morphing, and reaching across all or focusing on just one of these forms, historical periods and geographical demarcations in a heteroglossic meta dialogue about Indigenous representation" ("Introduction" 3).

For the purposes of this study I risk offering a definition of Indigenous cinema that is broad enough to allow for the inclusion of what I argue constitute important Indigenous films. I am careful at the same time not to make the definition so broad that it could become meaningless. The films under discussion have in common that they include some but not necessarily all of the criteria one can establish to characterize and define Indigenous films. With only one potential exception, the authors of the source material, writers, adapters, and/or screenwriters of the primary films examined in this study are Indigenous. Adhering to this criterion has resulted in the necessary and appropriate exclusion of several films. Especially noteworthy but excluded non-Indian "Indian" films include *Dance Me Outside* (1995), based on stories by European-Canadian author W. P. Kinsella; *Clearcut* (1991); Michael Apted's *Thunderheart* (1992) and his documentary about the controversial arrest and sentencing of Leonard Peltier after a shooting of two FBI agents, *Incident at Oglala* (1992). The study also excludes Chris Eyre's *A Thief of Time* (2004), based on a Tony Hillerman novel, even though in addition to its being directed by Eyre it stars many well-known Indigenous actors. Also excluded is the film *Flags of Our Fathers* (2006), despite the fact that it has a twentieth-century setting (the Second World War) and arguably provides a certain depth and complexity to the character Ira Hayes, played admirably by Adam Beach.

Indian roles should be played by Indians, and such is the case with the films in this study, with just the few exceptions discussed below. Another important selection criterion for the films included here is that Native actors are performing in films that center on Indigenous characters and primarily develop what can be termed Indigenous issues. The films have a contemporary, as opposed to a pre-twentieth-century, setting. Considering the heritage of the directors of these films is more problematic than some of the other relatively straightforward considerations. Auteur theory of course places huge emphasis on a single person, usually the director, as the one who creates and controls the film and would clearly argue that for a film to qualify as Indigenous, the director must be Indigenous. Dissidents will argue, however, that there exist many other, equally important influences on the creation of a film, especially in that film, unlike the novel or short story that so often serves as its source material, is very much a collaborative enterprise. Thus, while not meaning to discount the importance of the social identity and heritage of the director, I maintain for my purposes here that several of the films I examine constitute Indigenous film even though the directors themselves are not Indigenous. Those films include Richardson Morse's *House Made of Dawn* (1972), Kent Mackenzie's *The Exiles* (1961; DVD 2008), Stuart Margolin's *Medicine River* (1994), and Jonathan Wacks's *Powwow Highway* (1989). As will become apparent in the chapters devoted to these films, there are important reasons for including them in such a study, even though the directors are non-Native.

The study does not concern itself with trying to include huge Hollywood blockbuster Westerns that are set in the nineteenth century or before, even though they might include some of the characteristics mentioned above. A film's temporal setting is of major importance, even though here again there will be exceptions, notably, for example, director Chris Eyre's *Trail of Tears* (2008), a PBS documentary. In *Indianizing Film*, Freya Schiwy makes the point that activist Indigenous filmmakers "use video to bring key issues of concern to indigenous communities to the screen, locating them squarely in the present" (11). Despite their claims to sympathetic portrayals of tribal people, we can readily discount such major-studio, mass-market, non-Indigenous blockbusters as *Little Big Man* (National General Pictures, 1970), *Dances with Wolves* (Orion, 1990), *The Last of the Mohicans* (20th Century Fox, 1992), or *Pocahontas*, (Disney, 1995). Such films tell stories that leave "stereotyped visions of Native life intact and the radically unequal relations between European Americans and native Americans unquestioned," as Shari Huhndorf argues in the context of *Dances with Wolves*. This movie, she maintains, "actually reinforces the racial hierarchies it claims to destabilize," and "starkly evokes the conquest of Native America, the precondition of the birth of the white nation, only to assuage the guilt stemming from that painful history" (3, 4). Locked within their limited temporal setting, these Hollywood blockbusters inevitably deny the Indigenous characters any post-nineteenth-century existence.

Such mainstream Hollywood films, because of their huge popularity and box-office successes, deny Native filmmakers a share of the market and with it the ability to speak in their own voices beyond the smallest of audiences. Perhaps most pernicious is that such blockbusters coopt the stories and tell them from non-Indigenous perspectives. It is, thus, all the more important that Native films establish themselves and offer counternarratives that tell their own stories. It might be fair to say that Chris Eyre speaks for many Native filmmakers when he maintains that there is "nothing wrong with honoring, but I think we've existed too long as Hollywood Indians" (Chaw). The sheer number of Native productions, especially since about the 1980s, demonstrates that this reversal of the gaze is indeed underway.

Indigenous Actors

Self-representation is a form of resistance and is necessarily a fundamental aspect of Indigenous film. Naturally, a commitment to self-representation mandates that Indigenous roles be played by Indigenous people. The issue of casting is especially important to Indian film when one recalls that Indian parts of any significance in so many Hollywood Westerns were, and sometimes still are, played by non-Indians. One of the best-known non-Indian actors repeatedly taking Native roles is Iron Eyes Cody. Born to Sicilian emigrants, he became an iconic embodiment of the nineteenth-century American Indian. To cite just a few others of the virtually countless specific incidences: Debra Paget plays the unnamed "Indian girl" in *The Last Hunt* (1955). Henry Brandon plays the character Scar and Beulah Archuletta plays Wild Goose Flying in the Night Sky in *The Searchers* (1956). Sal Mineo plays Red Shirt, Gilbert Roland plays Dull Knife, and Dolores del Rio plays Spanish Woman in *Cheyenne Autumn* (1964). Asian American actor Aimée Eccles plays Sunshine in *Little Big Man*. In *A Man Called Horse* (1970) Greek actor and 1964 Miss Universe Corinna Tsopei plays Running Deer, and Australian actor Judith Anderson plays Buffalo Cow Head. The title character in *Ulzana's Raid* (1972) is played by Mexican-born actor Joaquin Martinez. Ted Jojola characterizes the tendency for such casting: "In spite of Hollywood's attempts to 'correct the record,' the movies of this period all basically had one thing in common—'Indians' in the leading roles were played by non-Indians" (14). But little has changed, and the list goes on. As recently as 2005 in *The New World*, the Quechua-Huachipaeri (Peruvian) and Swiss actor Q'orianka Kilcher plays the Algonquin character Pocahontas, for example; and in *The Lone Ranger* (2013), with an estimated production budget of between $215 and $250 million, the non-Indian actor Johnny Depp plays Tonto. This casting decision is doubly ironic and unfortunate in that in the original television series (1949–57) Tonto was played by Canadian Mohawk actor Jay Silverheels. In a 2003 interview with N. Scott Momaday (author of the source novel and screenwriter for *House Made of Dawn*), Joanna Hearne asks what difference "it makes to have Native actors in Native roles." Momaday responds that he thinks "it's a good thing because . . . Native actors can have an understanding of the cultural depth of the role. I think it's perfectly possible for a non-Indian to play an Indian remarkably well, but I think that the Indian has an advantage in understanding, if the part truly defines an Indian essence—the Indian actor is going to understand that better than a non-Indian actor. I think we're going to see some remarkable Indian actors. We're already beginning to" (Hearne, "N. Scott Momaday Interview").

There are notable Indian films that I include in this study, it must be admitted, that could be considered problematic when it comes to casting. In *House Made of Dawn*, to take an obvious example, the very prominent role of Tosamah, Kiowa Priest of the Sun, is played by the non-Native actor John Saxon. Director Richardson Morse comments that in order to have some experienced people as actors wherever possible he "went with John [as Tosamah]." But because he is non-Indian, declares Morse, "it was a mistake. Not that John was bad, John did a good actor's performance" (Hearne, "Richardson Morse Interview"). Another important and in this regard perhaps also problematic film is *Powwow Highway*, in which A Martinez plays the Cheyenne character Buddy Red Bow. It is not clear that Martinez has any Native heritage, although on one website he does self-identify as Blackfoot (Martinez). Concern about casting based on an actor's heritage raises another important question: to what extent is it legitimate to be too rigid in response to the issue the casting of Indigenous people for Indigenous roles despite tribal heritage? Critics have denigrated the film *The Doe Boy* (2001), written and directed by Randy Redroad (Cherokee), for example, because the young Hunter lead is played by a non-Indian actor, Andrew J. Ferchland. In an interview with Michelle Svenson, Redroad responds to that particular criticism by noting that in principle he agrees with the argument that Indian people should take Indian roles, but he argues that sometimes experienced actors can be extremely difficult and expensive to find, and besides, he states further, "in this movie it didn't matter because it's about a mixed character, so it's kind of its own disclaimer" (Svenson).

The question about the necessity and importance of Indians in Indian roles is further complicated given the almost complete lack of attention paid to specific tribal heritage and identity in casting choices in narrative fiction films by Native American filmmakers themselves. The two leads in *Smoke Signals* (1998)—in which their Coeur d'Alene identity is declared in the film and maintained as thematically important throughout—for example, are played by the Coast Salish actor Evan Adams and the Canadian Saulteaux actor Adam Beach. The father Arnold, also Coeur d'Alene in the film, is played by Cayuga actor Gary Farmer, who had played a Cheyenne man in *Powwow Highway*, and a presumably Lakota man in *Skins* (2002). Similarly, none of the three leads in *Naturally Native* (1998) are Viejas, even though identity questions serve as an overarching thematic element in this particular film: the characters are acted by non-Mission Indian actors: Valerie Red-Horse (Cherokee/Sioux), Kimberly Norris Guerrero (Coville/Salish), and Irene Bedard (Inupial/Cree). Bedard is perhaps most widely known for her performance as the voice of the seventeenth-century Algonquin title character Pocahontas in

Disney's animated film. Tribal identity is important enough a theme in *Naturally Native* that the Viejas character Connie, played by Cherokee actor Sheri Foster, rudely and forcefully challenges two characters about their assertion that they are Viejas.

One can argue in such contexts that it is especially remarkable then that in a film like *House Made of Dawn*, despite its own casting issue, the two Pueblo characters (Abel and the grandfather) are played by Pueblo men. Larry Littlebird, who plays Abel in the film, points out cultural differences in the context of Indian and non-Indian actors playing Indian roles: "In the Pueblo culture there are things that are just correct in the sensibilities. It's ingrained in them, in the people. We have an unspoken understanding of presence. And that presence, if it's going to be brought onto the screen, has to play itself. You cannot duplicate it" (Hearne, "Larry Littlebird Interview"). This element of cultural, tribal specificity, this particular understanding of presence that is, is lacking in the casting of most all North American Indigenous film. In a discussion session at the National Museum of the American Indian's film festival in March 2009, after the screening of Chris Eyre's *Trail of Tears*, an installment of the PBS We Shall Remain documentary series, Cherokee actor Wes Studi expressed his delight in having had the very rare opportunity to assume the character of a Cherokee man, Major Ridge, in the film. What is important in this context is that he stressed the rarity of such an opportunity.

There can often be undeniable political and economic advantages associated with one's tribal status, and in the ways noted above there can be important aesthetic and political advantages to Indians' playing Indian roles in film. In sum, it is easy to make the general statement but much more difficult to draw fine, specific lines when it comes to casting an Indigenous film. Perhaps we can find helpful the comment by the character Marvin (Gordon Tootoosis) in *The Doe Boy* and measure not by blood but by the stories that come out: "Everyone wants to know how much blood runs through an Indian. It's kind of hard to tell, unless you cut one of us open and watch all the stories pour out." The stories themselves as well as who gets to tell them and from what perspective, then, are what must remain crucial deciding factors.

Adaptation

Most of the films under discussion in this study are adaptations of literary works or screenplays by Indigenous writers: N. Scott Momaday (Kiowa/Cherokee), Thomas King (Cherokee), Adrian Louis (Paiute), Sherman Alexie (Coeur d'Alene), Gerald Vizenor (Anishanaabe), Randy Redroad (Cherokee), David Seals (Huron), and Valerie Red-Horse (Cherokee/Sioux). That is to say, since most of the source material is Native, it is already potentially somewhat subversive or hostile to the limiting and reductive mainstream depictions of

Indigenous people. The film adaptations can further serve to break the hold the mainstream has over history and culture and its resultant hold over the viewer. As Julie Sanders writes in *Adaptation and Appropriation* (2006), for instance, in adaptation "there are as many opportunities for divergence as adherence, for assault as well as homage" (9). And it goes almost without saying that this study favors such film theorists as Robert Stam who argue against the perpetual reinscribing of "the axiomatic superiority of literature over Film" (Stam "Introduction," 4). As Stam argues in *Literature and Film* (2005), for example, there is a need to reconceptualize adaptation and to become "less interested in establishing 'vertical' hierarchies of value than in exploring 'horizontal' relations between neighboring media" ("Introduction" 9). Brief discussions concerning adaptation choices, as will become apparent in subsequent chapters, do explore some of the horizontal relations between film and source material and can, I hope, augment a viewer's understanding of and appreciation for particular films. *House Made of Dawn* chooses a contemporary setting and dispenses with entire plot lines and characters. In *Harold of Orange* (1984) some elements of the screenplay do not make their way into the film even though some critics find exactly those absent elements crucial to explaining and understanding the film. *Powwow Highway* follows the general plot outline of the source novel, but offers a significantly altered personality of one of the principal characters. And *Smoke Signals*, based on episodes from short stories by Sherman Alexie differs in important ways even from the screenplay, which Alexie also wrote. It can be helpful in a few instances to consider the source material for the films under discussion, but in general one must acknowledge that the films themselves stand on their own, with or without overt recognition of their relations to written media, such as source novels, short stories, or screenplays.

Talking Back

Several scholars of Indigenous film argue that these productions are of necessity continually in dialogue not only with mainstream culture in general but very specifically with Hollywood and especially with the Hollywood Western as a genre. Houston Wood discusses Indigenous films from around the world in his study *Native Features*, and he notes somewhat generally that these films "share not content but rather a similar relationship to the dominant cinematic traditions that they, to various degrees, oppose" (2). Leuthold argues more specifically that Native Americans seek to "control their own public image" in an effort "to counteract five hundred years of white people's imagery of Indians, including consistent misrepresentation in Hollywood Westerns" ("Native" 153). When asked why he makes films, Zacharias Kunuk, director of *Atanarjuat (The Fast Runner)*, replies, "I see it as talking back" (*Reel*).

One can indeed characterize the dialogue between Indigenous film and mainstream film as a form of talking back, as Marubbio suggests when she writes that "visual sovereignty talks back to the residual legacy of colonialist and neo-colonialist actions toward Indigenous peoples. It is a mechanism through which Indigenous filmmakers and communities reply to histories of oppression, misrepresentation, and silencing by outsiders" ("Introduction" 4). The outsiders have been mainstream politicians, military personnel, and clerics, of course, but they have also been Hollywood directors and non-Native screenwriters who have circumscribed American Indians and restricted them to the conventional, limited, and stereotypical roles they have been forced to assume. They have played these roles in Hollywood Westerns, and the roles have plagued Native peoples since the very beginnings of the film industry. Whether explicitly or implicitly, Native North American films also respond to the long history of ethnographic film about Indigenous peoples, but until recently only rarely by those peoples. As Knopf argues, "Indigenous filmmakers are constantly in some state of dialogue with Western ethnographic filmmaking and with classical narrative filmmaking and its epitome, Hollywood narrative cinema" (xiii). The titular character in *Harold of Orange* codifies this notion with the brief statement he makes inside a museum: "Those anthropologists invented us" (*Harold*). In countering this "invention," Indigenous cinema must talk back as it offers correctives.

Adrienne Rich argues for the importance of "the act of looking back, of seeing with fresh eyes, of entering an old text from a new critical direction. . . . It is an act of survival." She continues, "We need to know the writing of the past and know it differently than we have ever known it; *not to pass on a tradition but to break its hold over us*" (278, 279, my emphasis). In this essay, entitled "When We Dead Awaken: Writing as Re-Vision," Rich refers to women's writing specifically, but what she argues can be seen to pertain to American Indian filmmaking as well: we need to know the films of the past, one can contend analogously, not to continue a Hollywood tradition, but to break its hold. I argue that American Indian films achieve this, in large measure, by talking back to Hollywood both explicitly and implicitly. Crucially, however, at the same time they talk back, they move beyond the very limiting portrayals Hollywood offers as well as the limitations that mere talking back would impose on their own productions. It is this struggle for self-determination, for self-representation, and toward a form of visual sovereignty that marks the living and continuing tradition of American Indian film.

A major component of establishing visual sovereignty must include filmic presentations, challenges, and refutations of the many stereotypes imposed on Indigenous peoples as represented in photographs, ethnographies, and Hollywood films, especially because of the long-term ubiquity of such (mis)representations. One goal of Indigenous film, therefore, as Marubbio points out, has to be "to challenge public memory; and to refuse the stereotypes of the Indigenous primitive so cherished by [Hollywood] Cinema" ("Introduction" 2). Indigenous North American film is necessarily so positioned that it must continually talk back to mainstream, non-Indigenous film and filmmakers as a part of its being a vehicle for self-representation. It must encounter and counter the age-old stereotypes perpetuated and reinforced by mainstream Hollywood cinema, and it must repudiate such cinema. Jacqueline Kilpatrick makes the argument that for "dialogue to truly exist, the represented subject must be able to talk back," and she suggests how films "written, directed, and/or acted *by* Native Americans" might enable this dialogue (xvi). The very title of Native filmmaker Beverly Singer's monograph, *Wiping the War Paint off the Lens* (2001), implies the need for Native filmmakers to challenge and refute stereotypes that have long spoken for and about Indigenous people: "Indians have been misrepresented in art, history, science, literature, popular films, and by the press in the news, on radio, and on television. . . . What really matters to us" as Indigenous peoples, she argues, "is that we be able to tell our own stories in whatever form we choose" (1, 2). Clearly, this need for dialogue is ever present, because, as Smith contends, "the idea of contested stories and multiple discourses about the past, by different communities, is closely linked to the politics of everyday contemporary indigenous life" (33).

There is also a need to talk back to Hollywood on a purely urbane, economic level. Indigenous film is inevitably low-budget film and therefore cannot compete economically with Hollywood's horrendously budgeted, mass-marketed, highly advertised films. As Barry Barclay argues in the context of New Zealand, for example, "modern nation states regularly raise taxes, directly or indirectly, to subsidize feature film production in their own territories. Indigenous peoples cannot raise their own taxes" (11). To drive the idea of economic imbalance home, one can compare two American-made films. John Woo's 2002 blockbuster *Windtalkers* (starring Adam Beach and Nicholas Cage), had an estimated budget of $115 million and opened on nearly two thousand screens nationwide. The film made $40 million on its opening weekend and totaled $77 million worldwide. In stark contrast, the Indigenous film *Skins*, directed by Cheyenne-Arapaho Chris Eyre, opened that same year on but nine screens and grossed $23,000. At its most widely distributed, it showed on sixteen screens; its total gross was about $238,000. As another example, one can consider Michael Mann's *The Last of the Mohicans*, with its production budget of $40 million. The film grossed $75 million in the United States and another $35 million in rentals. Its advertising budget alone is reputed to have been somewhere between $15 and $20 million (see Fox). Meanwhile, Chris Eyre's 1998 film *Smoke Signals*, which was produced on a budget of an estimated $2 million, remains one of the most widely distributed and most lucrative of American Indian films. It opened in October 1998 on five screens and grossed $43,000. Its total gross is $6.7 million, obviously a small fraction of what blockbusters earn.

There are also important political reasons underlying the need for Indigenous film to talk back to Hollywood. Barry Keith Grant argues that making films outside Hollywood "inevitably means confronting Hollywood, which dominates international cinema, on an aesthetic as well as practical level—that is, by working simultaneously with and through Hollywood genres" (321). Grant refers to Brazilian political filmmaker Glauber Rocha who, writes Grant, "once remarked that any discussion of national cinema must necessarily begin with Hollywood" (321). The very title of a foundational postcolonial text, *The Empire Writes Back* (1989), incorporates the centrality of the notion of a marginalized group talking back to the dominant colonial culture: such cultures, the authors maintain, "emerged in their present form out the experience of colonization and asserted themselves by foregrounding the tension with the imperial power, and by emphasizing their differences from the assumptions of the imperial centre" (Ashcroft, Griffiths, and Tiffin 2). According to Smith, the project of her book *Decolonizing Methodologies* (1999) has to do with "researching back, in the same tradition of 'writing back' or 'talking back,' that characterizes much of the post-colonial or anti-colonial literature. It has involved a 'knowingness of the colonizer' and a recovery of ourselves, an analysis of colonialism, and a struggle for self-determination" (7). To combat the illusionism and (mis)representation intrinsic to dominant cinema, proposes Annette Kuhn, counter-cinema "speaks from politically oppositional positions or concerns itself with subject matters commonly ignored or repressed in dominant cinema." It pairs "oppositional forms with oppositional contents" (160, 161).

Some of these films offer the viewer oppositional pedagogical moments within their own fabric as a means of countering dominant cinema. These moments constitute a part of the talking back in general in that they reclaim an Indigenous perspective lost because of the long-term and ubiquitous presence of Hollywood's non-Native points of view. Indigenous films often include several educational or pedagogical moments for the non-Indian, the nontribal, or the uninitiated viewer as a part of that corrective. The educating or reeducating of nontribal viewers is especially pertinent since, again, Hollywood cinema and dominant culture in general have for so long and so spectacularly (mis)represented Indigenous peoples. But even in addition to instances of talking back or re-visioning and of correcting misperceptions, these Indigenous films often "create a learning place," to use Lewis's terminology (183), for the audience. In some instances, the viewer notes that these films are quite adept at crossing or challenging genre borders. A fiction film like *Skins*, for example, relies heavily on the documentary genre to create such a learning space at the same time it creates for the viewer a sense of verity and realism. Conversely, Victor Masayesva's *Imagining Indians* (1992), primarily a documentary, includes a recurring narrative fiction plot around which the documentary's interviews and film clips are organized, thereby suggesting the impact of extrafilmic repercussions of Hollywood depictions on Native peoples. In yet other instances, films like *Naturally Native* and *Tkaronto* (2007) seem virtually to stop the action to offer explanations of Indigenous culture or issues (such as dream catchers, the widespread use of Indian sports mascots, or the ceremonial use of eagle feathers). These educational moments would not be necessary for specific tribal audiences but are necessary for a viewer schooled exclusively in Hollywood presentations of Native people and culture, and they thus can be seen to embody instances of conscious opposition.

Intertextuality

Intertextuality can serve as a potent means of talking back. Indeed, it should come as no surprise that a common thread running through many of the Indigenous films under discussion here is their shared use of intertextual references to Hollywood or other mainstream visual media. These references can serve as points of departure, as ways to challenge and refute stereotypes, and as means of talking back. Most explicitly might be their evocation of particular Westerns, such as the reference the character Victor makes in *Smoke Signals* when he actually names *Dances with Wolves* or when Thomas in the same film names the actor John Wayne. Other, less overt instances of intertextuality occur in *Powwow Highway*, in moments when the film makes only implicit, but I think unmistakable, reference John Ford's film *Cheyenne Autumn*. Randy Redroad's film *The Doe Boy* can be seen to make ironic visual reference to Michael Mann's *The Last of the Mohicans*. Not limiting itself to Westerns, Rodrick Pocowatchit's *Dancing on the Moon* (2003) names and reverses some of the plot elements of *The Wizard of Oz* (1939). Filmic use of and reference to visual media in addition to film constitute another prevalent form of intertextuality. That is, in addition to calling out of specific Hollywood movies, the Indigenous films call attention to other historical visual (mis)representations. They make explicit use of "ethnographic" photos such as those by Edward Curtis, for example, or the paintings by George Caitlin. The films make visual reference to these portraits either explicitly or implicitly as a means both to subvert and move beyond them.

In the contexts of intertextuality and self-representation, these films recognize and acknowledge their own use of and response to photography and other visual-image-making issues concerning Indigenous peoples. Several of these films, that is, exploit the artifice of filmmaking and/or picture taking and call specific attention to filmmaking itself. In both Sherman Alexie's *The Business of Fancydancing* (2002) and Valerie Red-Horse's *Naturally Native*, for example, the directors depict as a part of the plot Indian characters actually doing the filming. The self-awareness exemplifies Fourth Cinema, in a sense, in that such instances demonstrate the filmmakers' insistence on the importance of telling one's own story by holding and focusing one's own camera. In this way, the filmmakers very literally and self-evidently control the gaze. Overt recognition of the camera can also be complexly ironic, as in *Imagining Indians* when a character begins scratching and effacing the very camera lens that depicts and thus makes possible her rebellious act. This self-conscious use of film and photography, I argue, forces an awareness on the viewer and insists on a somewhat critical rather than merely a passive response to the viewing experience.

The Motif of Death, Life, and Survival

In addition to evoking specific Hollywood films and other mainstream visual images, Indigenous North American film also often makes thematic inter-textual reference as a part of its presentation of oppositional contents. One remarkable and recurrent theme is evident in the presentation of Native characters who die within the film or shortly before the film's action. Paradoxically, however, these deaths actually contest the long-standing Hollywood insistence on the death and vanishing of American Indians. The prominent action of Native Americans throughout the history of Hollywood Westerns is to die. "'Clutch your chest. Fall off that horse,' they directed. That was it. Death was the extent of Indian acting in the movie theater," declares a character in a chapter entitled "The Plunge of the Brave" in the novel *Love Medicine* by Chippewa writer Louise Erdrich (123). This sort of representation of Indians in Hollywood film works two ways. First, until just the past few decades virtually the only place to see American Indians on screen as Indians was in Hollywood Westerns; and second, as Jane Tompkins suggests, Westerns were almost always defined by the presence of Indians in them. In her book on the Western as a Hollywood genre, *West of Everything* (1992), she writes that "one of the things that lets you know when you're in a Western is the presence of Indians" (7). Ironically, Tompkins herself does not actually devote any space in her study to Indians in Westerns, a lacuna that she does acknowledge. For Kirkpatrick, Indian characters in mainstream film are "proto-American allegories" because they are so limited and stereotyped; she continues, "These proto-American allegories were conveniently vanishing" (3). Stuart Christie maintains that "with origins in nineteenth-century representations of 'the noble savage,' this alliance of discourse and technology persists in representing tribal identities and cultures as artifacts of their own inevitable disappearance" (52).

Anyone who has seen just a few Hollywood Westerns can agree that a very common role of American Indians is to die at the hands of members of the dominant, majority culture, usually embodied in a settler/rancher, a cowboy, or a soldier of the United States Cavalry. Such films are of course too numerous to begin to list. The individual Indians on screen in Hollywood Westerns die, but because they are most often nameless, often faceless, and because they lack anything that would mark them as individuals, their individual deaths represent at the same time the death of the entire culture or group. Put another way, as Indians in so many of these Westerns are used as the representation of conflict that must be overcome by the European Americans in that West, their individual deaths and general defeat signifies the erasure of the entire culture. In these films Indians are vanished. As Edward Buscombe writes for example, in John Ford's film *Stagecoach* (1939) the Indians "are presented en masse, appearing suddenly out of the landscape, a force of nature not characters in the drama" (95). And as a force of nature to be overcome, like a blizzard, they storm down upon the principal characters, but once the cavalry arrives to vanquish them, they disappear from the film both literally and figuratively.

Because so many American Indians are always already dead or dying in Hollywood movies, especially Westerns, one might expect American Indian film to repudiate such representations of dying by avoiding them, but in fact a great many of these films actually also portray the death of an Indian character, but these representations actually confront and repudiate Hollywood rather than reinscribe the common trope of vanishing Indians. I argue that the Indigenous films acknowledge the imposition of the dying or vanishing Indian portrayed by Hollywood in order to break the hold it has and to move beyond it, to counter the absence of Indigenous characters with their presence. This turn is especially unexpected because in filmic terms the characters die or are already dead. Hollywood vanishes them, and Indigenous film brings them back. An interviewee in Victor Masayesva Jr.'s documentary *Imagining Indians* makes this point emphatically: "The Indian filmmakers, I would imagine, you know, we would concentrate on life, life itself" (*Imagining*).

Even in the context of the motif of death and dying, that is, many of the films discussed here move beyond mere refutation of Hollywood's insistence on dying Indians and a vanishing race. The plot may well often include as a central component the death of an Indian, but that death is inevitably situated and contextualized. These are not nameless, faceless characters who simply appear out of the landscape, chase a stagecoach, and fall from their horses to die. These are people, these films insist, who have families and lives, and they have an influence that reaches beyond their literal deaths. These films inevitably focus on and stress the impact a character's life has on those who survive the individual. These films inevitably turn their focus to those Native people who survive the film's ending, often the children and grand-children of the deceased. Whatever their references to and evocations of the past, these films are ultimately interested in the future, and they insist on and actually demonstrate and embody continuance and survival.

Organization

While acknowledging thematic connections from chapter to chapter, the study is organized by individual film rather than by theme or topic. This ar-rangement allows for detailed, in depth analysis of the specific Indigenous films under discussion, and thereby insists that each film merits full attention in its own right. Although the book is devoted primarily to feature-length narrative film, there are exceptions. The first chapter offers a discussion of a documentary, *Imagining Indians*, directed by Victor Masayesva Jr. (Hopi). Even this film, however, is not exclusively a documentary. It includes a fic-tional narrative framework, which consists of a Native American woman's visit to a non-Indian dentist. Masayesva's documentary about the extras who played in Hollywood Westerns and have survived to talk about their expe-riences repeatedly interrupts the narrative. The second chapter argues that even though Kent Mackenzie, the director and writer of *The Exiles* is non-Native, the film is worthy of consideration in the present context because it deals with contemporary (late 1950s) urban Indians, and the actors (none of whom were professionals) are Native Americans and contributed to the creation of the script. In a postscreening discussion, Chris Eyre identified director, writer, and producer Mackenzie as a "non-Native filmmaker who made an Indian film" (Eyre). The chapter looks at how Mackenzie uses Curtis stills and voice-overs to create a complex film that explores the issues of mid-twentieth-century relocation and urban life for American Indians.

The third chapter turns to a discussion of *House Made of Dawn*, arguing that like the novel by the same title (1968), the film marks an important mo-ment in the history of the respective genres in the context of American Indian arts and letters. Although the director, Richardson Morse, is non-Native, the novel and screenplay are written by N. Scott Momaday (Kiowa/Cherokee), and, with the one notable exception of John Saxon playing Tosamah men-tioned above, the actors are Indian, even to the extent that Pueblo men take the roles of Pueblo characters. As in the novel, the film portrays the death of a Pueblo elder whose influence affects the entire film. Chapter 4 offers an analysis of the Gerald Vizenor's non-feature-length film, *Harold of Orange*. The chapter interrogates Vizenor's adaptation of trickster from written into visual form.

The fifth chapter presents a discussion of *Medicine River*, a feature-length, made-for-television, relatively mass-market film produced by the Canadian Broadcasting Company in which the death of the protagonist's mother can be seen to motivate the plot. The film deals with First Nations themes and is based on Thomas King's 1989 novel by the same title. King (of Cherokee and Greek heritage) wrote the screenplay as well as the teleplay, and he has a small speaking role in the film. This chapter explores non-Native director Stuart Margolin's use of photography within the film to create a filmed story that is highly aware of itself as film. Although Jonathan Wacks's film adaptation of the novel *The Powwow Highway* (1979) by David Seals (Huron) has been called "a film by non-Native Americans" (Wood 20), I maintain in chapter 6 that the film nevertheless deserves a place in this study for several reasons. It can be seen as a twentieth-century Indigenous response to any number of Westerns coming out of Hollywood since the beginning of the industry; for example, it has a contemporary setting, and through intertextual references it evokes and refutes some common Hollywood tropes and offers an instance of counter-cinema.

Chris Eyre's film *Smoke Signals* marks a pivotal moment in the history of American Indian film. The director, actors, and screenplay writer are all Native. Despite its uniqueness, however, I argue in the seventh chapter that like several other films under discussion, *Smoke Signals* also portrays a lead character who dies relatively early in the narrative. This character's death motivates the plot, and his influence is felt throughout the entire film. Chapter 8 considers *The Business of Fancydancing*, suggesting again that one character's death early in the film motivates the plot. The film focuses on the death and funeral throughout but ultimately turns to a focus on those who survive the individual's death. The ninth chapter points out that the same year as *Smoke Signals*, but to much less fanfare, Valerie Red-Horse coproduced, codirected, and acted in the Indian-funded film *Naturally Native*. Even though it is a feature-length narrative film with an Indian cast and is written, directed, produced, and funded exclusively by American Indians, it never received and still fails to receive the attention doled out to *Smoke Signals*. Whereas Eyre's film is very male in subject and orientation, *Naturally Native* is very female. In these ways this somewhat neglected film deserves attention and recognition as groundbreaking and innovative. It challenges many of the stereotypes of Indian women and/or the absence of Native women in both Indian and non-Indian "Indian" film at the same time it seems to reinscribe various mainstream cultural norms.

Chapter 10 turns back to director Chris Eyre and his first feature following the success of *Smoke Signals*, with *Skins* (2002), a film based on Paiute writer Adrian Louis's 1995 novel by the same title. A documentary-style opening sequence coupled with a filmic (diegetic) newscast midway through the film situates the death of a principal character, Mogie, and the workings of the trickster figure Iktomi as it lends an air of authenticity and realism to the plot of this film. In *The Doe Boy*, the subject of the eleventh chapter, director Randy Redroad offers a reversal of the standard Hollywood depiction of the death of an Indian, and he also challenges and undercuts the notion of blood quantum as a means to determine one's degree of Indianness. An Indian, he suggests through the film's recurring voice over, is perhaps best identified not by blood quantum but by story.

Like other films discussed in previous chapters, such as *Skins* and *The Exiles*, for instance, *Tkaronto*, the subject of the twelfth chapter, begins with a nod to the documentary. In the opening scene, for example, Jolene (Melanie McLaren, Ojibwa) interviews an Ojibwa elder, Max (Loren Cardinal, Cree), asking about his Indigenous or Aboriginal identity. Moving beyond this nod to the documentary, the film tells the story of two urban Aboriginals who seek to come to terms with their identity. In chapter 13 I turn to director Sterlin Harjo (Seminole/Creek) and his film *Four Sheets to the Wind* (2007). The film recalls such films as *House Made of Dawn*, *Smoke Signals*, *Skins*, and *The Business of Fancydancing*, in which the death of a main character motivates the plot and stands as thematically central.

A Note on Terminology

At one point in Shane Belcourt's film *Tkaronto*, the character Jolene complains to Anishinaabe elder Max that she doesn't know how to pray: "I feel like I should know how to do this, you know. I'm Anishinaabe. My parents are First Nations. My ancestors were First Nations. Isn't this something that all Aboriginal people should know how to do?" (*Tkaronto*). Jolene uses almost interchangeably the terms Anishinaabe, First Nations, and Aboriginal. At another point in the film, the character Ray will somewhat more carefully distinguish between his own Métis people, First Nations people, and Inuit people. As these two examples make clear, terminology in relation to identifying groups of Indigenous peoples can be tricky. Gerald Vizenor often prefers the term *postindian*, in italics, in part because he acknowledges that Indian, with its upper case *I* is a misnomer but in common use anyway. He also uses the compound-noun phrase "Native American Indian." During the 1960s and 1970s, perhaps the most politically radically antimainstream Native group identified with the phrase "American Indian Movement," either ignoring the term as a misnomer or using it ironically. In Rodrick Pocowatchit's *The Dead Can't Dance* (2011) the character Ray Wildhorse calls attention to the problematics of terminology, listing different options, Native person and Indigenous people, among them. According to this character, the terminology depends on what is "politically correct" (*Dead Can't*).

In short, no one term will suffice to include or identify some 300 million Indigenous peoples worldwide or the millions making up the 565 different tribal groups in the United States and Canada. I am therefore forced and resigned to being comfortable using the terms Indigenous, Native American, Native North American, American Indian, and Indian somewhat interchangeably throughout this study. When specific tribal affiliation is necessary or appropriate, such is of course noted.

ONE

He Was Still the Chief

Masayesva's *Imagining Indians*

His horse stumbled. And he got all wet, and got run over two or three
times. . . . The war bonnet was hanging way down there, and dripping
with water, you know, and buckskin outfit all wet. . . . "No," he says,
"I'm the chief," and he was still the chief when he got all wet.

—*Imagining Indians*

The documentary film *Imagining Indians* about Hollywood representations
of American Indians, directed by Victor Masayesva Jr. (Hopi), includes a
narrative, fictional frame that tells the story of a Native American woman's
visit to a dentist's office. This narrative plot, such as it is, revolves around
the dentist's chair, and the unnamed patient (Patty Runs after Swallow). She
sits in the chair surrounded by walls plastered with posters advertising classic Hollywood Westerns; she listens to diatribes against Native people on the
dentist's radio; and she endures the anesthetic, the drill, the pliers, and the
male, non-Native dentist's monologue about his having seen repeatedly Kevin
Costner's film *Dances with Wolves*. Unsolicited, he shares his thoughts about
that film and about how it has inspired him to establish a resort in order to
sell to non-Indians "Native spirituality" packaged as sweats and ceremonies.
Between the several brief scenes in the dentist's office, Masayesva intersperses
the stories of over thirty people who offer accounts of how American Indians
and American Indian cultures are and have long been imagined in film and
how those people and those cultures have been appropriated and consumed
in other Native art forms. In addition to the series of interviews, Masayesva
includes a few clips from selected Hollywood Westerns, movies such as the
silent-era film *The Battle at Elderbush Gulch* (1913), *The Plainsman* (1936),
and *The Last Hunt*. The one-hour film maneuvers the viewer by pulling in
several directions at once. Despite its fictional frame, it is indubitably a documentary whose subject is the different ways mainstream American culture,
especially Hollywood, has imagined, invented, appropriated, and coopted
American Indians and American Indian history and culture. Masayesva's
relatively early film anticipates similar documentary studies such as *Reel
Injun* (2009), directed by Neil Diamond, and the short, *I'm Not the Indian*

You Had in Mind (2007), directed by Thomas King. Both of these films, like Masayesva's before them, confront and refute Hollywood and other mainstream depictions of Indigenous peoples.

Masayesva's method as documentarian is conventional enough: he appeals to the authority of several of the men and women who worked as American Indian extras in different Hollywood Westerns, and he films the interviews and includes interspersed archival film clips as well as shots of posters of some of the films discussed. The film thus constitutes expository documentary, yet through its inclusion of the fictional plot as a framing device, it at the same time offers a generic hybrid that challenges the genre. The film also challenges and actually reverses Hollywood's discourse of the vanishing Indian. Several of the narrators in the documentary, that is, are literal survivors of the deaths they acted as extras in those films, and they often humorously recount those filmic deaths or experiences. In addition to reversing a prevalent and long-standing Hollywood discourse, Masayesva deconstructs other mainstream representations and images of American Indians, especially in his final sequence in which portraits of American Indians by George Catlin drop away like shattered glass and are replaced by the face of the dental patient character, who until this final moment has remained passive. In yet another ironic stratagem, Masayesva makes invisible the Hollywood blockbuster *Dances with Wolves* by refusing to show a single clip of that film. He deconstructs non-Indian (mis)representations of American Indians; and he privileges the former extras who acquire a voice and take center stage. The cumulative effect of these maneuverings and reversals, as this chapter argues, constitutes an important step toward establishing a visual sovereignty and insisting on and actually demonstrating American Indian survival despite longstanding Hollywood tropes.

Masayesva's film as documentary relies on visual images of the art of filmmaking to address, as Fatimah Tobing Rony writes, "the absurdity and indignity of dominant culture's appetite for images of Native Americans" (27). The documentary is concerned with demonstrating how the dominant culture imagines American Indians, especially as extras in mainstream Hollywood Westerns. As Masayesva himself says, "It was *about* imagining Indians, and *I* was part of that imagining. And I wasn't trying to absolve myself . . . I was implicating myself by having, by showing the technology, the filmmaking, the transparency *behind* the scenes" (qtd. in Rony 31). The documentary as documentary is belied or undermined, however, by the fictional narrative frame, a device that calls into question the validity of a genre that purports to frame reality and that colonizers and/or anthropologists have used for over a hundred years to represent Indigenous peoples around the world. Masayesva's film questions its own premise and offers the complications of myriad representational viewpoints.

Both the patient and the viewer hear a series of different recitations on the radio in the opening sequence of the documentary, and as far as the film lets the viewer or the dental patient know, these recitations could be present-day editorial comments read by a talk-radio guest or host. In that they are heard on the radio diegetically and without context, that is, they appear to be contemporary. But in fact, unbeknownst to the viewer, the texts consist of anti-Indian diatribes from previous centuries. The presentation of these apparently present-day passages suggests how pre-twentieth-century history of and inflexible mainstream attitudes toward American Indians remain very much a part of the present. With these passages Masayesva further complicates any easy distinction between fiction and documentary in his clever and disingenuous presentation of these passages without identifying the speaker or offering any context: "We must act with vindictive earnestness against the Sioux, even to their extermination, men, women, [and] children. . . . The Indian Bureau keeps feeding and clothing the Indians 'til they get fat and saucy, and then we are only notified that the Indians are troublesome. . . . I think it would be wise to invite all the sportsmen of England and America there this fall for a grand Buffalo hunt, and make one grand sweep of them all" (*Imagining*). These particular excerpts, heard over the radio in the dentist's office as if of one piece, are actually sentences combined from three different comments William Tecumseh Sherman made as Commanding General of the U.S. Army (1869–83). The first sentence is from a telegram he sent to Ulysses S. Grant on December 27, 1866. What Masayesva does not include in the excerpt is that Sherman follows the clause about extermination with this: "nothing less will reach the root of this case" (Simon 422). The next sentence, about the troublesome Indians, is from a different source, the House Reports (1874). Masayesva cuts the final clause of the original sentence, which continues the thought: "Indians are troublesome and are going to war, after it is too late to provide a remedy" (Utley 165). The sentence concerning the buffalo hunt comes from yet another source, the Sherman to Sheridan correspondence, and here Masayesva omits any contextual help: Sherman is concerned about the railroads, and maintains that "until the Buffaloes and consequent[ly the] Indians are out from between the Roads we will have collisions and trouble" (Athearn 197). Because of the omitted contextual material, the viewer has reason to assume that these particular nineteenth-century excerpts actually express late-twentieth-century attitudes. Furthermore, the radio texts anticipate and foreshadow much of what is to come in the films and film clips that Masayesva's documentary investigates. This anticipation is made immediately evident by the cut from the radio broadcast to one man speaking of his role, as discussed below, as an extra in *Dances with Wolves*.

In a subsequent scene in the dentist's office, the radio continues to blast, this time with a reading of excerpts from an "Oration at Plymouth," delivered in 1802 by then Massachusetts state senator John Quincy Adams. The passage the viewer hears, also unidentified within the film, concerns part of the future president's commemoration of the landing of the Plymouth pilgrims in 1620. Jedediah Morse would later quote this passage and use the argument in his rationalization of and justification for Andrew Jackson's Indian removal policy (see Morse 409). Adams's words come alive for the viewer of the documentary: "Shall the exuberant bosom of the common mother, amply adequate to the nourishment of millions, be claimed exclusively by a few hundreds of her offspring? Shall the lordly savage not only disdain the virtues and enjoyments of civilization himself, but shall he control the civilization of the world? Shall the fields and the valleys, which a beneficent God has formed to teem with the life of innumerable multitudes, be condemned to everlasting barrenness?" (*Imagining*). This passage, read almost as if part of a sermon, is followed by an excerpt from a few lines of a speech by Andrew Jackson in which the then sitting president attempts to explain and justify his administration's Indian Removal Act of 1830:

> Humanity has often wept over the fate of the aborigines of this country. And philanthropy has been long busily employed in devising a means to avert it, but its progress has never for a moment been arrested, as one by one have many powerful tribes disappeared from the earth. To follow to the tomb the last of his race and to tread on the graves of extinct nations excite melancholy reflections. But true philanthropy reconciles the mind to these vicissitudes as it does to the extinction of one generation of people to make room for another. . . . What good man would prefer a country covered with forests and ranged by a few thousand savages to our extensive Republic, studded with cities, towns, and prosperous farms? (*Imagining*)

Although the viewer does not hear it on the radio, a few sentences later in his actual speech, Jackson states that that a preferable country would be one "filled with all the blessings of liberty, civilization, and religion" (Jackson 115–16). One of the very painful ironies inherent in this presidential address and exposed by Masayesva's film is that Jackson attributes to mainstream American people and culture the very attributes it lacks in its bearing toward the Cherokee people and the members of other "civilized" tribes subject to removal in the 1830s: liberty, civilization, and religion.

Meanwhile, with the pernicious radio continuing in the background, the dentist chatters as he anesthetizes the patient and waits for the sedative to take effect. He describes having seen the film *Dances with Wolves*, commenting that "the whole sort of spiritual lifestyle you guys had is really very inspirational, very inspirational" (*Imagining*). The thought leads him to talk at the patient about the "higher consciousness resort" he has going with some other New Age people in Phoenix. The juxtaposition of radio broadcast and dentist's ignorant harangue certainly suggests that when it comes to main-stream attitudes toward Indigenous peoples, there is no separation of past and present. These radio broadcasts of words from a previous century provide Masayesva thematic links between the historical physical violence advocated by former U.S. presidents and military commanders—Adams, Jackson, and Sherman in these instances—and the violence represented on Hollywood's screen for over a hundred years. This physical violence is simultaneously juxtaposed with the violence done through the misrepresentation and commodification of American Indians near the beginning of the twenty-first century.

The radio broadcasts at first interspersed with crosscuts to interviewees' comments also add a verbal element to the mise-en-scène visual in the dentist's office, an office whose walls are covered with posters of Hollywood movies featuring American Indians, including *Taza, Son of Cochise* (1954) and *Captain John Smith and Pocahontas* (1953). The dentist's report of his own attempts to coopt what he (mis)understands to be the "spiritual life-style" of American Indians fuses the nineteenth-century attitudes toward the land evident from the radio with late twentieth-century attitudes concerning the availability of Indigenous spirituality. Masayesva thus offers examples through both the verbal and the visual of how Indians have been and continue to be imagined and treated and of how mainstream European America has always been at the same time dismissive and exploitative of American Indians. Neatly layered with the radio broadcasts is the dentist's numbing of the actual patient, which is merely another form of violence, preamble to the pulling of the tooth, a procedure that meanwhile renders the patient voiceless.

Early in *Imagining Indians*, the dentist holds up to the light an x-ray slide of his patient's tooth, and at the instant he does so there is a match on action cut, in a sense, to an interview that concerns the (mis)treatment of American Indian extras in film, specifically during the filming of *Dances with Wolves*. The crosscut to Marvin Clifford as he begins his account of working as an extra in that film is thus implicitly paired with the dentist's holding the x-ray film up to the light; similarly, Clifford holds up to the light an analogous x-ray, a verbal picture of what goes on behind the scenes as experienced during his work as an extra. The documentary then makes an explicit match on action cut: in the opening moments of Clifford's interview sequence, a child in the background turns on a television, and on the television screen the viewer sees the same Marvin Clifford, this time wearing a Washington Redskins cap, beginning his account. Through this metafilmic match, Masayesva again calls attention to the artifice of film and of his own complicity. That it is Clifford on the television screen is also an instance of Masayesva's reversal of the normal emphasis in such a scene. Typically, especially in such contexts, the viewer could expect to see an old black-and-white Western on a television that would remain in the background during Clifford's account. Instead, as the actual informant begins to tell his story, the Indian man himself, the extra, becomes not only the authority figure as interviewee, but at the same moment becomes the star of the television show. Clifford dominates the television screen, and Masayesva thus completes the reversal. The Hollywood film and its star become marginalized, and an extra takes center stage; his story becomes central; Clifford (re)writes the history.

Masayesva includes no clips from or posters of the film *Dances with Wolves* itself. That particular film becomes the "invisible other," so to speak; much spoken of and alluded to and thus almost palpably present, but at the same time kept invisible. By strategically keeping any visual reference to this blockbuster completely absent, Masayesva further privileges the roles of the American Indian extras at the same time that he forthrightly diminishes the value of Costner's film. Clifford mixes humor and chagrin as he relates his stories about working as an extra. Expecting a Greyhound-type charter bus with comfortable seats to get to and from the site of the filming, for example, he describes instead the old, white school bus that arrives to take him and the other extras to the set. He makes a joke about the skimpy clothing, the "G-string," he and the others have to wear during the shoots, and he notes that it was a long day on horseback. He is more serious when he describes the horses themselves:

> The horses we had, I'll say that too, was, were really green-broke horses, you know. I grew up around horses, and I know horses, and those horses weren't very good horses, you know. And, um, I told that David right away about that. I said, "You know David, these horses aren't broke too good." And he said, "Well, we got them from a local rancher, and he says that they're quality horses," you know. I said, well, you know, I just kinda said, to myself mostly, "Well, I know horses and these horses ain't worth a crap, man, you know." And the thing about it was, is, we were riding them bareback, and it just had a rope around their noses, with just one rope, riding green-broke horses, and we're running amongst people and everything, full gallop, downhill. (*Imagining*)

By presenting such a viewpoint at the outset of his documentary, Masayesva immediately turns the tables on the mainstream understanding of the hugely popular blockbuster. One of the interviewees late in the documentary comments that the film remains "all his [Costner's] story. And Native Americans are all props. . . . We provide the stage." The viewer does not "ever get to know what the Indian feels about those two people coming . . . to come and be part of the tribe" (*Imagining*). By reversing the perspective or point of view, Masayesva challenges the viewer to rethink not just the one film but the entire enterprise of Hollywood's attitude toward and exploitation of American Indian extras in Westerns.

Clifford's interview is on occasion overlaid with panels containing newspaper clippings. One headline insists "Indian Extras Got Treated Fairly." With this filmic device, Masayesva offers the viewer a juxtaposition of Clifford's sometimes humorous oral narrative with the written newspaper accounts that offer a much different version of the issues Clifford discusses. The clippings present not only what seems contradictory, given Clifford's narrative, but they also appear to be overly defensive reactions on the part of the press and the film's publicity people. Clifford includes a story of a woman coming with a pail of water, but that water is literally for the dogs rather than for the extras, who, according to Clifford, were not provided any drinking water:

> And here this lady comes up, a younger white lady comes running up and she's got a little bucket like that and she comes from way over there where all the cameras are and stuff are because Costner was shooting his scene over here you know and we're in the background and this lady comes running up like that and she has a little bucket like that for water and there's water in that bucket and she comes running over there and she goes up to them dogs and she takes the water to the dogs, you know, and I, we're sitting there, I look down, and I say "Hey, blank the dogs, man; give us that water." (*Imagining*)

The newspaper clipping accompanying this part of the story challenges the firsthand narrator's account: "Clifford's complaint of a water shortage was disputed by TIG's craft service assistant. Also, the anonymous extra working said water was available" (*Imagining*). Whether or not there was actually sufficient drinking water made available to the extras, the impact of the sequence within the documentary serves to ensure that issues of concern to the Indian extras are front and center. They are important, as substantiated by the very existence of a newspaper response to their concerns. Masayesva so manipulates it that the viewer of this documentary loses all sight, both literally and figuratively, of Costner and what might be considered the main action of that particular film. It is as if the specific film no longer matters. What matters instead is that the extras are real people, people who have been to some degree misled and mistreated, and perhaps most importantly, American Indian people who have clearly survived, both figuratively and literally, against all odds, the final scenes of so many such Westerns. They have neither died nor disappeared.

The interview sequence's final newspaper clipping is perhaps the most poignant because it is the farthest reaching. The viewer sees this excerpt from the newspaper: "'If Clifford did not understand what he was signing, why did he sign the papers?' Haas asked. 'He is educated and should have known better'" (*Imagining*). Underlying this statement by an otherwise unidentified Haas is an ironic echo or evocation of centuries of treaty signing. By showing to the viewer the visual of Haas's statement, Masayesva is able on a certain level to subtly link the broken promises of the filmmaker (Costner) with broken promises by the U.S. government, made manifest in hundreds of broken treaties. Much of American Indian history after contact with Europeans is, after all, about the loss of land through treaties and broken treaties, and this theme of land loss, of course, underlies the action in Costner's film as well. As Masayesva's interviewee Rennard Strickland puts it, "The theft of so much land must be rationalized. Films are a part of the process of rationalizing the frontier theft of Native Americans' rights and land. What you have worked out on film is the ritualized justification of what at its kindest can be called the greatest land theft in history" (*Imagining*).

In a humorous scene just after Clifford has talked about his participation as an extra in *Dances with Wolves*, another interviewee comments on a character's hair. Without naming the character—Stands with a Fist (Mary McDonnell)—Karmen Clifford, who worked as an extra in the same film, wonders why the actor's hair is not long and braided if the woman has been living all these years with the Lakota people. When she is told by a woman sitting beside her that Stands with a Fist is supposedly in mourning and so might have cut her own hair, Karmen Clifford laughs, and says, "I obviously didn't see the film. [They all laugh.] I was in it though" (*Imagining*). Karmen Clifford's comment has the effect of further marginalizing the actual film. Not only is there confusion about the authenticity of the depiction of the film's lead female actor, the film itself, this context implies, is not even worth seeing by someone who was actually in it.

Masayesva's documentary does not make any explicit statement about connections between the mistreatment of the extras during the filming and the general use of American Indian roles on the screen. But such mistreatment and the parallels between such forms of mistreatment are inescapably apparent in the oral account that Charles Sooktis gives of the filming of a particular attack scene in Cecil B. De Mille's *The Plainsman*. Sooktis worked the scene as an extra, and he relates how the Indians were to gallop down a river into the barrage of gunfire coming from a small number of soldiers, including Wild Bill Hickok (Gary Cooper), on the embankment, well ensconced and protected behind fallen trees.

There has been some confusion among scholars about this moment in Masayesva's film and what happens in the scene in *The Plainsman*. According to Jacquelyn Kilpatrick, for example, in this unnamed "old De Mille film . . . Masayesva shows us the actual footage as *the old man* [whom Kilpatrick does not name] tells, in his own language as well as in English, of 'wild Indians' riding horses as fast as they could down a river for the filming. There was a wire strung just under the water, and when the *unsuspecting* Indians reached it, their horses went down, and many Indians as well as their mounts were hurt" (Kilpatrick 211, my emphasis). The "old man" Kilpatrick refers to is the interviewee Charles Sooktis, and according to his account the extras riding in this scene knew full well to expect the trip wire. As Sooktis states twice in the interview, some of the other extras warned the leader of the charge that there was the trip wire. In another discussion of the documentary, John Purdy writes that "In Masayesva's film he interviews a member of the Northern Cheyenne who played in the scene of a Cecil B. De Mille movie (I believe it was *Cheyenne River*) in which Gary Cooper and his troop are barricaded on a riverbank waiting for the attack" (173). According to the *Imagining Indians* credits, the De Mille film in which Cooper is barricaded is indeed *The Plainsman*, not a film called "Cheyenne River." After casually acknowledging that he is not sure of the film's title, Purdy reports on the interview itself in which an actor recalls the filming of the specific attack scene. Of the Cheyenne actor leading the attack, Purdy writes that "what he didn't know at the time was that the film crew had rigged a trip wire under the water so that when Cooper and his troops 'opened fire' the horses of the Cheyenne out in front would be tripped" (173). As mentioned above, in Masayesva's documentary, Sooktis states twice, unequivocally, that Little Coyote, the "chief," is indeed warned about the trip wire and that he nevertheless insists on riding in front. Little Coyote is thus one of the first to go down. Indeed, the delightful humor in the interview arises in large measure from Sooktis's account of how Little Coyote insisted on riding out front, even though he had been warned about the trip wire and even though it meant that he would fall and risk being trampled by the horses galloping behind his own.

During the verbal account of the filming of the scene, the documentary cuts to a clip of the attack scene itself in which the Indians make their suicidal ride down the middle of the river toward the small military brigade crouched behind their barricade. Evidently finding the absurd logic of the plan of attack in the first place not worth calling the viewer's attention to, Masayesva intricately layers the meanings in this sequence so that several things are going on at once. As Joanna Hearne reads this scene in the documentary, it is "a complex negotiation of authenticity on the set" in that Sooktis's account seems mostly interested explaining how it was important to Little Coyote that he be cast as the chief even though he was warned about the trip wire. "'No,' he says, 'I'm the Chief. I been Chief of the Northern Cheyennes for many years'" (*Imagining*). Little Coyote thus disregards De Mille's statement that anyone could be chief and ride out front in this scene. Little Coyote refuses to relinquish authenticity and authority in this way. He will ride as chief in the scene because he is chief in reality, regardless of the consequences.

On another level is a fine humor inherent in the story about Little Coyote's falling in the water. As Sooktis tells it, "he had—war bonnet, all the buckskin outfit, all—he had too many things in his hand! He had a sword, he had a bow and arrow, and—and a tomahawk. . . . And they got to that wire that was strung across the, under water. His horse stumbled. And he got all wet, and got run over two or three times. And you know how the chickens look when they get wet—the war bonnet was hanging way down there, and dripping with water, you know, and buckskin outfit all wet" (*Imagining*). The viewer sees the actual black-and-white footage of the horses and riders stumbling during this narration, and in this way, the humor of the account is complicated by the visual information demonstrating that horses and riders may well be risking injury in these falls. Little Coyote, for example, is actually "run over two or three times." Sooktis insists on the humor again, however, when he embeds the comment about himself as one of the extras in the context of that scene: "Good thing I was behind—or one of the last ones, you know." And again in the coda, in which Sooktis, delightfully deadpan, highlights the point of what Little Coyote had said after was suggested to him that he let a younger man play the chief just for the one scene: "'No,' he says, 'I'm the Chief.' And he was still the Chief when he got all wet, you know." Although much of acknowledging the actual danger in such a scene is lost in the humorous retelling, that danger does underlie the story through the combination of Sooktis's mentioning of the trip wire and Masayesva's showing the clip of the riders and horses falling.

Joanna Hearne argues that Sooktis "re-frames the *Indian charge* scene through voiceover and suggests a complex negotiation of authenticity on the set. . . . Sooktis is more interested in his own community's politics than in the film's Hollywood-based stars or director. The usually anonymous extras become the most important figures as they struggle to make the film more accurate in its representations of the tribe's social organization" (Hearne, "John" 202, original emphasis). The narrator in this instance implies that Little Coyote simply refuses to accept or participate in the film's fiction; he refuses to contribute to the inauthenticity of De Mille's film. On still another level, throughout the entire sequence looms the inescapable implication that here again, according to the fiction of *The Plainsman*, the slaughter, the ultimate demise, and the final vanishing of American Indians are inevitable. Yet in Masayesva's presentation of De Mille's Western, the actual Indian actor survives that battle and is in a good position to tell his story about it. He thus actually takes control of the record.

Through the entire sequence narrated by Sooktis and through the many other references to Hollywood Westerns, Masayesva artfully engages issues of authenticity, mistreatment of extras, humor, and the stereotype of the vanishing Indian. He challenges and actually reverses the dominant, mainstream narrative. In a different but applicable context, Freya Schiwy writes that Indigenous "documentaries privilege the indigenous subject as expert in his or her own right, and docudramas and fiction shorts counter the way race and gender have intermeshed in the patriarchal gaze of empire" (Schiwy 11). One certainly sees this countermove in the way Masayesva sets Sooktis *the extra* and *his* story front and center while the white soldiers in the film become marginalized. The interviewee narrates, tells his own story, and controls and shapes the history much like Clifford does in his narration. In so doing Sooktis offers a treatise on dignity and authenticity that transcends the artifice of film in general and of the Western specifically. The Indigenous narrator thereby challenges the pretended historical veracity and realism of the genre, and at the same time he demonstrates his fine and subtle sense of humor. The "vanishing Indian" actually does not vanish at all. He has once again survived the scenes of slaughter and motif of disappearance so often at the center of the Hollywood Western. Both Clifford and Sooktis sit comfortably before Masayesva's camera, relating their experiences to other Indians and ultimately to all of the Indian and non-Indian viewers of the documentary.

Masayesva's documentary points out the mainstream culture's lack of respect for and the brutality against American Indians in and on film as made manifest through radio, poster, and film. As the filmmaker details, this brutality carries over into religion and the sacred as well. He makes this point explicit by cutting from one of the scenes in the dentist's office to an interview with Clement "Sunny" Richards as he talks about Skinwalkers and other Navajo spiritual beings. Richards describes the powers and cultural significance Skinwalkers have, and he laments their cooption and commodification: "I think Hollywood's gonna promote the Skinwalker now. . . . They're gonna go inside into the ceremony now. . . . It's just a sellable thing, and they're gonna sell it. It's gonna sell" (*Imagining*). With the turn to spiritual exploitation, Masayesva broadens his scope; he moves from film exclusively to demonstrating how mainstream culture imagines and then co-opts all things "Indian," including cultural artifacts, even those made or manufactured for sale to tourists. In her discussion of the film, Beverly Singer emphasizes Masayesva's attention to the "Santa Fe Market" and the issue of Hollywood's filming on the Hopi reservation, arguing that filming and "replication of popular images of Indians for commercial purposes—whether in films or other forms of culture—contributes to a loss of respect for culture, confused identity, and weakened beliefs about what it means to be a Native American" (7). She implies, though does not state as much outright, that the Hopi tribal government's vote to allow filming in exchange for payment—even though Hopi elders opposed the filming of revered places—is one way through which Masayesva demonstrates that decline of culture. According to Laurie Whitt in another context, "cultural imperialism . . . serves to extend the political power, secure the social control, and further the economic profit of the dominant culture. The commodification of indigenous spirituality is a paradigmatic instance of cultural imperialism" (140).

Masayesva himself has written of the struggle to maintain what he calls his essential self away from the imagining and coopting that goes on and has gone on for ages. "We Hopis often find ourselves the subjects of tourist cameras. The reason is simple. As Southwest Indians we are on display, always: on napkins, on sugar and salt packets, on Fred Harvey tours and brochures, sometimes in rare library collections, but most often on postcards. As tourist attractions we remain as available as the inimitable prong-horned jack-rabbit, the rare jack-a-lope. And yet it is a fact that, although we are inundated by collectors of Indian images, we somehow keep our essential selves away from the camera" ("Kwikwilyaqa" 10). Steven Leuthold argues that "when Masayesva points to the 'sacred' as the basis of a Native American aesthetic, he is singling out content as a source of aesthetic unity; many videos are about native religion and spirituality. . . . The notion of an aesthetic based in the sacred points to the normative character of the emerging indigenous video genre" (*Indigenous* 123). Although the notion of the attempt to define an overarching "indigenous aesthetic" might make one uncomfortable, one can nevertheless appreciate Leuthold's contention that the sacred is an important part of Masayesva's own aesthetic. In an essay in a volume on Hopi photographers, for example—written before the making of *Imagining Indians*—Masayesva notes that "refraining from photographing certain subjects has become a kind of worship" ("Kwikwilyaqa" 10). Clearly this aesthetic has remained with him as he edits and produces his 1992 documentary. He does not offer any clips from *Thunderheart*, for example; thus, as with presentation of *Dances with Wolves*, the mainstream films remain in the background, secondary in importance to the Indigenous stories of the people who participated as extras or as crew members and who recount their experiences working with those films.

One of the interviewees, not clearly identified in the credits, a man who worked as a set carpenter for Michael Apted's *Thunderheart*, witnessed the filming of that film's Ghost Dance scenes. He speaks of the inappropriateness of filming a Ghost Dance at all, but he finds especially egregious the fact that the filmed dance is incorrect. During this narration, the documentary crosscuts not to a clip from *Thunderheart* but rather to stills of the aftermath of the 1890 massacre at Wounded Knee, a massacre that resulted in part from the practice of the Ghost Dance. The interviewee has this to say:

> No matter how they do it, it still ain't right because doing a Ghost Dance in a movie, that was a spiritual thing back in Wounded Knee, and them people they gave their lives, and in the movie they were using powwow music for Ghost Dance, and they were dancing like Sun Dancers and it wasn't even right. I felt so low; I felt so bad watching them practice doing a Ghost Dance, and it's not even right. You know, even if they have the right songs, the right dance, the right tree, the right everything, it still doesn't make it right. Still doesn't make it right. (*Imagining*)

In addition to pointing out the inappropriateness of the filming of a Ghost Dance in the first place, then, Masayesva emphasizes that the very filmic technique signals the film's failure to offer any historical accuracy. Not only does the film *Thunderheart* profit by exploiting the sacred for the screen, it serves as another example of how Indians are (mis)imagined, invented, kept separate from the very nineteenth-century history in which the films and popular consciousness forces them to remain. Robert Burgoyne makes this point when he writes that "Native Americans are now being appropriated as cultural progenitors" (54). Masayesva implies that the Ghost Dance has been appropriated in every sense of the word: the director Michael Apted makes use of the dance without the moral right, certainly, but insofar as his film *Thunderheart* is supposed to based on actual historical fact, the director also takes exclusive possession as he denies the Ghost Dance its historical, sacred, and legitimate contexts. This film is released in 1992 (the same year as Masayesva's documentary), not in (say) 1913 when *The Battle at Elderbush Gulch* was released or the 1950s, when *Taza, Son of Cochise* or *John Smith and Pocahontas* and countless Westerns were made. The relatively late release of the film in the context of the ways it exploits American Indian people and culture makes it of even graver concern. Despite its being set in the 1970s instead of the 1870s, for example, and despite its anti-Western themes, as Masayesva makes clear, *Thunderheart* remains problematic.

Insofar as it includes a fictional dentist-office plot, *Imagining Indians* is to a certain extent a narrative fiction film, and as such it can even be said to reverse the typical Western plot of an Indian maiden attacked by the white male character and often eventually killed or left to die. Masayesva reverses this traditional plot element as he depicts an Indian woman in the dentist's chair, not literally tied but in a sense tortured and anesthetized by the white, male dentist as he examines an x-ray, fires up his drill, and eventually pulls a tooth. The dentist assaults the female patient with his drill and pliers, keeping her silent. Throughout the entire ordeal, the entire film, she does not speak a single word. Even more invidiously, perhaps, the dentist debases and demeans her through his ignorance and concomitant arrogance. Ultimately, however, the patient rebels. She first attacks the dentist himself with his own dentistry tools, very literally the master's tools, and then, through Masayesva's metafilmic move, she scratches out (whites out) the lens of the camera that represents her, the very camera that records her actions and makes any of the story possible. As Elizabeth Weatherford states emphatically, "the dental patient herself drills into the camera lens (Masayesva's camera!)" (Weatherford and Masayesva 51).

In an essay comparing Masayesva and Leslie Marmon Silko, Karen Jacobs offers a fine close reading of this final scene, drawing attention to how the patient's actions are "so economically an exemplary representational conflict" (297):

Scratching the lens. *Imagining Indians.* Documentary Educational Resources.

the patient rapidly cycles through the gamut of representational possibility, beginning with an "X" that she marks on the glass that both frames and encloses her. The X is a letter and also a symbol, connoting a simplified signature as well as a crossing out of meanings; it is also an image of a gun's crosshair which captures us, the film's viewers, in its frame. With the next horizontal line she draws, however, the X evolves into an emerging spider's web of marks—an image which has powerful resonances as a figure for Native American storytelling. (298)

Jacobs suggests that the patient's actions enable the dissolution of the interspersed images of several of George Catlin's portraits. Like the glass of the lens, these images "crystallize and fall away" (298) as they literally pixelate and dissolve. Finally, the patient places her hand over the scratched lens, establishing a momentary identification before forcing the entire visual field to go blank. In this way, Masayesva refuses to allow his viewers to maintain any simple reading of representation. Although he might seem to advocate one's taking charge and control of whatever might appear within the visual field, he at the same time suggests that doing so includes the very real possibility of destroying his own opportunity to imagine Indians, to set the record straight. After the patient destroys the Catlin images and the camera itself, the screen goes black and the film ends with "voice-overs in several different Native-American languages," voices accompanying the blank screen, and as Rony argues, "knowing one's language and having a connection with one's community are essential requirements for the Native-American filmmaker" (31). I would add that such a requirement, ironically, risks voiding or disallowing the very medium of film, the medium Masayesva uses to make that very point.

Masayesva makes it possible for a viewer to read the film as a story about a young American Indian woman's visit to her non-Indian dentist, a woman who—in the course of her visit—relives or visualizes many of the ways that American Indians have been imagined and exploited on screen, in other media, and in the marketplace. One of the ways in which Masayesva suggests this possible reading is through his use of sound bridges between cuts to and from the dentist's office. Sound or musical continuity can serve to "bind a series of otherwise disparate shots together, thereby reinforcing the principles of the sequence" (Buhler, Neumeyer, and Deemer 323). After an early interview, for example, as the film cuts back to the dentist's office, the laughter of the women interviewees from the previous scene carries over into a close-up of the dental patient's face, a sound bridge that can be seen to imply that the laughter comes from within the patient's head. Masayesva's fusing of documentary and narrative fiction film is doubly empowering. The director takes the control away from Hollywood at every turn. Just as the interviewees ultimately depict and actually construct history, the patient maintains the meaning-making power as she overturns a metonymy of the culture that oppresses and silences. Like the actors interviewed throughout, she not only survives the end of the film, she triumphs.

TWO

Into the City

Ordered Freedom in *The Exiles*

I've always wanted to go, get away from my people there, and all
that, and go someplace where somebody will maybe, ah, make me
feel different and be happier. That's why I'm glad I came out to
Los Angeles. — *The Exiles*

In the course of a postscreening conversation during part of the Film Indians
Now! series in Washington, D.C. (November 28, 2008), Melissa Bisagni, film
and video program manager at the National Museum of the American Indian, stated that Kent Mackenzie's film *The Exiles* is "essentially a Native
film" (Bisagni). Following up on her comment, Native filmmaker Chris Eyre
as respondent identified director, writer, and producer Kent Mackenzie as a
"non-Native filmmaker who made an Indian film" (Eyre). Although the filmmaker is non-Native, his lead actors, none of whom were professionals, are
Native Americans. They contributed the basic information upon which the
film is based, and they influenced Mackenzie's script. Given that they impro-
vised and scripted as the filming proceeded, they essentially had input into
the writing as well. That is, one could consider the film to be at least on some
levels cowritten by Native Americans. *The Exiles* offers in this sense an honest Native perspective and shows the subtleties and complexities of the lives
of several American Indians in Los Angeles during the late 1950s. It has a
contemporary setting and deals specifically, almost exclusively, with American
Indian themes.

The group of actors (Homer Nish, Tommy Reynolds, Yvonne Williams,
and others) agreed to have Mackenzie film them as they reenacted their move-
ments on a typical Friday night, creating a sort of night-in-the-life narrative.
The plot of *The Exiles* thus follows several different individuals for about
twelve hours, from a Friday evening until about dawn the next morning.
Yvonne, who is pregnant, comes home from shopping, cooks pork chops for
her husband, Homer, and his friends, goes on her own to a film, and spends
the night at her friend Marilynn's place, half a block down the street from
her own apartment. A second plot follows Homer and his friend Rico as
they leave the Café Ritz bar together, play some cards, return to the bar and

Coming back from a night on Hill X. *The Exiles*. Screen Capture. Milestone Films.

get into a fight, before Homer joins his friends and acquaintances on top of Hill X for drumming, singing, dancing, and more drinking. A third plotline follows Tommy, another friend of Homer's, as he spends his evening and night pursuing a woman who alternately pushes him away and embraces him. They also end up on the hilltop. The film ends as Yvonne, from her friend's window, watches Homer, Tommy, and some of the others return home just at daybreak Saturday morning.

In the opening moments of *The Exiles*, before the action of the film as it were, Mackenzie juxtaposes shots of several Edward S. Curtis photographs with shots (as stills) of the principal actors in his own film. Although Curtis took many of his photographs in his studio in the early twentieth century, completing his massive multivolume photographic study *The North American Indian* in 1930, the photographer writes that his work would represent the subjects as they existed in some pristine, pre-twentieth-century past. The sepia prints are thus meant to offer glimpses into and thereby preserve what Curtis saw as dying cultures. His photographic study, he asserts, is of "a people who are rapidly losing the traces of their aboriginal character and who are destined ultimately to become assimilated with the 'superior race.'" A few pages further on, he writes that "the information that is to be gathered, for the benefit of future generations, respecting the mode of life of one of the great races of mankind, must be collected at once or the opportunity will be lost for all time. It is this need that has inspired the present task" (Curtis 1: xiii, xvi–viii).

Mackenzie's use of the Curtis photographs serves to remind the viewer of how ubiquitous such images of American Indians are. And because of this ubiquity, the style and content of the shots certainly suggest exactly what it is that mainstream Americans might think of when they consider American Indians. In such imaginings the Indigenous North Americans exist exclusively in the nineteenth or early twentieth century; they typically ride on horseback; they remain stoic; and they live a simple, primitive, sepia-colored life. In other words, Mackenzie's use of the Curtis photographs seems to play directly into major, mainstream stereotypes of American Indians. According to Randolph Lewis, in another context, beginning in the 1850s non-Indigenous "portrait photographers began taking shots that prioritized their own needs for salable images, deciding what was salable on the basis less of indigenous realities than of hegemonic narratives about Native people as an exotic or vanishing people" (174). These hegemonic narratives are the very images that Mackenzie's film ultimately refutes, and as part of that refutation the filmmaker juxtaposes the several Curtis photographs with photographs of the modern-day actors in the film itself. In addition to portraits of the actors, he offers several shots of the contemporary tenement houses in the Bunker Hill area of Los Angeles, where the film is set. These juxtapositions immediately and powerfully challenge stereotypes in that the actors and their places of residence are no longer lost in a temporally distant past or a geographically remote area; instead these people are suddenly recognizable as the viewer's contemporaries and neighbors. Nor are they culturally so different or distant: they wear the same clothes and have the same haircuts as the viewer. They do not live on reservations in teepees or hogans as depicted in the Curtis stills but rather in the tenement house next door to or down the street from where the viewer might live.

The differences between the Curtis stills and the shots of people and places of contemporary Los Angeles are substantial and powerful, yet the transition itself from the Curtis photographs to the photos of the actors is very subtle, made so by MacKenzie's use of smooth dissolves. Viewers do not necessarily—indeed, they cannot at first—recognize Yvonne as one who will figure as a main character in the film to come. Nor can the viewer even be certain that she is a contemporary, even though her photograph is clearly not from the Curtis files. Several similar extreme close-ups of some of the other actors follow the shot of Yvonne, and they come in rapid succession: Homer, Tommy, and Mary, for example. By their clothes and haircuts, they are ultimately recognizable as the viewer's contemporaries, and thus these filmic juxtapositions have the effect of demonstrating emphatically that Native Americans still exist in the United States almost half a century after Curtis's declaration that the Indians were disappearing from the continent. The voice-over accompanying this series of photos corroborates the visual assertion: "What follows is the authentic account of twelve hours in the lives of a group of Indians who have come to Los Angeles, California. It reflects a life that is not true of all Indians today but typical of many" (*Exiles*). Following the introductory portraits and as the opening credits begin to roll, there are cuts to shots of several Bunker Hill tenement houses where the film is set. These shots echo yet contrast with the Curtis stills of teepee villages the viewer has just seen. One effect of the juxtapositions is to transform Curtis's nostalgic look at a teepee village or at a group of people on horseback against the backdrop of the stone walls of Canyon de Chelly into a mid-twentieth-century urban residential neighborhood peopled with young, vibrant American Indians.

Mackenzie's use of the Curtis photographs in a sense anticipates the use to which Masayesva puts paintings by George Catlin at the end of *Imagining Indians* thirty-some years later. In Masayesva's documentary, as discussed in the previous chapter, the shots of the Catlin portraits break up or pixelate into dissolves of shots of the dental patient as she scratches at the camera lens. Masayesva employs a sort of match on action shot sequence: with each of the dissolves the patient's face replaces one of Catlin's images. In this sense she both literally and figuratively survives any attempt to make her disappear behind images of nineteenth-century Indians. It is as if through her actions the dental patient destroys the images at the same time she destroys the camera lens, thereby taking complete control of the image making. Similarly, the use to which Mackenzie puts the Curtis photographs implies that his actors are not hidden behind or defined by the stylized and ubiquitous images of a previous era. In many ways Catlin's pre–photographic era paintings are analogous to Curtis's photographs from the late nineteenth and early twentieth centuries. Both artists offer stylized images of Native Americans from a previous era in an effort to provide anthropological studies of what they consider vanishing peoples and cultures. And both Masayesva and Mackenzie replace such images with contemporary, living Indigenous actors.

Mackenzie anticipates Masayesva's approach in *Imagining Indians* in another way as well. He challenges the stereotypes that result from the especially powerful because ubiquitous photographs like Curtis's, and he simultaneously implies that the contemporary American Indians he is filming are worthy of memorializing. In *On Photography* Susan Sontag writes that "to photograph is to confer importance. . . . [T]here is no way to suppress the tendency inherent in all photographs to accord value to their subjects" (28). Like Masayesva, who puts the often unidentified men and women extras who play roles in Hollywood westerns front and center in his documentary, Mackenzie takes individuals from the tenements of inner-city Los Angeles and gives them names, personalities, and realistic, comprehensible motivations. As the heroes or protagonists of their own film, they take on an importance that no straight documentary would allow them. This aspect of Mackenzie's film starts with the initial filming of the Curtis stills that metamorphose into photographs of the actors.

One could perhaps assert that there is a troubling similarity between what Mackenzie does with his film in the late 1950s and what Curtis does with his photographs. In a sense, the filmmaker does indeed gather and preserve information about a carefully selected group of American Indians. Just as Curtis supplied clothing, accessories, and a studio setting for many of his photographs, Mackenzie carefully selects his subjects and his setting. The actors dress up, as it were, for the shoot. At the same time, however, one of the startling effects of the way Mackenzie uses the Curtis photos belies such an assertion. Mackenzie's use of the photographs can be seen to challenge Curtis's very premise, a premise and attitude that survives even in the headline of a contemporary review of *The Exiles* in the *New York Times*: "A Cinema Saga of the 'Vanishing American'" (McDonald). The headline gets it wrong, of course. These Americans are not vanishing. They are neither fading into oblivion nor becoming lost in a distant past. Indeed, the film makes the present of their presence emphatically clear. They are walking the same streets as the mainstream viewer, living in the same neighborhoods, frequenting the same bars and other locales, listening to the same radio programs, watching the same movies and television programs, and shopping at the same markets.

Along with the juxtaposition of the two sets of photographs, Mackenzie's film interweaves a sound bridge to link two different eras: the era that Curtis's photographs simulate and the era that Mackenzie's film presents. The sound bridge consists of a steady, low drumbeat that accompanies the shots of the Curtis photographs, music that continues during the shots of the stills of the cast and of the Bunker Hill neighborhood. With the transition to modern Los Angeles, however, what seems at first an almost clichéd "Indian" solo drum beat suddenly becomes drumming accompanied by voices and jingles. The nondiegetic sound of the opening sequence thus links the two eras, and simultaneously the soundtrack anticipates the end of the film when the actors, some of whom wear bells on their legs, convene on top of Hill X to drum, sing, and dance. What the audience first hears simply as establishing, mood-setting background music accompanying the Curtis photographs (nondiegetic sound), then, turns out to be just the opposite: very vibrant drumming and singing that accompanies the photograph shots of the actors themselves. At the end of the film, this music is accompanied by other diegetic sounds: the honking of automobile horns, the people's laughter, and the friendly noise of their greeting one another late at night after the bars have closed.

A third means through which the film immediately bridges the gap between past and present is with its use of a documentary-style voice-over. As the film begins, even before the opening credits, an unidentified male voice-over accompanies the shots of the series of Curtis photographs: "Once the American Indian lived in the ordered freedom of his own culture. Then, in the nineteenth century, the white man confined him within the boundaries of the tribal reservation. The old people remembered the past. They witnessed great changes. Many of their children stayed on the reservation, but others of a new generation wandered into the cities" (*Exiles*). The use of the verb *to wander* to describe the effects of the urban relocation plan of the 1950s and 1960s is of course problematic, suggesting as it does that relocation and termination policies resulted in completely voluntary and fortunate moves from different reservations into various urban centers across the West and Midwest. The term *exile* of the film's title seems much more appropriate. Relocation was not necessarily a happy choice: "For most the decision to relocate was not a selection between various viable life alternatives but rather a desperate last resort," maintains Larry Burt (89), for example. Despite the problematic word choice and the images that such a word summons, the voice-over coinciding with the shot of a photograph of the face of Yvonne, a contemporary Indian woman, does bring the viewer both visually and aurally immediately from a past that the Curtis photographs evoke into the mid-twentieth century. Simultaneous with the voice-over statement about "a new generation" emigrating to the cities, a dissolve takes the viewer from a shot of a Comanche woman beside her cradled baby, zooms to an extreme close-up of the baby (Curtis 19: *A Comanche Mother*), and then dissolves to a close-up shot of the face of one of the actors in *The Exiles*. Maintaining a graphic continuity, similar close-up shots of several of the other actors come in rapid succession.

These juxtapositions of the old with the new suggest yet another tension in the film: the combination of two genres. Mackenzie evokes the genre of the documentary in several ways: he uses the Curtis shots to set a context at the very opening; he provides an initial male voice-over, which offers a verbal equivalent of an establishing shot; he makes liberal use of the camera's apparently candid street shots; and he chooses black and white for the filming. At the same time, the film's plot counters this documentary promise by developing a narrative film. In actual fact, Mackenzie's actors agreed to play "themselves in scenarios based on their experiences" (Straus), and the choice of black-and-white film was as much a result of economics as an aesthetic choice, "produced with an initial budget of the $539 in the filmmaker's savings account" (Goldsmith). But the film provides a creative reenactment of a night in the lives of several relocated urban American Indians, and as such it stands between two genres. Like Masayesva's film, Mackenzie's too is a documentary and narrative fiction film hybrid.

Mackenzie's use of sound functions as one his of his framing devices. That is, the opening is linked with the closing through similar sound as mentioned above. Still another of the film's framing devices is Yvonne's narrative. She has the first of the film's several extended interior monologues as well as the last, and in both cases, she is either actually shopping or window shopping. The film's final shot is from her perspective as well. According to a reviewer's conversation with the director, the material for these interior monologues was "culled from hours of tape that Mr. MacKenzie [*sic*] had made with Yvonne, Homer, and Tommy discussing their real lives, ambitions and feelings" (McDonald). The film proper opens with shots of Yvonne walking through an open market, and the viewer sees the produce and fish stands as the camera often focuses on the prices of items such as potatoes or fish. These shots are accompanied by Yvonne's monologue as voice-over. She introduces herself, in a way, by thinking aloud about her baby and how she wants the best for that baby. She speaks of her dreams and her aspirations, especially her hopes for a good life for the baby, and that best includes her raising the child in the city and providing opportunities that she maintains she never had growing up in San Carlos, Arizona: "I don't know what to do sometimes, now I'm having so much trouble. And sometimes I feel that I'm happy where I'm at because I have that little baby coming, and I always wanted a little baby. At least I'm getting one thing I want that was a little child of my own. I don't think I want to take the little baby back to San Carlos. I'd rather have him raised out here. I want him to speak English and try and maybe go to college or become something. I would like the baby to have the things I didn't have in my life" (*Exiles*). Given that Yvonne speaks this interior monologue while the film captures visually the scenes of the marketplace, the subtext here is that her child will perhaps be able to buy some of the products that her mother can look at but evidently cannot afford to buy.

Mackenzie shows Yvonne to be somewhat distanced from the mainstream hustle and bustle of buying and selling at the market in that although she does carry a bag of groceries, the viewer does not see her actually buy anything. Back at the apartment she again remains aloof, keeping a distance from Homer and his mostly idle male friends; she cooks for them but does not eat with them, nor does she partake in their joking around. While cooking, she muses on their aimlessness and her own sense of isolation and dissatisfaction:

> Well, if the boys weren't hanging around and staying at the house all the time, he [Homer] would stay home. At least Homer did try to look for a job, but the rest of the guys I don't think they really tried for a job. I see them here almost every day. I wish a lot of times he'd stay home a lot, but he doesn't. And he asks me if I want to go anyplace, down to the theaters or down to shop. He'd usually take me along, but he'd drop me off, and he don't pick me up when I ask him to. (*Exiles*)

The theme of Yvonne's social and financial isolation is evident again in the theater where she goes to spend the evening while the boys are out on the town. According to the marquee Yvonne watches a Western, *The Iron Sheriff* (1957), and that film was indeed playing at the theaters when Mackenzie was filming. The one passage of the film that the viewer hears is a male voice saying, "I mean it lady: I only got ten bucks left in the world" (*Exiles*). The passage is especially poignant in that although *The Iron Sheriff* is lighted on the marquee as Yvonne enters the theater, the lines she hears are not from that film; rather Mackenzie seems to have chosen them intentionally to make the point about money. The idea of tight economic circumstances is reinforced when the viewer hears the concessions jingle that comes on at intermission yet sees that Yvonne remains sitting. She apparently does not get up to go buy any of the advertised candy or popcorn.

There is an important thematic and structural logic to the fact that Yvonne is supposed to be watching a Western, albeit *The Iron Sheriff*, a Western with no Indian plot or character. That it is a Western is appropriate not only because "Westerns reach the height of their popularity" during the 1950s, but also because they have always been far and away the dominant medium and genre for depictions of American Indians. Furthermore, even though some of the popular Westerns of the era did tend to show "more sensitivity towards the history and social problems of their Native American characters" than others (Hilger, *From Savage* 98), the films were by definition set in the nineteenth century and any significant or speaking roles were played by non-Indians. They thus doubly insist on the disappearance of American Indians. Despite their being set in the past, however, some of the thematics of these Westerns have a contemporary ring to them. One such theme has to do with the principle of assimilation, a principle underlying urban relocation policies. In her study *Making the White Man's Indian*, Angela Aleiss writes that after the Second World War Hollywood was ready to depict "Indian/white brotherhood," as a means to signal "that tolerance was now Hollywood's weapon against frontier discrimination as well as the solution to hostile race relations" (81). Aleiss refers to *Broken Arrow* (1950), arguing that beneath its "appeal for reform was a plea for Indian assimilation into white society. Hollywood Indians could now stand alongside the movie's white heroes, provided they compromised their heritage" (81). Two of those non-Indian Hollywood Indians standing beside the film's white heroes are Cochise (Jeff Chandler) and Morningstar (Debra Padgett). But by 1956 and John Ford's *The Searchers*, argues Aleiss, all that changed: with that film, "peaceful Indian/white frontier relations were shattered. Gone were the postwar ideals of tolerance and brotherhood. . . . [T]he movie's box-office success established a turning point: Indians became society's victims and faced a life of frustration and alienation on both the Western frontier and in America's urban centers" (101).

The Iron Sheriff is not the only Western that Mackenzie uses intertextually. When Homer accompanies his friend Rico to the latter's apartment, everyone in the small tenement apartment is watching what appears to be a Western on the television. It is certainly no coincidence that at the moment the two men are in the apartment so that the viewer is thus privy to that private space, a Western plays on the television. The viewer does not see the television screen but does hear one particular excerpt: "That'll teach the moon-faced 'Injun' to have more respect for his betters" (*Exiles*). With its associations and specific reference to Indians, such an intertextual moment calls the contemporary viewer's attention to the uniqueness of Mackenzie's film. America's movie-going public was enamored with Hollywood Westerns and their reductive and stereotypical depictions of American Indians at this time, and at the very height of their popularity Mackenzie challenges the ethics and legitimacy of these widely distributed movies. *The Exiles* is simply very different from what the public would have been used to in the late 1950s and early 1960s. The contemporary audience would have been familiar with the depictions of Indians of another era in popular Westerns on television and in the movie theaters, but not as neighbors. Mackenzie's film thus reemphasizes that these characters are indeed "Indian" and they do indeed live in modern-day Los Angeles.

Mackenzie's use of the Curtis photographs and references to mainstream Westerns are nods to the past, but his use of other media insists on the present. Part of the film's diegetic sound, for example, includes contemporary hit-parade music, including tunes by The Revels. According to Steven Rosen, who does some rewarding digging concerning the film's soundtrack, among the film's "other accomplishments was a thrilling and innovative rock 'n' roll soundtrack, featuring unknown raucously celebratory instrumentals and a few wistful ballads presented as if they were the day's biggest hits. They were heard as coming from radios and barroom jukeboxes, part of the natural, ambient environment of L.A. at the time" (Rosen). The characters are shown to be listening to the mainstream pop music of the day, and the soundtrack thus demonstrates how Mackenzie takes the trouble to carefully distinguish his characters from those stuck in the nineteenth century of Hollywood's Westerns and set them in the era contemporary with the early days of rock and roll.

After watching the movie, Yvonne window shops as she makes her leisurely way toward her girlfriend's apartment where she will spend the night, while Homer and the others are partying on Hill X. The viewer is again privy to her thoughts through an interior monologue. This time she looks at merchandise such as shoes, watches, jewelry, and dresses. She seems to be focusing on shop-display items that are clearly out of her price range, and thus the film might imply her economic entrapment. But if not being able to buy is on her mind at all, she doesn't share any such thoughts with the viewer. Instead, the accompanying monologue suggests that her thoughts are not on material goods at all, and the viewer gets an account something much less tangible, her past and her hopes for the future:

I don't remember much from when I was a child, after my mother died or even before. But right now it isn't so bad as when I was a child. And I've always wanted to go, get away from my people there, and all that, and go someplace where somebody will maybe, ah, make me feel different and be happier. That's why I'm glad I came out to Los Angeles. Well, all my life I wanted to get married in the church and wanted to wear a wedding gown, you know, not too many people, but I wanted to get married in a church, and be blessed, have a nice house. And I wanted two little girls and two boys. That's all I wanted just four kids. I used to pray every night before I went to bed and ask for something that I wanted, and I never got it, or it seems like my prayers were never answered. So I just gave up, and now I don't hardly go to church or don't say my prayers sometimes. Well, I stopped going to church and all that already, but I haven't started drinking or hanging out around Main Street yet. I know that will never come for me. I want my baby, and I want to raise him up myself. I think I could do it. I don't know; I have to wait and see. (*Exiles*)

In the background accompanying Yvonne's monologue is the city street, and especially prevalent as part of that mise-en-scène are the neon signs. As Yvonne thinks about the praying she has done and stopped doing and about how it seems her prayers have seldom been answered, a neon sign that reads "Gloria" is strikingly visible in the background. In that her thoughts return to the baby and to the assertion that she wants to raise the baby by herself, the film recalls her earlier monologue in which she mentions that she is happy to be pregnant: "At least I'm getting one thing I want," she says early in the film, "a child of my own" (*Exiles*).

Yvonne's narrative suggests tension between what she thinks and hopes and her living situation with Homer, and the film includes parallel interior monologues from Homer, the father of Yvonne's baby, and from Tommy, a mutual friend. Homer's monologue creates a similar sort of tension between what the viewer sees and what Homer asserts about his life in Los Angeles. Through his monologue, he insists that he is happy to be in the city, or at least that he prefers the city to the reservation, but he does acknowledge that his life is going nowhere. It is almost as if the characters want to believe one thing and take the viewer in one direction while other elements of the film take the viewer in another. Homer insists verbally that he prefers to be in the city, yet everything about his actions suggests otherwise. *The Exiles* as a film seems to suggest otherwise as well. This counter-suggestion is perhaps most evident in the sequence involving Homer's first monologue, a monologue that begins as he sits in the bar, Café Ritz, with several of his friends:

It's the same thing all over and over again. I sit there and listen to them talk over and over, you know, to them talk over the same subject. Guys want to tell you about their troubles and all that. Especially when they get high, you know, they tell you about, you know, how much money he lost or who took his girl out or something like that, you know, and that's old stuff. When I want to go in a bar I don't like to just sit around, you know, I like to, you know, have some kind of excitement, you know, get in a fight or something, you know. (*Exiles*)

In the course of his monologue, Homer recounts his experiences of quitting high school and of joining the Navy. He maintains that he thought joining up might help him because he had begun to drink so much, but he confesses that it actually "made it worse." Then he came to Main Street in Los Angeles where he has made friends: "Then I met this girl from home, you know, same tribe. So after that, every weekend, every chance I get I come down there. I was pretty bad off too, you know, when I was, got discharged, drinking every day, man, never miss a day."

In this monologue, Mackenzie is able to contrast Homer's life in Los Angeles with his earlier life in Arizona:

Well, me, I grew up in Valentine, Arizona. You can hardly see it on a map, and we used to sit by the store, you know, in front of the trading post, and make fun of, you know, laugh at the tourists as they'd come from somewhere, you know, wearing Bermuda shorts and all that and cameras, and some of them used to take pictures of us, you know, sitting around there. Soon as they'd get through taking the picture we'd go up there and get some money off them.

That was good, them days. My dad worked there for a hospital. I went to a public school there, I guess, for five years, I guess. (*Exiles*)

As the viewer listens to the monologue, which clearly suggests a preference for his Arizona home, Homer and his friend Rico walk out of the Ritz bar, into another establishment where Homer gets a letter from home. The two of them then walk to a liquor store. The tension suggested by the contrast between Homer's former and present situations is intensified and corroborated by the letter he gets from home and the visual flashback that the letter provokes.

As a filmic device, the flashback enables the viewer to see what Homer thinks as he reads the letter. The flashback also provides the filmmaker a means to suggest the contents of the letter, as well as to show the viewer what might actually be going on at home. This flashback provides the film its one and only scene outside the city, evidently on the reservation, the place Homer would call home, or what was home before he left for the navy and the city. The scene of home is framed with the shots of Homer standing outside Royal Liquor, reading the letter from, as he says, "back home." He opens the envelope to find a photograph of an unidentified couple, perhaps his parents. As he leans against the liquor-store window, reading the letter by the light from inside, he remembers or visualizes home, which he has identified as Valentine, Arizona. The letter includes a return address of Peach Springs, visible to the viewer. The two towns are actually within a few miles of each other, both on Route 66, just west of Flagstaff.

The Arizona scene itself recalls the opening moments of the film, as it begins with a dissolve from the photograph Homer is holding to a shot of the man pictured in that photograph. He sits in the shade of a large tree, shaking a rattle, and singing. Two women, Homer's mother and sister perhaps, or mother and grandmother, listen to the old man and playfully toss pebbles at him as he sings. Two children run out of the house, laughing and chasing each other, trying to splash each other with water. A visitor comes by on horseback and speaks briefly with the man with the rattle before riding off. As the camera follows the man on horseback, the viewer hears the song, and as the camera zooms out, widening the angle and offering a somewhat romantic extreme long shot of the man on horseback set against a mountainous Arizona landscape, the singing continues. Thus, the initially diegetic sound of voice and rattle becomes nondiegetic, accompanying the man on horseback as he rides away. He recedes to where he is well out of earshot, but the audience still hears the music. Given its long focal length and subject matter, the shot recalls one of the opening shots of the Edward Curtis stills: the Indians on horseback beneath the towering cliffs of Canyon de Chelly, just as the snapshot of the couple enclosed in the letter recalls the opening sequence and juxtaposition of Curtis photographs with portraits of the actors themselves.

The juxtaposition of the urban with the rural enables Mackenzie to demonstrate the thoughts that the letter from home brings Homer, and the flashback scene works to underscore the film's recurring tension between city and country, between the two ideas of home. Even though Homer insists verbally that he prefers to be in and to remain in the city, visually the flashback implies otherwise. With the Arizona scene the film suggests an idyllic home from which Homer is obviously distanced or alienated from and nostalgic for. The power of the flashback results from its stark contrasts: the Arizona scene is shot in bright daylight, which contrasts vividly with the nighttime and artificial light of the city. The family members in Arizona sit and play in shirtsleeves, suggesting warmth as opposed to the chill of the city night suggested by the jackets that everyone wears. The old man's singing and shaking of his rattle sound a dramatic contrast to the city's traffic noise and the music of radios and jukeboxes. The Arizona scene exudes contentment and fulfillment. There is humor, laughter, and good-natured fun among family members. The children are playing, running, laughing. A friendly neighbor or relative drops by. The urban scene, in contrast, is peopled by strangers and characterized by drinking and carousing.

The effect of the flashback is especially telling in its visual and aural contrast, but even through his monologue, Homer suggests a level of discontent in the city. As he and Rico walk to Rico's place to get some cash for their card game, Homer continues his monologue, as if talking to himself, again hinting at a nostalgia for a better place, a better time: "My people mostly roamed all over the place, two, three hundred years ago. Before the white man came in, you know; well, they used to move all over the place, all over the canyon, you know, from the canyon up and then back down again, you know; they did a lot of farming around there, corn, squash, and I guess they lived mostly off the land, you know, all kinds of, you know, berries and all that. I'd rather be in that time, than, you know, in this time now" (*Exiles*). Homer perhaps paints a rather romantic picture here, but as a reflection of what he is thinking, the passage is clear. He cherishes an impossible dream of returning to the land. Instead of attempting in any way to realize his dream, and instead of spending time with Yvonne, who is carrying his child, he spends the night drinking, losing at poker, fighting with friends and strangers, and observing others doing the same.

Interspersed with Homer's evening at the poker table and Yvonne's time at the movie theater are scenes of Tommy's evening and night with his friend Cliff and two women from the bar, Mary and Claudia. They meet in the Café Ritz and then leave to go dancing. When they stop at a gas station, Tommy offers his monologue. Again, the monologue serves as a means for the audience to get to know the character, and it also serves to heighten the tension between what the character says about his having a good time in the city and the filmic depiction of that time.

> I figure a person that lives their regular lives in a worse world than I do, because that, they want to live the way I do, but they just can't do it. And look at me: I wanted that regular life, you know, my poached eggs, and, you know, Ovaltine and stuff like that in the morning, and then, ah, get in bed at certain times or have somebody kiss me every night, you know, or have somebody that I trust. I'll take care of myself. I can make it good; I can make it bad. It's up to me, you know. As long as I feel strong the way I always feel, well, it'll never get me down. And I know when it does. I seen my, I seen my days, I seen good days. I get my kicks.
>
> So that's the way it is down there, you know, just like a merry-go-round, and just wheel and deal you know, just go round and round. You meet your buddies, and, you know, you start drinking and next thing you know Monday rolls by, and Tuesday, and then I'm still going, and it keeps going on, you know, from day to day and months. Before you know it, man, a year's gone. And it's still the same. Just like when you go to jail it's the same thing. When I'm in jail, I don't worry about it, 'cause I can do time in there. I mean, time is just time to me. I'm doing it outside so I can do it inside. (*Exiles*)

Mackenzie interrupts this monologue several times with scenes at the gas station as Tommy walks around, talking to Cliff, buying gas and cigarettes with Mary's money, and finally driving off and rather heartlessly abandoning her. The scene itself is an example of the kind of life Tommy is living. He and the others are boisterous and having a seemingly good time throughout it all, but as in other such scenes, in this scene there is an undercurrent of dissatisfaction and frustration.

Tommy curiously equates jail time and non-jail time, and his sense of doing time is reasserted, as it were, at the end of the film when he insists that everyone will get together to do precisely the same thing the next night. That is, Tommy twice insists that the coming Saturday night will be very much a repeat of the Friday night that the characters have just experienced and that the viewer has just witnessed. As the people are leaving Hill X at dawn, he says "I'll see you guys tonight, about the same time." And then, just as he and his friends are arriving back at Bunker Hill in the city, he says, "Tonight we'll start all over again, okay? I got a couple of dollars left. Okay?" (*Exiles*)

Except for this denouement set at dawn in a Bunker Hill alley near Homer and Yvonne's apartment, the final sequence of *The Exiles* takes place late at night on top of Hill X. In another monologue, Homer describes part of the appeal of spending time there: "The bars close at two o'clock in the morning, you know, most all the Indians meet right after two too and then, ah, Indians like to get together where they won't be bothered, you know, watched or nothing like that, and we turn loose, want to get out there and just be free, you know, where nobody won't watch you and nobody won't bother you or nothing where nobody's watching you, every move you make" (*Exiles*). As Homer shares these lines with the viewer, he is still on Main Street, sitting in the car watching the goings-on along the street in front of the bars. The viewer gets to see what is going on late night on Main Street. The police are pictured on patrol, and one officer twirls his billy club as he stands outside a bar. Several policemen are busy arresting a drunken man; they force him into a squad car. Also interspersed with Homer's comments are background dispatches from the police radios. Though none of the characters the viewer meets is in trouble with the police this Friday night, Tommy does make clear that he has been in jail, and the suggestion is clear that anyone of them, with the exception of Yvonne, could be in a literal jail at any time. Given the interlacing of Homer's comment that the police are "watching every move you make" with the shots of the police in action, it is clear that it is the police who are watching the Indians. Hill X is, thus, all the more a sanctuary, a place to be free of them, a place "outside of" (*Exiles*) and away from the city, if only for the remainder of one night.

Even though all three characters from whom the viewer gets monologues—Yvonne, Homer, and Tommy—insist that they want to stay in the city and that they prefer being in the city to being at home on the reservation or on the land, much of the nonverbal aspects of the film work against that insistence. In this sense the film is ambiguous and captures the complexities and conundrums the relocated American Indians face. If they have not exactly *wandered* into the city, they have come, for the most part, voluntarily, and they want their coming to work out; there will inevitably be some nostalgia and perhaps a little regret, but all three of them know that they must carry on. Where the film leaves no ambiguity is in its depiction of contemporary American Indians with very real, immediate concerns. Their lives, this film insists, cannot be all that different from the lives of many of their non-Indian neighbors. Stuck in an urban present, they yearn for a better yet urban future.

Mackenzie's seventy-two-minute independent black-and-white film has much in common with a film made a decade later, based on N. Scott Momaday's Pulitzer Prize–winning novel, *House Made of Dawn*. Both films offer glimpses of the lives of several American Indians who have relocated to Los Angeles. In the context of the relocation program of the 1950s, N. Scott Momaday states in an interview with Joanna Hearne that "nothing much had been done with that" (Hearne, "N. Scott Momaday Interview"). Momaday can make the statement in part because it is hardly possible that either he or Richardson Morse, who directed the film version of Momaday's novel, was aware of Kent Mackenzie's *The Exiles*. Although it circulated at some festivals, it simply was not distributed. The filming of *The Exiles* predates *House Made of Dawn* (the novel) by a decade, and the release of the film (1961) predates the film of *House* by about a decade also. Nevertheless, the two films complement each other in important ways. Like Mackenzie's film, the film version of the novel addresses some of the results of urban relocation as it presents mid-twentieth-century Indian characters who are, to differing degrees, stuck in the city, away from home.

THREE

The Native Presence in Film

House Made of Dawn

The Native presence, when it's allowed to express itself,
is very powerful. I knew that that's what was going on, and it helped
me to be encouraged. I know that movies can be made about Indians
and they're going to look different, they're going to sound different,
and this is the beginning of it.

—Larry Littlebird, in Hearne, "Larry Littlebird Interview"

N. Scott Momaday published his novel *House Made of Dawn* in 1968, and
in 1972 non-Native filmmaker Richardson Morse directed a film adaptation.
The respective receptions of novel and film could hardly have been more different. The year after its publication, the novel won the Pulitzer Prize for Literature and has been in print and widely available ever since. In addition to
clearly launching Momaday's own literary career, the novel initiated "what is
called the renaissance of American Indian literature," according to LaVonne
Ruoff, who also writes "Momaday became the most influential American
Indian writer in the late 1960s and early 1970s. . . . [His novel] provided
an example that several later Indian novelists followed" (*American Indian*
76). Kenneth Lincoln defines an American Indian literary renaissance from
the publication of Momaday's novel. Scholarly acclaim and critical attention grew every decade for thirty years after the novel's publication. Including a few book-length studies, the *MLA Bibliography* lists twelve scholarly
works devoted to the novel in the 1970s, twenty-three in the 1980s, more than
two dozen in the 1990s, and another dozen or so in the first decade of the
twenty-first century.

In contrast to the novel's success and centrality in the world of American Indian literatures, the film adaptation, produced by first-time director-producer
Richardson Morse at his own expense, could not find a distributor; and after
a few initial screenings to small audiences, it was essentially shelved. Momaday reported in an interview in 1975 that the film "has never been distributed" (Morgan 54), and as Jacquelyn Kilpatrick writes in 1999, "In attempting to locate a film copy of *House Made of Dawn*, researchers generally
have serious difficulty. It is simply not available. . . . It seems to have simply

'vanished' from all but a few university video libraries" (182). The film is finally more widely available, but as Morse himself reports in a 2005 interview, "it was quite totally unseen for damn near 30 years" (Hearne, "Richardson Morse Interview").

As a result of its relative obscurity, the film has received very little scholarly attention. Nancy Schmidt lists the film in the mid-1970s as an example of "using films as the core of an anthropology course," and includes it in the section on "Intersocietal Relationships" (34), but she is able to incorporate it into her syllabus only because there was a special screening at her university, not because the film was otherwise available. In the introduction to a section called "The Indian in the Film: Later Views" in *The Pretend Indians* (1980), Gretchen Bataille and Charles Silet mention but do not discuss the film in any detail, noting that it "is available but has been shown only to limited audiences." The authors do make the important argument, however, that it is an Indian film:

> [b]ased on a Pulitzer Prize–winning novel written by a Kiowa Indian, directed and produced by Harold Littlebird [*sic*] and featuring many new Indian actors, this film demonstrates what can be done despite a low budget and a lack of "Hollywood" experience. Although the film may receive criticism on selected technical issues or resentment from some Native Americans who would have preferred that the religious peyote ritual be omitted, it is generally a fine film which visually presents Native American experiences as something other than the usual fare of "cowboys and Indians." (73)

That neither Beverley Singer nor Kirsten Knopf mentions the film in their respective studies is further indication of its relative obscurity. Rollins and O'Conner provide the film a sentence or two (14, 23), and both Hilger and Kilpatrick devote a few pages to helpful plot summaries, but neither offers further analysis of the film. (See Hilger, *American* 143, and *From Savage* 253–55; and see Kilpatrick 180–82).

House Made of Dawn, although not an award-winning film nor widely distributed in its time, stands out now, in retrospect, as marking an important moment in the history of American Indian cinema. It can be seen to qualify as an Indigenous film, as Bataille and Silet note, and it thus constitutes one of the very first feature-length American Indian fiction films—even though the director is non-Native and the non-Native actor John Saxon plays the crucial role of Tosamah. As an Indian film it is groundbreaking on several levels: it is based on a novel written by an American Indian writer who coauthored the screenplay; with exception of the role of Tosamah, American Indians play Indian roles (even to the extent that Pueblo men take the roles of Pueblo characters); it includes instances of Pueblo language use; it has American Indian issues at its center; and it has a contemporary, twentieth-century setting.

As such, *House Made of Dawn* signals or at least reflects a major step in the history of film. Analysis of it therefore offers insights into many concerns important to discussions of subsequent American Indian cinema generally.

This chapter addresses some of these concerns. The film's limited distribution is indicative of the very limited availability and accessibility of so many Indigenous films in general. The casting underscores the importance of Indigenous actors taking Indigenous roles, and the directing by a non-Indigenous director calls attention to issues surrounding the ethnic identities of producers, directors, and writers in the context of Indigenous film. The adaptation from novel to film raises questions about notions of fidelity and the role of source material in telling an Indigenous story on film. The temporal setting suggests ways in which Indigenous film does make use of contemporary history. The setting also suggests an insistence on an Indigenous way of viewing that history. The location shooting implies the fundamental centrality of the land, of a sense of the homeland, and of the connection between place and identity. Like many films with Native Americans as their subjects, *House Made of Dawn* raises issues concerning the filming of the sacred or the ceremonial. Depictions such as those of Indian characters' drinking or of their participating in ceremonies invite conversations about the extent to which Indigenous cinema either reinscribes or challenges stereotypes engendered and perpetuated by Hollywood film and other media of mainstream culture.

With these topics come related thematic concerns. The early 1970s saw the production of many so-called liberal or anti-Western films, such as *Little Big Man*, *Soldier Blue*, and *A Man Called Horse* (all 1970); *Ulzana's Raid* (1972); and *The Outlaw Josey Wales* (1976). Such films turn the tables on the typical Hollywood fare of Indians as props or mere savages, and they promise fuller, more detailed and sympathetic portraits of their Indian characters than were available to viewers of the classic Hollywood Westerns. Some of these films even purportedly tell the stories from an Indigenous point of view, often vilifying the non-Indian oppressor rather than the Indians. These films from the 1970s often use nineteenth-century Indian massacres as thinly veiled allusions to the horrors of the war in Vietnam. But as the film titles themselves suggest, these films are still finally concerned with the non-Indian heroes; and in each case, the setting remains nineteenth century. *House Made of Dawn*, in contrast, sets the viewer down in the midst of the twentieth century and features American Indian characters throughout. Morse's film also includes thematic elements common to several other, later Indigenous North American films, notably its presentation at the outset of the death of an elder whose presence and influence is felt throughout, despite that death. This representation allows the film to talk back to Hollywood's insistence on the vanishing Indian at the same time it presents the possibility of breaking Hollywood's hold. As

Momaday himself tells Gretchen Bataille in an interview, "The days of the befeathered Indian chasing John Wayne across the screen are gone, and it's good that they are" (66).

The credits list both Richardson Morse and N. Scott Momaday as authors of the screenplay, but Momaday maintained in a 1977 interview that he actually had "very little to do with the film" (Bataille 65). In another interview, Momaday recalls to Hearne that he "wasn't in on the actual filming . . . wasn't on location much of the time" (Hearne, "N. Scott Momaday Interview"). According to Morse, in stark contrast, Momaday is not quite accurate in recalling the authorship of the screenplay. The director relays that he wanted Momaday to do the screenplay from the very beginning; indeed, he maintains that is one of the reasons he was able to buy the movie rights in the first place: "One of the things that perhaps appealed to Scott, and that let him give the rights to somebody who was so totally inexperienced, was that I wanted him to do the screenplay." And further, according to Morse, Momaday did indeed do "the writing of the screenplay. And as I recall, he would bring pages to me, and then I might have ideas or might not have ideas, and he might try a slightly different direction or tell me why we shouldn't go in a different direction. But I have a sense that certainly 90% of what was put down on paper was originally put down by Scott, with then maybe some editing coming from me" (Hearne, "Richardson Morse Interview"). Whether or not he had much to do with other aspects of the film, Momaday does acknowledge at one point that he did contribute significantly by preparing the screenplay and thus by determining how and what ideas of the novel would be put on film. He maintains that he also had a voice in choosing the locations for the shooting: "I had something to do with determining where the filming should be done. I was familiar with the landscape of the novel and could be helpful in pointing out various locales." Momaday also points out that he "was happy with the film that was made. The external photography was good; the way the race and the man running worked as a thread throughout was well done" (Bataille 65).

Not everything about the film pleased Momaday, however: "The acting was not particularly distinguished, but I'm not sure that distinguished acting was called for in the parts" (Bataille 64). In none of his interviews does Momaday allude to the fact that a non-Indian plays the part of Tosamah, nor does he mention that he would like to have played that part himself. Given the potential of this production to make an important statement about American Indian film, Tosamah, played by accomplished non-Native actor John Saxon (*The Appaloosa*, 1966; *Joe Kidd*, 1972), constituted an unfortunate casting choice, but not because Saxon does not do a decent job with the part; rather, reviewers object to a non-Indian's taking an Indian role, and such an important, central role at that. As Jacquelyn Kilpatrick writes, "perhaps if the part had been played by a Native American actor such as Chief Dan George or Floyd Westerman, the message would have come through more clearly in the film version" (182). In a 2004 interview for the Smithsonian's National Museum of the American Indian, Morse comments that casting Saxon "was a mistake. Not that John was bad. John did a good actor's performance. But Scott would have been much better, especially in the sermon, which he read brilliantly" (Hearne, "Richardson Morse Interview").

Except for the role of Tosamah, the Indian parts are played by Indian actors, and Morse comments that "there are some marvelous performances in it—especially Jay Varela, who plays Benally" (Hearne "Richardson Morse Interview"). The Pueblo man Larry Littlebird plays the protagonist Abel, and his "real-life" Pueblo grandfather Mesa Bird plays the character of Abel's grandfather, Francisco, unnamed in the film (the character is listed simply as "Grandfather" in the credits). In response to a question about the importance of Indian people taking the roles of Indian people, Larry Littlebird responds, saying that, from his perspective,

> the difference is, for example, in the Pueblo culture there are things that are just correct in the sensibilities. It's ingrained in them, in the people. We have an unspoken understanding of presence. And that presence, if it's going to be brought onto the screen, has to play itself. You cannot duplicate it. . . . [Non-Indian actors] can learn mannerisms and they can learn colloquialisms and they can learn ways of speaking that are peculiar to these people. But when they're viewed on the screen, they stand out rather than speak from the content of Pueblo people's history, thousands of years of being. And so those are the sensibilities that I think filmmakers wanting to tell stories of Native American people have to be aware of. (Hearne, "Larry Littlebird Interview")

Littlebird's attitudes concerning the significance of Indigenous acting anticipate those of Māori director Barry Barclay, who uses the term *interiority* to get at the idea of Indigenous sensibilities in Indigenous film. He maintains that with the idea of interiority something "is being asserted which is not easy to access" (Barclay 7), but part of the idea is that for these filmmakers and/or actors the location of the shoot is their ancestral home, as Littlebird comments. And on their own ground, as it were, they control the sensibilities. In addition to this somewhat amorphous and intangible idea of Indigenous sensibilities expressed through acting, there is the obvious and more overtly political sense that when Native people play the roles of Native characters on screen they are in a position to tell their own stories. They gain access to the means of self-representation. They take control of the nuance of telling and of the story itself. And as argued in the contexts of *Imagining Indians* and *The Exiles*, their very presence in a film with a contemporary setting makes manifest their survival and refutes one of Hollywood's dominant tropes, that of the vanishing Indian.

Although the film is based on a Pulitzer Prize–winning novel, viewers cannot necessarily ask that *House Made of Dawn*, or any film based on a work of fiction, simply reproduce the novel. Fidelity to an original text or straightforward reproduction is not what films based on novels are about, ultimately. Indeed, the number of differences in the two media alone disallows fidelity. According to Francesco Casetti in the context of adaptation theory, for example, "we are no longer confronted with a re-reading or a re-writing: rather, what we are dealing with is the reappearance, in another discursive field, of an element (a plot, a theme, a character, etc.) that has previously appeared elsewhere" (82). Furthermore, as R. Barton Palmer maintains, "An exclusive view of the adaptation as a replication closes off its discussion not only *per se*, but also *in se*" (2). André Bazin makes a similar point, maintaining that "all it takes is for the filmmakers to have enough visual imagination to create the cinematic equivalent of the style of the original, and for the critic to have the eyes to see it" ("Adaptation" 20). According to Linda Hutcheon, "an adaptation is a derivation that is not derivative—a work that is second without being secondary. It is its own plamipsestic thing" (9). Speaking about the adaptation of his novel in an interview with William Morgan, Momaday himself seems also to see a film adaptation being free from maintaining some essentialist fidelity to the source. He reports, "I think the film dealt honestly with the novel. It isn't a representation of the whole novel, but it deals fairly with a part of the novel. The producer once said to me that he could make eight different films of the book" (Morgan 55). Film theorist Robert Stam echoes this sentiment when he argues that "a single novelistic text comprises a series of verbal signals that can trigger a plethora of possible readings" ("Introduction" 15). It is instructive to touch on and compare a few of the most obvious differences between the novel *House Made of Dawn* and the film in the context of adaptation theory. Comparisons between the two are especially worthwhile in this instance because of the film's obscurity in contrast to the novel's immense success and relative popularity. Because of the film's relative inaccessibility, one comes to the film *House Made of Dawn* almost inevitably already being familiar with the novel and wanting to see the film because of the novel. This order stands in contrast to viewers of many film adaptations of novels.

Many of the points of comparison between novel and film have to do with characters and plot elements that Morse and/or Momaday omitted as they were making the film, yet the concept of *difference* is certainly preferable to *omission* in this context. It is important to note, for example, that a character very important to the novel does not find her way into the film at all, and that the film offers a streamlined plot. Perhaps the most important character and corresponding plot element that are not a part of the final cut of the film are those involving the character Angela Grace St. John. She is absent not because Momaday did not see a place for her in his screenplay, however. He wrote her into in the original script, but, according to Morse, all her scenes were cut during editing with Bill Brame: "I know there were certain scenes like all the scenes with Angela, who was played by Lee Meriwether—that are no longer in the film. And it's too bad because it's some of the best work Lee's ever done" (Hearne, "Richardson Morse Interview"). One can see in retrospect a subtextual irony in Angela's not making the final cut. In contrast to its Hollywood precursors, this Indigenous film disappears the would-be significant white character. She vanishes so completely in fact that she never even makes an appearance in the first place.

Another important character in the novel, another non-Indian, is Father Olguin. He has only a very small role in the film: he appears briefly in the opening sequence when Abel wakes him before dawn to tell him that Francisco has died. He also has a very brief voice-over as the viewer hears, but does not see, part of Abel's trial. One of Olguin's arguably important functions in the novel, in contrast to his being displaced in the film, is that he provides much of the historical perspective. In the novel, it is through Olguin's reading of an old, non-Indian priest's diary that the reader gains historical perspective and a sense of context for the novel's present action. Through this history the reader learns that the albino, Juan Reyes, is himself a Pueblo man, for instance, a heritage that the film does not clarify but which is thematically central to the novel. And through these journal entries the reader discovers much about the grandfather's past, especially how he has come to know and understand evil: "for evil had long since found him out and knew who he was" (Momaday 59–60). Drastically limiting Olguin's role also results in the film's ignoring the issue of the clash between the Pueblo and Christian religions, important to the novel, but very understated in the film. The extremely limited role of the non-Indian Father Olguin results in the film's privileging the Indian perspective.

In addition to differences in the cast of characters, there are also differences in plot sequences and related thematic issues that go with them. Most immediately apparent is that Morse offers a different temporal setting. The novel's action occurs in two distinct time periods: the summer of 1945, when Abel has just returned from having fought in World War II; and 1952, when Abel has gotten out of prison and has been "relocated" to Los Angeles. The film, in contrast, is set essentially a generation later, making Abel a veteran of the Vietnam War and his sojourn in Los Angeles somewhat arbitrary. One significant result of this difference in setting is that it greatly diminishes the emphasis—so apparent in the novel—on federal relocation and termination policies of the 1950s and early 1960s. In one interview Momaday offers a justification for the change in temporal setting: "In order to reflect the time span and the convolutions of time in the film one would have had to make a very long and complicated film," he says (Bataille 65). But in another, later interview he implies that the temporal setting of his novel was important, suggesting that he does indeed miss it in the film: "I think that was something that I was working with, an urban Indian, in a sense. And that was a new thing, you know, the 'Relocation' program, the '50s. Nothing much had been done with that, and it was such a reality" (Hearne, "N. Scott Momaday Interview"). The change in the temporal setting was primarily a practicality rather than thematic choice, however. It made filming easier and much less expensive, as there was no need for elaborate sets and vintage automobiles, for example.

One of the results of the film's Vietnam-era setting, Momaday implies, is that the idea of Indian urban relocation of the 1950s and 1960s loses much of its meaning. The main action of the film begins with shots of Abel arriving in the city, for example, as a voice-over explains why he is there: he has killed another man and has thus presumably come to the city after he has served his time in prison. According to a voice-over: "Abel, we feel it would be best for you if you were relocated in Los Angeles" (*House*). The character Tosamah in the film also alludes to the relocation policy, incorporating it into his sermon on *the word*: "Brothers and sisters, you have come here to live in the white man's world. Some not by choice but relocated by the white man" (*House*). Because taken out of its historical context, the issue as presented in the film becomes an ahistorical anachronism. Even though urban migration was still going on into the 1970s, it was significantly different from what it was in 1952 when it was part of the termination policies of the Truman and then Eisenhower administrations.

The federal government initiated the so-called Urban Indian Relocation Project in 1952, a program whose purpose was to encourage Indians to leave their reservation homes by relocating to such cities as Chicago, Denver, Salt Lake City, and Los Angeles. The program provided funding for the establishment of offices in these and other cities and provided a staff of social workers whose mission it was to help those who were relocating with their difficult transition from reservation to city. The program promised the newcomers temporary housing, an offer of four-weeks' start-up money, and help finding jobs and more permanent housing. The government did not keep all its promises, and one of the unlooked-for results of the initiative was the evolution of Indian ghettos in these cities: "Since accommodations had to fit within the bureau's aid package and Indian incomes, many ended up in lower-class neighborhoods. Tribal leaders frequently received complaints from relocatees or their families and how 'most in the first place went to skid row sections' or were moved into 'slum areas'" (Burt 90). During the early 1960s, with a democratic president and a new commissioner of Indian Affairs, Philleo Nash, "the BIA changed the name of the program [from 'relocation'] to 'employment assistance' since the name relocation had been so closely linked with the termination policies that by this time had become controversial and discredited. The bureau also began to place more emphasis on job training" than it had done previously (Burt 95).

Many aspects of Abel's experiences in Los Angeles in the film remain representative of Indian urban migration in general, even though the film offers a doubly ahistorical account of relocation. The transition to urban living was difficult, however, whether it took place in the early 1950s or two decades later, as the film presents it. And in this sense, Abel remains representative of one trying to negotiate these difficulties. Larry Burt points out that "for most the decision to relocate was not a selection between various viable life alternatives but rather a desperate last resort" (89). Those relocating, whether in the 1950s or the 1970s, faced difficulties finding housing and steady and satisfying work; they encountered racism and discrimination on the job and in the community; they experienced difficulties establishing their own communities because oftentimes fellow tribal members were scattered into several different cities across the country. Burt notes that relocation officials often intentionally sent people to the cities most distant from their reservations in order to discourage them from returning (see Burt 91). The film definitely succeeds in making these issues clear.

The difference in temporal setting between novel and film does not adversely affect the film's fidelity to the spirit of the source material. The point remains that Abel lands in Los Angeles and finds himself unable to keep his job or stay out of trouble with his racist employer or to avoid run-ins with the corrupt policeman Martinez. According to Burt, "cultural dislocation was perhaps the greatest problem. The fast-paced, competitive existence in cities represented a dramatic departure from the collective tribal world to which most were accustomed" (91). In this regard, completely independent of the novel, the film does a solid job of representing the serious difficulties Abel faces in trying to adjust to an urban life and lifestyle.

Abel's status as a veteran of the Vietnam War allows Morse to align his film with some of the very popular anti-Westerns of the era, and the setting had very practical benefits for the filmmaker as well. The careful and protracted attention Morse pays to the novel's peyote ceremony scene is yet another indication of the way he capitalized on the culture of the early 1970s. The peyote scene is a relatively small part of the novel; it occupies a proportionally much greater and therefore more central place in the film. The scene runs just over ten minutes in the seventy-seven-minute film, but it takes up only 5 pages of a 212-page novel. In other words, whereas barely 2 percent of the novel is devoted to the peyote scene, nearly 13 percent of the film is so dedicated.

Inclusion of the peyote ceremony in the film, as in the novel, raises the issue of when and how a film can be said to transgress when it appropriates the sacred and ceremonial. Such issues are especially prominent, in films like *A Man Called Horse*, with its depictions of a sweat lodge, and *Thunderheart*, with its (mis)representations of the Ghost Dance, for instance.

When asked about the emphasis the film places on the peyote ceremony, Momaday responds merely that it was important for the scene to be done imaginatively "because the peyote ceremony itself is highly imaginative and very dramatic. It is an artistic consideration more than anything else" (Bataille 65). As to whether or not depicting such a tribal ceremony is appropriate in the first place, Momaday seems feel that the film remains on the windy side of the controversy: "There are ineffable qualities of Indian religious experience; there are sacred areas that are sacred because they are private, and those are unavailable to us. There are always questions of that kind, whether you are making films or writing books" (Bataille 65). In other words, it seems as if Momaday does not feel that he inappropriately revealed anything that should have remained unrevealed. In a broader sense, he skirts the issue altogether when he asserts that in making films about American Indians, "we shouldn't worry about the representation of the cultural realities; that should be secondary to the idea of making an exciting, creative, and inspirational film" (Bataille 66).

As Momaday's comment makes clear, issues of religious freedom were very much at issue in the 1960s and 1970s. According to Alvin Josephy Jr. and his coauthors, "protesters and Indian leaders on reservations and in urban Indian communities demanded native cultural and religious rights" (Josephy, Nagel, and Johnson 209). The protests ultimately helped to spur passage of an "American Indian Religious Freedom Act" (August 11, 1978). The peyote scene thus implies a reference to and a comment on an important historical moment; it concerns the participants right to "believe, express, and exercise the traditional religions," as well as retain the right to the "use and possession of sacred objects, and the freedom to worship through ceremonials and traditional rites" (210). The film makes no overt reference concerning the legality of the peyote ceremony in the early 1970s, when it was illegal, even in the context of a religious ceremony.

Elements of the peyote scene relay important information to the viewer within the film itself as well, and it is thematically important. Depiction of the ceremony offers Morse another opportunity to depict Abel's voicelessness and his general inability to fit in, even among his male peers. It demonstrates emphatically Abel's inability to speak, and in this context, Momaday comments that "it is so important, there is an urgency to express his spirit, and he can't, he has no voice. That's done in the film all right, that's realized maybe especially in that Peyote scene" (Hearne "N. Scott Momaday Interview").

The scene shows contemporary Indian men practicing a ritual that is "traditional" but that is also clearly a borrowing from recent, non-Indian culture. The spittoons seem to be ordinary tin cans for example, and except for Tosamah, who has painted his face ceremoniously, the participants are unadorned and wear street clothes. During the ceremony, they express their concerns with their new urban environment, and their being together suggests a spiritual community formed in that environment. Through its several long takes and close-ups, the filming of the ceremony focuses intensely on the participants' faces, thereby hinting at their emotional states, the demonstration and depiction of which is a challenge to the Hollywood stereotype of a stoic Indian. Both Ben and another participant, for instance, show themselves to be so emotionally caught up in the ceremony and their own thoughts and prayers that they come to tears.

The film opens with a sequence in which Abel sits at his grandfather's deathbed, the very plot element with which the novel ends. Morse's choice to film the novel's final events as the opening sequence neatly defines the entire film in that that choice enables the filmmaker to emphasize and privilege the grandfather's dying and imply that the death motivates the plot. Most immediately, the viewer knows that the grandfather's death inspires Abel's run, but because the entire film can be understood as a series of this runner's flashbacks, it becomes clear that the elder's death has a significance. Thus, even though the grandfather dies within the first few seconds of film time, he is present throughout. A series of flashbacks enables the viewer to see the old man save the young boy Abelito from a rattlesnake and identify the albino as "Diablo," the embodiment of evil. The grandfather teaches the boy to hunt, and the viewer witnesses the adult Abel interact with him as they work side by side, cleaning a saddle, cleaning a bridle, and drilling turquoise. Although he dies in the opening moments, he speaks the film's final words in a voice-over. The words are especially important because they inspire Abel to rise and continue running after he has fallen.

Morse clearly challenges the stereotype of the vanishing Indian imposed by Hollywood cinema by insisting on the grandfather's presence and significance throughout Abel's youth and adulthood, even though he at the same time depicts the literal death of the individual man. Even in this literal depiction, however, Morse is able to challenge the mainstream, specifically by displacing or sublimating the dominant culture's Christian religion. Once Francisco dies, Abel walks to a wall hook and removes a turquoise necklace to place on the dead man's chest, turquoise perhaps made of the stone the viewer will see him drilling later in the film. Abel removes the necklace, but the camera lingers on the wall hook from which hangs a cross. This filmic moment calls attention to the essential uselessness of the cross in the ritual Abel is performing. Only after laying out the turquoise and performing a ritualistic cleansing

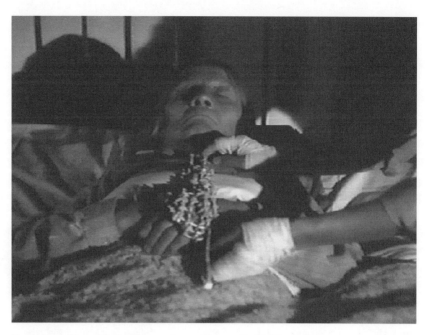

Death ritual. *House Made of Dawn*. Screen Capture. Firebird Productions.

of the body does Abel walk to the church to wake the priest and inform him: "My grandfather has died; you must bury him" (*House*). In this context a putatively Christian burial seems of little importance in comparison to the Pueblo ritual Abel performs. To reinforce the significance of Pueblo rather than Christian ritual, the film turns immediately from the church with its dim artificial light and follows Abel as he prepares for the dawn run. He takes bandages from his hands and smudges his face, arms, and chest with ash; he walks to the ridge, and as the sun breaks over the mesa, he begins to run. The film thus cues the viewer to see the grandfather's death as the impetus for Abel's healing, suggested by the removal of the bandages, as well as for his participating in the dawn run.

Abel has a series of flashbacks that the film presents as if they are the thoughts he has while he runs, and these flashbacks constitute essentially the entirety of the film. The film weaves together two main plot strands from this point. One strand concerns Abel's life on the reservation: his growing up with his grandfather, his losing the rooster-pull contest to the albino man, and finally his killing the albino man in a quasi-ceremonial encounter. The other plot strand, the main plot, so to speak, concerns Abel's time in Los Angeles: he arrives, meets Milly the social worker and two fellow American Indians, Ben Bennally and Tosamah; he falls in love with Milly, who reciprocates his affections, and he runs afoul of Martinez the corrupt policeman, who beats him badly. Ben and Milly realize that Abel is not able to cope in the fast-paced city, and together they convince him to "go home." The final scene in Los Angeles is of Abel boarding the bus to leave the city. The film ends, like the novel, as it begins: Abel is running across the mesas of his homeland.

Virtually the entire film, like the novel, can be understood as series of Abel's flashbacks as he runs, and his actual running frames the film. There are layers of flashbacks within the main Los Angeles experience, itself a flashback. When Milly asks Abel about his military service, for example, he flashes to a scene in which he is squatting with two others, presumably on the reservation. One of them asks him whether he killed anybody in the war, and he flashes back to a scene in which he remembers shooting someone. The next shot brings him and the viewer back to the two men on the reservation, before the next shot returns him to the office where he sits with Milly, who has just asked him the question about his military experience. This layered temporal complexity of the flashbacks underlies the structure and enables the film to offer a powerful sense of the influence of the past on the present. Indeed, the film makes manifest that the past palpably affects Abel's present. The film provides a contextual, inferred explanation for the man's voicelessness, for example. He is no more able to talk to Milly about his war experiences than he is able to talk to his two friends on the reservation or to his new acquaintances at the peyote ceremony.

As noted above, Momaday finds the running and the photography two of the film's greatest strengths, especially because they offer the viewer a sense of the landscape in New Mexico where the filming was done. Another aesthetically pleasing moment in the film, both visually and aurally, is not in the novel at all. In the novel it is not clear that Abel is even present at the peyote ceremony, but he is present in the film's rendition. During the peyote sequence, Abel tries unsuccessfully to speak. The shot begins with a close-up of his face, his mouth is open, tears run down his face, but he is unable to speak. The shot dissolves to a long shot of a Los Angeles highway at night. Accompanying the dissolve is a sound bridge, Ben singing. As the camera zooms slowly to medium close-ups of the two characters, Abel recognizes and then sings the song Ben has been trying to remember. As Abel sings, another dissolve overlays three images: medium close-up of Abel as he sings, long shot of the L.A. highway, and the grandfather working a hand operated jewelry drill. This shot introduces another flashback, this one to a time before the rooster pull. After the conversation between Abel and his grandfather, who speaks exclusively in Pueblo, left untranslated, there is yet another dissolve bringing the viewer back to Abel with Ben in Los Angeles as he finishes his song. In this way, the film offers a brilliant counter to Abel's voicelessness. He cannot speak, but he can sing, and sing beautifully. Littlebird has this to say about the scene of Abel with his grandfather:

It's so typical, because there's silence. There's silence. They're involved in their own activities, yet they're sitting side by side, and it isn't until awhile that they begin to speak to each other, and the old man speaks to Abel. This is what I mean about those sensibilities—he so understands the relationship between grandfather and grandson. He starts teasing Abel about cleaning this bridle for the horse. Abel's been gone for awhile, and the old man's got a new horse that he doesn't think this young kid is going to be able to ride, and he starts teasing him about it and it's just wonderful. There's a relational context that's so steeped in care and love for his grandson, but it's not, "Oh, grandson, I'm so proud of you!" which is what you typically see on the screen (Hearne, "Larry Littlebird Interview").

The overlay and juxtaposition of scenes of singing and working demonstrate the fellowship and friendship between Abel and Ben and between Abel and his grandfather, respectively. There is the suggestion of camaraderie and goodness inherent and embodied in these shots.

Other scenes contrast visually and thematically with this one. Through crosscutting, Morse effectively associates and links the forces of evil represented by a rattlesnake, the albino, and the corrupt policeman Martinez. These forces are of critical thematic importance to both the film and the novel, and the film manages to summarize the symbolic importance of evil through the use of several brief montage sequences. Early in the film, for example, a shot of Abel's grandfather shows him pulling the young Abel away from a coiled rattlesnake moments before it strikes. From the perspective of the grandfather, the viewer sees the snake strike but miss. It then slithers away toward the cornfield. Morse cuts from the snake to a shot of the albino dressed in black and wearing dark glasses; he is apparently standing at that same moment in that cornfield. The parallel editing clearly implies the proximity of snake and albino, both spatially and temporally. And the director further emphasizes this coexistence with the match between the snake striking and the albino smiling, almost as if the man has the teeth of a viper. The cut cues the viewer to associate the rattlesnake and the albino, obviously an association of symbolic and thematic importance. When the child Abelito asks who that man is, the grandfather replies in Spanish, "Diablo," the devil. At this point in the film, the viewer has also already witnessed the rooster-pull competition and so has already seen the albino beat Abel with the rooster. This incarnation of Diablo has gained the right to choose a contestant to beat with the "pulled" rooster by virtue of his victory, and he selects Abel from among the other competitors. Momaday recalls his feelings about creating the albino character for the screenplay: "I was very much interested in the Albino, and I thought that came off pretty well. It was visually really good, you know—to see him was to understand the power that he exercised over Abel and Francisco. Just visually he was good. It was important to me that he was played well, that it was there in its authenticity" (Hearne, "N. Scott Momaday Interview").

Through juxtaposition of scenes and use of a graphic match, Morse emphasizes the close association between the corrupt policeman and the albino, as well as the similarity in their relationships with Abel. In a Los Angeles bar, Abel, Ben, and Tosamah sit at one table among many others, as all enjoy themselves. Martinez walks in, and at this point the entire bar goes silent. The viewer already knows the policeman to be corrupt because he has taken money from Benally, and with his billy club he has whacked the hands of the unsuspecting Abel. The viewer also knows him to be racist in that he singles out Indians. Dressed in his navy blue uniform and policemen's cap, Martinez walks into the bar; he looks around, greets Benally with his sneer, and walks out. The film juxtaposes this scene with a flashback scene in which Abel kills the albino. In this scene, Abel is at a bar on the reservation. Rather than Martinez entering in his dark blue policeman's uniform, the albino man walks in, dressed completely in black: black hat, shirt, and trousers. The juxtaposition of scenes, the match cut, and the characters' manners, dress, and actions all serve to recall Martinez and definitely to call attention to the close thematic association between the two. The graphic match, as it were, connects these two scenes and certainly cues the viewer to see the connection between the two forces of evil in Abel's experience. Just as the viewer already knows Martinez to be a corrupt cop, the viewer also knows the albino to be associated with forces of evil. And both the albino and Martinez beat Abel.

Morse juxtaposes scenes of Abel's killing of the albino man with an eagle's attacking a rattlesnake. Here again he makes clear to the audience through visual cues that there is an inextricable link between the albino and the snake. The montage sequence is especially effective because the film has already cued the viewer to associate the albino with the snake through a previous flashback. In this duel scene (reminiscent of countless such scenes in Hollywood Westerns), the lighting is especially effective: Abel follows the albino out the door of the bar into the night, and they fight under artificial light. Throughout their nighttime encounter, however, Abel has visions of the eagle attacking the rattler in bright, desert sunlight. Morse is thus able to break the continuity through the use of light and action. The cuts alternate between two humans fighting in near darkness to two nonhuman animals fighting in bright sunshine. The contrast suggests that the eagle hunt is a perfectly natural and legitimate action; something that does not need the cover of darkness. In a sense the juxtaposition through match cuts can be seen to legitimate, at least in Abel's eyes, the killing of the albino man. As Tosamah describes the encounter, Abel simply cut himself "up a little snake meat there in the sand" (*House*).

Morse makes clear through such scenes the associations between evil and the albino, and between the albino and Martinez. In another scene he then depicts the corrupt policeman brutalizing Abel. As he had done in reaction to the albino man, Abel attempts to avenge an earlier beating; this time, however, he is drunk and completely ineffectual. Martinez easily knocks him down, kicks him in the ribs, and grinds a boot heel into the back of his hand. Whereas Abel's killing the albino man ultimately lands him in Los Angeles after a prison sentence, his fight with the policeman results in his leaving the city to return to the reservation. The two fights thus serve as framing devices as they relate Abel's battles against forces of evil.

Morse juxtaposes Abel's encounters with Martinez with crosscuts to scenes of his running, and twice those running scenes cut to scenes of Abel and Milly together. Since the film is essentially from Abel's perspective or point of view, the viewer assumes that when the camera shows Abel running it is because he is conscious of his running. When the viewer sees a flashback, it implies that Abel is recalling episodes from his past as he runs. In this sense, the film leads the viewer to imagine that Abel momentarily forgets that he is running as he becomes lost in thought. It is as if his consciousness of the run inspires good memories, laughing and loving Milly, for example. As those flashbacks build in tension, they switch to thoughts of Martinez and the physical and mental pain that policeman inspires and causes, at which point Abel's thoughts return to the run and to a consciousness of his running, and ultimately to the pain he experiences as he runs.

As Abel lies almost unconscious after Martinez beats him, the camera zooms to an extreme close-up of the injured man's face. His mouth is on the ground, and dirt clings to his wet lips. This close-up anticipates a later shot when, in the final running scene, Abel stumbles and falls. With another extreme close-up, the viewer again sees Abel's face on the ground, dirt again clinging to his wet lips. Whereas after his beating in Los Angeles Abel is for a long time unable to get to his feet, after he falls during his run he is able not only to stand up but to resume running. The viewer hears the voice of Abel's dead grandfather, at this point, speaking to him in Pueblo (Keresan) and translated simultaneously. The grandfather tells him that he too had run, that he too had fallen and thought he could not go on, but he had gotten up and had continued running: "Abelito, once I ran on the road at dawn. I ran with all my strength. I ran until my whole body seemed to burst open with pain. And I did not think that I could go on. And then the pain was gone and still I was running. And something was running with me and in me. And that year I killed seven bucks and seven does" (*House*). Remembering or hearing his grandfather's story inspires Abel to get back to his feet and to begin running again. The camera pans back for a distance shot of Abel running, and the runner transforms himself into a younger, long-haired man, wearing only a breechclout. As this man runs, the viewer hears the final translated words of the grandfather: "Those who run are the life that flows in our people"

(*House*). Thus, by means of the grandson's run, inspired by the death of the grandfather, the film insists on the life of the people.

A summary is in order here as a means of recounting and calling attention to the several ways in which *House Made of Dawn* the film can be said to break new ground and thereby serve as exemplary of several of the characteristics this study will draw on again and again in discussions of subsequent films. Both the source novel and the screenplay are written by an American Indian. With one exception the principal actors are Indigenous, and their indigeneity imbues the film with a unique sensibility. The film includes the use of a Pueblo language, and keeps Indigenous issues at its center. The contemporary setting insists that American Indians have survived into the twentieth century, and the film thus challenges Hollywood representations of dying Native people and cultures. Thematically as well, the film challenges Hollywood by presenting an Indian man who dies on screen but who neither falls from a horse nor vanishes. He dies of natural causes, and his presence is felt throughout the entire film. Indeed, his death represents survival.

FOUR

A Concordance of Narrative Voices

Harold, Trickster, and *Harold of Orange*

The trickster in the oral tradition, however, would overturn the very printed page on which his name has been printed. And certainly the trickster would blur the television screen.

—Gerald Vizenor, "Trickster Discourse: Comic," 69

The thirty-minute film *Harold of Orange*, which won a Film in the Cities competition, premiering in Minneapolis on May 17, 1984, is set in Minneapolis–St. Paul, one of several urban areas to which American Indians were relocated throughout the middle of the twentieth century. But this film offers a reversal of the relocation stories told in *The Exiles* and *House Made of Dawn*. Unlike *House Made of Dawn*, which is in large measure a story about how the city defeats the protagonist before forcing him home, *Harold of Orange* depicts a group of reservation men, the Warriors of Orange, who descend upon the city only long enough to exploit the mainstream system before loping back to the reservation with the loot, as it were. The film tells the story of Harold Sinseer (sincere, sin seer) (Charlie Hill) and his group of friends, the other Warriors of Orange, as they travel from the reservation to the city to present their proposal to a foundation grant agency for a (bogus) pinch-bean coffee enterprise. After introductions in the agency's boardroom, the presentation before the board members, by the self-identified Trickster Harold, consists of a school bus ride through the city with three stops: a naming ceremony in a parking lot, a visit to a university anthropology department's museum, and a softball game in a city park. The plot is rounded out with a return to the boardroom before the Trickster Warriors ride home to the reservation.

In this chapter I argue that *Harold of Orange*, directed by Richard Weiss, allows Gerald Vizenor (Anishinaabe), the author of the screenplay, to challenge and talk back to mainstream attitudes toward American Indians. Vizenor's targets of special interest are dominant, mainstream articulations of history and culture. Vizenor thus manipulates the viewer in part by overcoming what might be seen as the inappropriateness or impossibility of creating visual, representational images of the trickster. The film undermines the dominant culture's false images, or what Vizenor calls simulations, by actually presenting them, but presenting them on his own terms. The film borrows and coopts for its own purposes such quintessentially European American institutions as boardrooms, parking lots, softball games, museums, and television and radio Westerns. The medium of film allows Vizenor the opportunity to confront and transcend dominant (mis)representations and (mis)understandings in a coopted version of the dominant culture's own visual culture.

Harold is continually on the move in what might be called typical trickster fashion: he sidesteps an old college girlfriend, the non-Native Fannie Mason (Cathleen Fuller), to whom he still owes money; he maneuvers the board's director into lending him the money he owes Fannie; he "shape-shifts" at the softball game by changing team T-shirts; he turns a racist board member's stereotype about Indian drinking to his own advantage to seal the grant deal; he manages to repay Fannie without incurring any debt himself; and he escapes successful and unscathed back to the reservation.

From the outset, *Harold of Orange* takes several occasions to insist that the Warriors generally and Harold specifically constitute tricksters. The opening intertitle provides this pertinent information: "Now, Harold and the Warriors of Orange, *tribal tricksters* determined to reclaim their estate from the white man, are challenging his very foundations" (*Harold*, my emphasis). The film's theme song, sung by Native artist Buffy St. Marie, is called "Trickster," and the viewer *sees* Harold climb out of the car and self-identify as a trickster: "We are the Warriors of Orange, *tricksters* in the new school of sociocupuncture" (*Harold*, my emphasis). Late in the film, Fannie calls Harold a "rotten trickster," and in a voice-over as the bus leaves the city near the end of the film, Harold reminds the viewer once again: "We are *tricksters* in the best humor" (*Harold*, my emphasis). At the same time the film takes such care to establish Harold as a trickster, the actual physical corporeality, the human representation, of Harold is also established from the very opening sequence when the strictly verbal description of the intertitle is made manifest by the visual depiction of Harold, the man. What the viewer sees on screen is pretty much what Vizenor writes as a part of the screenplay: "Harold has a round brown face and black hair. His cheeks are full. . . . He is dressed in a ribbon shirt and brown leather vest. He gestures with his lips in the tribal manner when he speaks" (*Harold* [screenplay] 297).

The character Harold is only one of many tricksters to be found in the works of Gerald Vizenor, one of the most prolific of American Indian writers and one who has composed in a wide variety of genres. Novelist, poet, essayist, playwright, critic, historian, and journalist, Vizenor is also a screenwriter, and among readers of American Indian literature, this author is well known for his complex presentations or representations of trickster figures. As LaVonne Ruoff contends, the "trickster/transformer figure from Indian oral literatures pervades Vizenor's recent work" ("Gerald Vizenor" 45). Some of his tricksters include Cedarfair and Zebulon Matchi Makwa (Wicked Bear) in *Darkness in Saint Louis Bearheart* (1978); Martin Bear Charme in *Earthdivers* (1981); Griever in *An American Monkey King in China* (1990); Stone Columbus in *The Heirs of Columbus* (1991); Mother Earth Man, Zebulon Matchi Makwa in *Landfill Meditation* (1991); Bagese the wild bear in the city in *Dead Voices* (1992); and Harold in *Harold of Orange.*

Despite or perhaps in part because of the great number of trickster figures who make appearances throughout Vizenor's written texts, the trickster himself/itself remains elusive. Anishinaabe poet and scholar Kimberly Blaeser maintains that "Trickster is . . . imaginative energy" ("Trickster" 51), and according to Louis Owens, Vizenor's "mixed-bloods and tricksters become metaphors that seek to balance contradiction and shatter static certainties" (225). Alan Velie argues that "to Vizenor trickster is first and foremost a sign in the semiotic sense, a sign in a language game, a comic holotrope. This means that Vizenor conceives of trickster as a product of language, who must be seen in a linguistic context" (131). Elizabeth Blair writes that in Vizenor's postmodern texts "language—not reality, identity or truth—is preeminent" (76). That is, according to these literary scholars, Vizenor's trickster remains a verbal construct, whether spoken or written. Vizenor himself suggests as much in the introduction to *Trickster of Liberty*, writing that "the trickster figure is comic nature in a language game, not a real person or 'being' in the ontological sense" (x). In "Trickster Discourse: Comic and Tragic" Vizenor explains that "the trickster arises in imagination and the trickster lives nowhere else but in imagination" ("Trickster Discourse: Comic" 68), and in yet another trickster essay, a different essay by the same title, Vizenor writes that "the trickster is a communal sign, never isolation; a concordance of narrative voices" ("Trickster Discourse," 1990, 284).

With regard to his own and others' articulated conceptions of the trickster, then, Vizenor certainly faces a very specific challenge in turning to film with *Harold of Orange*: if the trickster exists only in language or only in imagination, as a word warrior, how then does one adapt the figure to film, which necessitates a visual, referential character? The adaptation challenge is much different from the challenge the Morse-Momaday team faces in adapting *House Made of Dawn*. For Vizenor, the challenge is not so much what to include or omit in adapting a verbal into a visual text, or how to best represent a man and his situation in the community, but rather how to depict visually any character at all. According to James Ruppert, the "very nature of cinema presents Vizenor with a problem" ("Imagination" 225). The trickster, the shape-shifter, the elusive word warrior, as a verbal construct exclusively, can remain sufficiently abstract by the very nature of the strictly verbal medium. According to Vizenor, "Tricksters are real in stories but not in the flesh. Tricksters are not blood or material, but imagination. . . . The power of a trickster would be diminished, even abolished, by human representations" ("Trickster Discourse: Comic" 70). Any filmic depiction would thus seem to run counter to Vizenor's conception of the trickster, especially because, as Carl Plantinga argues in *Moving Viewers* (2009), representations of the human body and the nature of sound, image, and movement make "possible a sensual experience unique to the medium" of film (9). The advantages of making possible a sensual experience would appear to be disadvantages for Vizenor as he turns to filmic representations of the trickster because as Vizenor himself makes explicit, visual representations would seem to run counter to the very concept of trickster.

Vizenor often suggests how photographs or representational images can be very misleading and problematic, even in contexts of visual images or representations not specific to tricksters. The example of his discussion of visual renditions of Russell Means serves to underscore the apparent paradoxes he understands to be an inherent part of visual images of *indians*. In "Interimage Simulations," he points out the delimiting effects of photography, writing that "Native American Indians bear in their memories, sense of presence, and chance of solace in narratives *not on cameras*" (234, my emphasis). In that same essay, however, he seems to suggest that photographic renditions can at least transcend an ethnographic purpose: "Andy Warhol pictured the narrative closures of the obvious, and the most noticeable simulations of the *indian*. Indeed, his studio production of Russell Means is an artistic, not ethnographic, interimage simulation in several obscure dimensions: the absence of the other at a *massacre*, the pasticcio warrior, and the postindian poses of the American Indian Movement" ("Interimage," 233). In film too, according to Vizenor, the desires of Russell Means "to bear uncommon simulations were heartened as Chingachgook in the film *The Last of the Mohicans*" ("Interimage" 233). In the context of certain other representations, Vizenor finds depictions of Means more clearly unfortunate: "How ironic that the poses of certain radicals were the specious simulations of premodern *indian* cultures. The poseurs maintain the obvious, a cultural dominance that denies real native pictures, cultural variations, conversions, and modernity" ("Ontic Images" 165). The problems and the dangers of such photographs, insists Vizenor, are that they "become the *real*, the faux evidence of a 'vanishing race.'" Edward Curtis's photographs, for example, disallow "the actual presence of natives" ("Ontic Images" 165). In this sense, according to Vizenor, it seems the pose, the medium, and the context are more important than the photographed subject, yet the pose can be or can become an unfortunate simulation. In the essay "Ontic Images," Vizenor maintains that the "images in photographs are not the real, and not the actual representations of time or culture" (165). Granted, the images in photographs and film, no matter the fidelity to the "real," no matter how specifically representational, are not the "actual" or "real," but film theorists necessarily still struggle with the relationship between filmic representation and "reality." André Bazin argues, for example, that "only the photographic lens can give us the kind of image of the object that is capable of satisfying the deep need man has to substitute for it something more than a mere approximation. . . . The photographic image is the object itself" ("Ontology" 14).

What the viewer confronts in the sense of the physical or sensual reality of the character on the screen is the notion that film, as well as still photography, presents or depicts reality in a way somehow different from depictions in exclusively verbal texts, whether written or oral. Although there has been some disagreement among film theorists concerning what is to be understood as the "reality" of what is projected onto a screen, scholars do tend to agree that film does present to the viewer a more real experience, certainly more visceral, than what the printed word presents the reader. Both Siegfried Kracauer and André Bazin, for example, argue that film is essentially photographic" (Carroll 112). They both maintain that "photography and film exist to explore and expose a raw material of brute reality," and that that "brute reality is at the heart of cinema's appeal" (Andrew 137, 141). That appeal is a result of the putative realism of the genre. In his essay "The Ontology of the Photographic Image," Bazin writes that "the objective nature of photography confers on it a quality of credibility absent from all other picture-making. In spite of any objections our critical spirit may offer, we are forced to accept as real the existence of the object reproduced, actually *re*-presented, set before us, that is to say, in time and space. Photography enjoys a certain advantage in virtue of this transference of reality from the thing to its reproduction" (13–14). In *Theory of Film* (1960), Kracauer begins with "the assumption that film is essentially an extension of photography and therefore shares with this medium a marked affinity for the visible world around us. Films come into their own when they record and reveal physical reality" (ix). Vizenor himself turns to Roland Barthes to make a case for photographic realism. In a comment he makes in *Camera Lucida*, Barthes acknowledges that the image depicted in a photograph represents an overwhelming realism: "Photography evades us," he writes. "Whatever it grants to vision and whatever its manner, a photograph is always invisible: it is not it that we see" (4, 6). That is, we see the objects photographed. The implication, of course, is that part of the reason we do not see it when we see it is because we see the "reality" of what it depicts, the representational image depicted.

Gregory Currie defines what he terms "Perceptual Realism" this way: "We recognize that people, houses, mountains, and cars are represented on screen by exercising the capacities we have to recognize those objects, and not by learning a set of conventions that associate cinematic representations of these objects with the objects themselves" (328). According to Bruce Isaacs, more recently, "traditional pictorial realism refers to the degree of verisimilitude of the reproduction of the real object . . . but it also indicates a sense of the reproduction as *striving for* a realistic representation of the tangible object" (8). Further still, argues Isaacs, "cinema promises the possibility of the perfection of representative art: the revelation of truth and a profoundly humanist capacity for the illumination of nature and an essential reality" (9). Although some theorists take issue with the validity of the "realism" thesis, even in so doing, they acknowledge its pervasiveness. Richard Allen argues that realism in cinema is an artistic convention, but he admits that nonetheless the "minimum condition for a picture or drama to be experienced as a projective illusion is simply that the form be representational, that is, it must contain pictorial elements that a spectator can recognize as standing for individuals or types of things" (Allen 88). Noël Carroll suggests that "the illusion of reality" in art has a "pernicious effect" (90), but like Currie, he also recognizes the ubiquity of the thesis in the context of film studies.

Such an understating of realism underlies one of the significant differences between film and strictly verbal arts like novels and even screenplays such as Vizenor's. According to Robert Stam, characters, representations of people, "gain an automatic 'thickness' on the screen through bodily presence, posture, dress, and facial expression" ("Introduction" 22). By the same token, however, one of the evident disadvantages of film (in comparison with a strictly verbal text)—especially in the context of adaptation but also in the context of Vizenor's trickster characters—is that "film offends through its inescapable materiality, its incarnated, fleshy, enacted characters" (Stam, "Introduction" 6). Indeed, this incarnation accounts for much of the reason, argues David Freedberg in *The Power of Images*, that "early photographs were seen as realistic and arousing. . . . Moreover, they were seen and used as arousing *because* they were realistic" (352).

Theoretical concerns about the close relationship between photography and simulation can be seen to extend to visual depictions of the trickster as well. In writing about *Harold of Orange*, Robert Silberman addresses the issue of the filmic embodiment of the trickster: "In *Harold*, for the first time, this more dramatic conception of literature appears within an actual dramatic form, with real actors instead of written characters. In particular, there is a flesh and blood individual playing the trickster, with a real voice, rather than the voice of a fictional character or the narrative voice of the oral tradition struggling to maintain its freedom" (14). Despite his pointing out the uniqueness of the trickster's having actual human form, however, Silberman maintains that "it must be admitted that Vizenor's Indians remain unlike any real Indians; they are the Indians of his imagination, in which tricksterism rides the range" (15). The character Harold in the film is an Indian man with long dark hair; he wears a polka dot ribbon shirt and blue jeans; he speaks English, and although he subsequently dons a tie, the noose of the white man, and changes from white to red to white T-shirts at a softball game, he does not otherwise seem to do any serious shape-shifting. The viewer knows what he looks like from beginning to end. Very real. Very human. As a verbal construct, in contrast, even when described through physical characteristics or particular smells, it remains nevertheless, up to the reader to imagine, to visualize this shape-shifter in any given moment or shape. Once Vizenor (or the filmmaker) commits the concept of the trickster to existence as a projection on a screen, that trickster becomes necessarily more than an abstraction. He, she, or it has a physical or essential verisimilitudinous existence or presence that seemingly cannot be denied. Because of the powerful mimetic nature of film, the visual verisimilitude of screen world and real world, there is an immediate and very real correlation between Charlie Hill the actor and Harold Sinseer the character, that is, between the strictly human being and the trickster figure.

Confronting this issue of visual representations of the trickster, James Ruppert offers a very intricate argument about how Vizenor circumvents the potential problem of Harold's being depicted in film while still remaining a trickster. Drawing on C. S. Pierce (via Peter Wollen), Ruppert argues that rather than an icon (a representational figure) or a symbol (an arbitrary sign without physical resemblance), Harold is indexical. That is, Harold is to a trickster what a weathercock is to the east wind, for example. "At any one moment," writes Ruppert, "the existence of Harold doing or saying something creates its essence" ("Imagination" 227), and besides, posits Ruppert, the action of the film "is not realistic" (230). Ruppert finds the scene in the anthropology department central to the film and to his argument. He writes that the "scene in the Anthropology Department gives the viewer a visual representation of the indexical relationship. Harold the contemporary trickster stands on the artifact case while slides are projected on him the way meaning is projected on the indexical signifier" (228).

Ruppert's analysis is extremely helpful in the context of the screenplay, which provides just such instructions: "the ghost dance figures are projected on his face and body" (Vizenor, *Harold* 320). But those screenplay instructions do not find realization in the visual realm of the film. That is, the viewer of the film itself does not actually see, at least not consciously, these images of the Ghost Dance, or of Wounded Knee, or of Buffalo Bill's Wild West Show. In that these projections are written into the screenplay, they are supposed to be in the film, of course, but without reading the exclusively verbal words of the screenplay into the film beforehand and thus knowing that they are there, the viewer cannot actually make them out. Without the aide and knowledge of the written text, that is, the viewer simply does not see the images described. In other words, as a strictly visual medium the film it-self does not cue the viewer to understand Harold Sinseer the trickster as an "indexical signifier." That reading seems to come from the exclusively verbal text of the screenplay, rather than from the visual-verbal-aural text of the film itself.

Thus, as interesting and compelling as Ruppert's argument is, it relies heav-ily, almost exclusively, on the written words of the screenplay rather on the visual aspects of the actual film. In his discussion of the scene that takes place in the Anthropology Department's museum, for example, Ruppert writes that "Harold the contemporary trickster stands on the artifact case while slides are projected on him the way meaning is projected on the indexi-cal signifier. As the slides change, the relationship between Harold, the visual image, and the viewer changes. When images of the ghost dance are projected on Harold, he explains the power of vision to create a new world, a trick-ster world we presume" ("Imagination" 228–29). That knowledge of what the slide projector projects comes exclusively through the written screenplay, which reads in part as follows:

> Scene begins with a photographic slide of the ghost dance. Harold steps into the slide, the ghost dance figures are projected on his face and body; he appears to be in the dance. . . . Plumero operates the slide projector. . . .
>
> Slide change, death scene from Wounded Knee. . . .
>
> Slide change, Wild West Show broadside. . . .
>
> Slide change to a photograph of Paul Newman in *Buffalo Bill and the Indians*. . . .
>
> Slide changes to a portrait of Buffalo Bill Cody. . . .
>
> Slide change, scene of Harold bearing Fannie in his arms, like the pose of the statue of Hiawatha and Minnehaha.
>
> The statue is on the screen as the bus approaches and stops. (Vizenor, *Harold* 320–25 passim)

For the viewer of the film, in contrast to the reader of the screenplay, the slide images are not nearly so pronounced or distinct. One cannot, in fact, actu-ally identify them without knowing beforehand what one is seeing, and even then, with one or two exceptions, it is difficult to make out what is depicted. As Harold stands on top of the display case in the film, there is, to be sure, a screen *behind* him on which slides are projected, but they are not projected *on* him. There is no Plumero operating a slide projector as far as the viewer knows. The viewer cannot make out that the Ghost Dance is projected onto Harold's face, nor can the viewer make out definitively any shot of Paul New-man. Several other images from the screenplay are left out of the film: the iconic Hiawatha and Minnehaha statue, for example, is missing from the film altogether as is any shot of Harold carrying Fannie. Even what shots there are, as indicated in the screenplay, are so secondary to the presence of Harold standing on top of the glass display case that they would have to work almost subliminally. Even when one watches specifically for the slides (rather than watching the main action), it is very difficult to identify the images as described in the screenplay. Read this way, or rather seen this way, Vizenor's film is still beleaguered by the problem of a representational depiction of a trickster. Trickster remains very *iconic*, very much a representation of a flesh and blood human being. To all appearances he is a real person, a human being, in the ontological sense; he is a physical (or a celluloid) embodiment of Harold, but he is also already always the actor/comedian Charlie Hill.

Although not mentioned at all in the screenplay, one of the few extremely vivid and thus recognizable images that the viewer does see as Harold stands atop the museum display case is a well-defined and distinct shot from the film *Northwest Passage* (1940), a "Western" set in colonial northeastern United States. The shot in the slide is from the film's climactic massacre at Saint-Francis-du-Lac, Quebec, during which an artist turned soldier, Langdon Towne (Robert Young), bayonets one of the unarmed Abenaki villagers. Implicit in Langdon's conversion from artist to soldier is the metaphorical notion that whether as artist or as soldier he "disavows" the Indians, either metaphorically by (mis)representing them in his sketchbook or by very literally stabbing them with his bayonet. At the moment the viewer sees the shot of the character Towne with his bayonet at the unnamed Abenaki man's throat, Harold speaks these lines: "Those anthropologists invented us, and then they put our bones in these museum cases" (*Harold*). The filmic moment allows Harold, the trickster, the opportunity to suggest the stunning similarities between the attitudes behind the work that soldiers, artists, photographers, and anthropologists do. In the context of Edward Curtis, Vizenor writes that the "pictorial photographic images and representations of Indians disavowed imagic moments, cultural conversions, and the actual presence of natives" ("Ontic Images" 165). Curtis's photographs, Vizenor continues, "reveal only the simulations of the vanishing race. . . . Curtis created a simulation of a native absence and an ethnographic presence" ("Edward Curtis" 205). Analogously, anthropologists disallow the inherent rights and integrity of the human remains of Indigenous peoples, while soldiers literally kill them. The intertextual visual reference to *Northwest Passage* in the film *Harold of Orange* thus emphasizes the connection between what the artist does in creating simulations, what the soldier does in killing outright, and what the anthropologist does in separating artifact from context and ossifying it. These are all means, according to Vizenor's filmic moment, to disallow and disavow the actual presence of Natives.

The strictly filmic moment of Harold standing on the display case allows the trickster to fuse three different aspects of mainstream culture through the analogies between or similarities in means of oppression and exploitation. The moment serves another function as well. It suggests how Vizenor might overcome the apparent restrictions he himself places on depictions or representations of the trickster. That is, trickster takes seemingly disparate manifestations and implies that they actually represent the same phenomenon.

Despite the degree to which Harold can be read as indexical or the degree to which the images of the slide show have intertextual meaning, the challenge of *Harold of Orange* remains for Vizenor—as well as for the viewer—to come to terms with how one accounts for a visualized and visually discernable trickster when such a character is supposed to be pure imagination. To respond to this problem of representation, I want offer an analogy between the adaptation of the trickster from written text to film and the adaptation of the trickster from a strictly oral tradition to a written one. That is, I want to argue that the difficulty of presenting the trickster figure on film is in some respects analogous to the difficulty Vizenor faces in his writing when he seeks to adapt the trickster concept from an oral tradition to the written page. In his writings, Vizenor acknowledges that he is acutely aware of the oral-to-written challenge, maintaining at one point, "I don't think the oral tradition can be translated well, but I think it can be reimagined and reexpressed and that's my interest" (quoted in Bowers and Silet 49). Elsewhere Vizenor explains that his "writing" trickster from an oral tradition is legitimate because it constitutes an imaginative extension of the oral: "The trickster is a brilliant tribal figure of imagination that has found a new world in written languages" ("Trickster Discourse: Comic" 68). At the same time, however, and playing something of the trickster himself, Vizenor argues just a page later in the same essay, in the context of the visual image of trickster, that "The trickster in the oral tradition, however, would overturn the very printed page on which his name has been printed. And certainly the trickster would blur the television screen and trick the reader and the viewer to remember that the real world is imagination. . . . The new world, the trickster world, is struggling to find a place on the printed page" (69).

Vizenor addresses in some detail the problem of a written representation of the trickster figure in his novel *Dead Voices* (1992). At the end of this work of fiction in which the narrator—named Laundry—has met and heard a series of trickster stories from Bagese, a trickster herself, Laundry attempts to justify writing down the stories even though he has pledged not to. He offers this explanation: "Bagese, these published stories are the same as the wanaki pictures and the stones that you placed in your apartment to remember the earth, the traces of birds and animals near the lake" (144). The narrator reminds Bagese of as much from the beginning: "I was more than eager to remind her that the wanaki cards were an obvious contradiction to what she had told me. The pictures on the cards were the same as written words and could not be heard" (18). One conundrum here, of course, is that within the novel the wanaki cards themselves remain merely verbal constructs, words on a page, albeit they are words that describe a visual image.

Although Bagese and the narrator thus literally *see* the images on the cards, there are no actual nonverbal depictions for the reader to see; they remain exclusively verbal images, images that must be visualized in the reader's imagination, pictures of crows, squirrels, and preying mantises, for example. According to Douglas Dix and his coauthors, in the context of Bagese,

> the trick to the narrative lies in the elision of both tellers—beneath the containing texts of Laundry's translations are Bagese's own representations of fragments of an aural matrix of stories: the "shadow" Vizenor sees uncovered in "the ruins of representation." Vizenor's own use of the Earthdiver myth serves as a model for this process: the aural appears as recoverable through the construction of the printed text as fragments of the old world from the seeds of the new. (179)

In a sense, the conception of this "elision of both tellers" can serve as an articulation of how adaptation from the oral to the written—and consequently how an adaptation from an oral or a written trickster to one in film—might work.

The novel, as one of those tellers, contains the representations of the other teller, that shadow that accompanies oral to written or oral/written to film. At one point in the narrative of *Dead Voices*, for example, the narrator Laundry explains to the reader the paradox inherent in and the importance of the visual. He notes that Bagese "was a bear and teased me in mirrors as she did the children, and at the same time she said that tribal stories must be told not recorded, told to listeners but not readers, and she insisted that stories be heard through the ear not the eye" (6). A moment later he explains further that "the tricksters in the word are seen in the ear not the eye" (7). Yet at another point the narrator has the realization that Bagese "was a bear in the mirrors, an image that escaped me for several months" (15). The narrator thus realizes that, although she is a trickster, Bagese is also embodied as an image in a mirror. Vizenor here writes about the eye seeing the spoken versus the written word, a form of voluntary synesthesia.

Film theorist Christian Metz, who is also interested in mirrored experiences, is helpful here. In writing about identification in the cinema, he argues that what makes possible "the intelligible unfolding of the film . . . is the fact that the spectator has already known the experience of the mirror (of the true mirror), and is thus able to constitute a world of objects without having first to recognize himself within it. In this respect, the cinema is already on the side of the symbolic" (172). Further, suggests Metz, film itself "is like the mirror." In the course of his argument, however, Metz decides that it is also unlike the mirror in that "at the cinema, it is always the other who is on the screen; as for me, I am there to look at him" (171). The viewer, according to Metz, is absent, yet present through that absence, "absent from the screen, but certainly present in the auditorium" (173). The leap from seeing sound to visualizing or seeing what is signified by the written word is not a great one. On some level, that is precisely the challenge anyone who is adapting a novel to film faces, creating a visual reflection of the strictly verbal.

In an essay called "The Trickster Novel," Alan Velie turns to Mikhail Bahktin to help him grapple with or at least "examine what happens when trickster leaves the oral tradition and enters the novel" (121). In the essay he asks the question: "What is the result of placing trickster in the highly specific chronotope of the postmodern novel?" (133). If we read "chronotope" to mean (roughly) genre, it seems but one step from one genre to another, the trickster of oral or written tradition to cinematic tradition. Thus we can ask a new but related question: What is the result of placing the trickster in the highly representational genre of film? This question leads to another: What is film doing that a strictly verbal text is not doing or cannot do? According to Robert Stam, "cinema has not lesser but rather greater resources for expression than the novel [or the written word] . . . cinema offers synergistic possibilities of disunity and disjunction not immediately available to the novel. The possible contradictions and tensions between tracks become an aesthetic resource, opening the way to a multitemporal, polyrhythmic art form" (Stam, "Introduction" 20). The question then becomes this: to what extent does the film *Harold of Orange* take advantage of such potentialities?

One example of how *Harold of Orange* might utilize a polyrhythmic form is the use to which it puts Gioachino Rossini's "March of the Swiss Soldiers" finale of the *William Tell Overture*. This nondiegetic music accompanies the Warriors' bus as the viewer sees it heading into the city. Although at face value, merely a brief (twelve seconds) comic reference to *The Lone Ranger* radio and television theme music, the effect of this particular soundtrack is actually complex and multilayered. By this music, the Warriors of Orange, these Indians in motley and wearing neckties with their T-shirts, are inextricably associated in the viewer's mind with the Lone Ranger, accompanied by Tonto, of course, arriving to fight evil and rid the white settlements across the Western frontier of whatever miscreants might threaten the settlers' peace and prosperity. The film also contrasts the full orchestration accompanying the Warriors on their bus ride with the tinny reproduction on the wristwatch of one of the board members. In a crosscut, the viewer sees the racist board member Felty walk into the boardroom and say to his colleagues, "*Watch* this," meaning *listen to* this, whereupon he plays the tiny tinny version of the *Overture* on his wristwatch (*Harold*). Whereas the board members hear only

The Warriors of Orange. *Harold of Orange*. Screen Capture. Film in the Cities.

the poorly replicated, "fake" version of the theme music on the watch, the viewer hears the fully orchestrated, nondiegetic music that accompanies the shot of the Warriors' bus galloping into the city on its rescue mission.

As a result of this apparently simple use of *The Lone Ranger* theme music, the film achieves a reversal of roles in which the viewer is encouraged to see the board members (innocuous as they otherwise might seem) as the bad guys. That is, the mainstream members of the dominant society, the granting-agency board members, stand in opposition to the Indian ruffians who through the different renditions of this popular piece of music are aligned with the good guys, riding to the rescue. The effect is achieved through this synergism, a device unique to film in a way, to the possibility of combining simultaneously sound and visual image. The filmic moment of course relies on the viewer's being familiar with *The Lone Ranger* theme music and on having an awareness of the typical plot of the series from either the television or the radio, both of which used the same music. Understood in this way, Harold the trickster figure and the bus, the means of transport, analogous to Lone Ranger's horse Silver, become fused, they become one. In this sense, the hero Harold is able to shape-shift on screen and for a time abandon his human form. In that he is the one leading the charge, so to speak, the trickster becomes the bus itself as the music insists that what the viewer sees is the Lone Ranger on his silver stallion galloping into town on what must be understood in this context as a rescue mission. There is a wonderful irony underlying the moment in that Harold's mission is ultimately to rescue the otherwise helpless or hapless board members. That rescue consists of his freeing them of both their biases and their grant money. This reading again offers a reversal in that Harold becomes both rescuer and robber, as he is when he borrows money from the board director, Kingman Newton (James Noah), to repay his old friend Fannie.

Once the viewer allows for such shape-shifting on screen and despite the alleged realism of film, another way Vizenor challenges the viewer is through the trickster's potential multiplicity. In the film, in contrast to the screenplay, none of the other Warriors of Orange, the other tricksters, is named or called by name. In stark contrast, the film takes care to introduce and name the many board members. Kingsly calls Fannie by name, for example, and later he introduces her to another board member:

TED: Call me Veltie . . .
FANNIE: Call me Fannie, Veltie . . . (*Harold*)

Further emphasizing the importance of names, there is even a naming cere-mony, in which Harold gives Kingsley, Marion, and Fannie new names from the "urban spirits." This naming of the board members calls attention to the lack of names connected with the Warriors of Orange and thus the lack of differentiation among them. Harold informs the viewer that they are "trick-sters in the new school of sociocupuncture," and the suggestion, on a certain level, is that they constitute Trickster, or that the trickster is the Warriors. What seems to be individual responses from different individuals to different questions asked of them on the bus turn out to be responses from a single source: the trickster. In each instance the trickster challenges long-held beliefs about and (mis)representations of tribal peoples. The trickster questions the "land bridge" theory and questions pre-Columbian population theories. "We were here first," declares the trickster at one point.

By such shape-shifting, one can argue, the filmic Harold, the filmic trick-ster, continues to defy representation. He can remain just as elusive on screen as in print, and just as much a wonder. As Freedberg writes in the context of representation and reality, "representation is miraculous because it de-ceives us into thinking it is realistic, but it is only miraculous because it is something other than what it represents" (438). The novel *Dead Voices* and the film *Harold of Orange* can be said to have a striking commonality. The suggestion is that in the narrative that is the novel *Dead Voices* there is a doubling going on between the strictly verbal form and the visual di-mension of the story and of the trickster Bagese. Correspondingly, in *Har-old of Orange* the trickster assumes various forms, verbal in the opening theme song and intertitle and visual from the time Harold arrives in his automobile, immediately challenging the conception of the trickster as purely verbal construct.

The very existence of a filmic trickster demands that the viewer ask a fundamental question about genre, about film, about adaptation: Why privilege one form over another in the first place? Finally, none is innately more realistic than another, whether voiced, written, or pictured. As W. J. T. Mitchell writes in *Picture Theory*, "all media are mixed media, and all representations are heterogeneous; there are no 'purely' visual or verbal arts" (5). Mitchell also asserts that "the tensions between visual and verbal representations are inseparable from struggles in cultural politics and political culture . . . issues like 'gender, race, class,' the production of 'political horrors,' and the production of 'truth, beauty, and excellence' all converge on questions of representation" (3). Thus, whereas Masayesva in *Imagining Indians* feels that in order to reimagine Indians he must literally destroy the visual depictions painted by Catlin, Vizenor challenges and undermines false images or simulations by actually presenting them. Vizenor's character Harold is inseparable from the cultural and political struggles as well as from the verbal and visual struggles. Vizenor writes in "Anishinaabe Pictomyths" that "the figures painted on stone, on the face of granite, are more fantastic than any representations of natural motion or naturalism. There is no trace of face or hands in some visions and dream images, but explicit lines that show sound, voice, and heart" (180). These imagic presences, he argues, provide a sense of mythic survivance.

Through the ways in which it talks back to the mainstream culture but ultimately transcends that culture by both tricking and coopting its very foundations, *Harold of Orange* shares similarities with *House Made of Dawn*, the film, and Masayesva's *Imagining Indians*. The final scene is of the successful Warriors of Orange getting off the bus and noisily entering their coffeehouse. They have both triumphed in the city and left it behind them. Harold pauses before the door and speaks as if to the camera, calling attention to the camera. He tells the viewer that "the revolution starts" at this coffeehouse on the reservation, not in the cities (*Harold*). As *House Made of Dawn* ends with a young Indigenous man running through time for the life of his people, and as the dental patient overturns the establishment, past and present, in front of the camera at the end of *Imagining Indians*, so Harold the trickster triumphs over the past and the present, over limits of oral, written, or visual culture, as he survives into the future.

FIVE

I Don't Do Portraits

Medicine River and the Art of Photography

The group refused to stay in place. After every picture, the kids wandered off among their parents and relatives and friends, and the adults floated back and forth, no one holding their positions. I had to keep moving the camera as the group swayed from one side to the other. Only the grandparents remained in place as the ocean of relations flowed around them. —Thomas King, *Medicine River*, 214–15

Medicine River is a feature-length, made-for-television, Canadian Broadcasting Company mass-market narrative film, in contrast to the short film *Harold of Orange*, which was not necessarily intended for a mainstream audience in the first place, or to the films *House Made of Dawn* and *The Exiles*, which found no distributor. In other aspects, however, *Medicine River* shares many similarities with these others. Like them it deals with Indigenous issues and is based on an Indigenous-authored work, Thomas King's 1989 novel by the same title. King, of Cherokee and Greek heritage, also wrote the screenplay as well as the teleplay, and he has a small speaking role in the film. The Indian characters are acted by Indians, some well known, including Graham Greene, Tom Jackson, and Shelia Tousey; others nonprofessional, Jimmy Herman and Maggie Black Kettle, for instance. The film has a contemporary setting and takes place in the fictional Alberta town of Medicine River next to the reserve. Although the director, Stuart Margolin, is European Canadian, the film is otherwise in many respects Indigenous.

In addition to these generic characteristics, *Medicine River* shares thematic similarities with *House Made of Dawn* and many of the other Indigenous films discussed in other chapters, and this chapter explores these thematic connections and argues that the film's self-conscious use of and reference to photography and its depictions of Indigenous peoples offer means of talking back to mainstream representations and culture. As in *House Made of Dawn*, the death of an elder motivates the plot. The protagonist's mother dies before the action of the film, but her presence is felt throughout. That protagonist is Will (Graham Greene), a photojournalist who puts his career on hold to come to Medicine River for her funeral, albeit belatedly. He lingers, as he finds himself useful photographing several of the tribal elders, and although the film does not necessarily talk back to Hollywood explicitly, it certainly evokes and challenges mainstream non-Indian photographic (mis)representations of Native North Americans. Ultimately, however, the film transcends any limitations it places on itself in its effort to challenge mainstream representations by insisting on the connection between photograph and story.

Little has been written about *Medicine River* the film as opposed to the book, which like the novel *House Made of Dawn* has received substantial scholarly attention. Neither Houston Wood in *Native Features*, Kerstin Knopf in *Decolonizing the Lens of Power*, nor Beverly Singer in *Wiping the War Paint off the Lens* mentions the film, and Angela Aleiss in *Making the White Man's Indian* offers only a pair of sentences about it. Jacquelyn Kilpatrick offers a substantial reading of the film, in her book *Celluloid Indians*, arguing that the film shows "Native Americans in roles that depict them as they are—as contemporary human beings" (195). She also provides a lengthy summary and notes that that the film breaks ground for American Indian film, in this case Canadian First Nations film, in important ways:

> This film works as a mainstream movie because, in addition to its highly professional direction, photography, and script, it contains all the best-loved tropes—a love story, a lost boy returning home, bonding buddies, even a sports event. For a Native American audience it works in all these ways, but it also overturns old stereotypes of female subservience and the wise old chief, thaws out the time freeze, and underlines an essential difference in Native cultures—the "hero" in this film is not Will. The real protagonist in *Medicine River* is the tribal community. In Native American fashion, the individual is not the center of the story—it is the relationships between the members that are important. (206)

To Kilpatrick's list, I would add that *Medicine River* also challenges and overturns notions of the photographs of Indigenous people as necessarily limiting, demeaning, or stereotyping. The film addresses the controversy of ethnographic or anthropological photography by realigning or reestablishing the context of the photographs themselves, especially portrait photography. If it is typically or was formerly typically aligned with ethnography and anthropology in the Edward Curtis vein, for example, the camera in this film remains exclusively in the control of the Indigenous person Will, who very literally holds and operates the camera. In a Curtis-esque fashion, the film offers portraits of some tribal elders, but, as the viewer discovers, inseparable from these black-and-white images are the back stories of the individuals in them. It might be instructive to note that something similar is going on in the novel from which the film is adapted. As Stuart Christie argues, the novel offers "a compelling metanarrative of realist photography" (53–54). Stressing the importance of story and context in photographs in the essay "Ontic Images,"

Gerald Vizenor writes that the "imagic moment, or vision, is the story of the picture. . . . The imagic moment is the creation of an ontic sense of presence, another connection in a picture" (170). In this regard, the narratives or *stories* of Will's efforts to locate and photograph his subjects and the *stories* the subjects tell as they are being photographed add additional layers of contextualization and make further manifest the ontological, physical presence of the people photographed. *Medicine River* insists to the viewer that these people have presence not because somewhere some sepia photographs of them exist; rather, they have presence because they include their stories. The film thus argues that the photographs themselves are story.

The linking of story and photograph begins with the opening sequence, in which Will, the photojournalist, is a prisoner in Malawi. As he is being released, the commanding officer (Blu Mankuma) demands that this prisoner, Will, take his portrait. Just after the officer has thrown Will's assignment photographs into the fire, there is this exchange:

OFFICER: Perhaps you would like to take my photograph?
WILL: I don't do portraits.
OFFICER: Personally, I was in favor of shooting you.
WILL: Is that, ah, full face or profile? (*Medicine*)

According to Kilpatrick, King was not happy with this opening sequence. She writes that "King wrote the dialogue but was not particularly pleased with the addition of this razzle-dazzle introduction to his story" (247n16). This addition to the film has nothing to do with the novel, but as an establishing sequence for the film, it draws immediate attention to the significance of photography. The scene introduces Will as a "world-famous photographer," as Harlan Big Bear (Tom Jackson) dubs him. It calls attention to the politics of photography, especially the politics of censorship and control over who holds the camera and who decides what can actually be photographed in the first place. The viewer actually witnesses political censorship as the officer burns the war photos Will has taken, and in the context of this censorship, the sequence implies that film is important enough to need to be censored and that part of that need results from the possibility that film creates its own reality. Furthermore, the opening sequence insists that photography is literally a matter of life and death.

The opening sequence also suggests a politics of photography and makes clear that photographs as such are thematically important in the film. *Medicine River* acknowledges that it is self-consciously about film from the very first moments, and it demonstrates that the process of making or taking photographs, of making images, is absolutely critical on several different levels. The opening sequence makes evident, for example, that humor is to be a part of the film's rhetoric. Will insists that he does not do portraits, and then he immediately and humorously changes his mind once he is threatened. On the surface the exchange offers the toss-off joke implicit in Will's acquiescing without hesitation to the officer's insistence that he take his photograph. Beyond this surface-level joke, the exchange implies an adaptability or flexibility on Will's part, an adaptability that later in the film will be seen to serve the photographer well. Furthermore, there is the humor of a pun on the word *shoot*. The officer readies his pistol as he informs Will that he would like his photograph taken, and he thereby makes obvious one meaning of *to shoot*, to kill or execute with a gun. The use of the word suggests that even in war-torn Malawi, the Indigenous North American is oppressed by a dominant culture, although the film gives no indication that Will's being an American Indian makes any difference to the officer. The verb *to shoot* has another denotation, of course, and this is the sort of shooting Will does. This idea of shooting with a camera in contrast to shooting with a pistol reverses the hierarchy. The putatively oppressed man becomes the one in control. He holds the camera. He is the one who governs the shooting and thus the one who has the power to record and even to create the history. The importance of who holds the camera, this capacity to reverse the century-long mainstream gaze, so to speak, is evident throughout the film.

In his novel *Heirs of Columbus*, Gerald Vizenor argues that "humor has political significance" (166), and Kimberly Blaeser writes that "because historical stories, cultural stories, imaginative stories work to form our identity, the disarming of history through satiric humor liberates and empowers us in the imagination of our destinies." She continues, arguing that these Native writers "turn old forms inside out with trickster humor because they, too, know the powers of story and humor" ("New Frontier" 49). Humor in *Medicine River* is immediately overtly political in that it challenges a political hierarchy. Through its use of humor, one might argue, the film turns inside-out old forms, specifically old notions of photographs of Indigenous North Americans. In contrast to the ethnographic stasis and traditional forms of (mis)representation evident in photographs by Curtis, for example, the photographs in *Medicine River* capture the stories of their subjects with their images. The viewer of the film comes to know the stories of the photographs, comes to realize that the stories make the photographs possible, and in this way the photographs themselves refuse stasis. Indeed, the very medium of a motion picture imbues the stills with a form of movement, and that movement further underscores the photographs' vibrancy, suggesting that the stills actually change depending on context. Blaeser offers an account of American Indian fiction that is applicable in this context. She writes that what she finds

> most compelling and ultimately the most rewarding are those [representations of history by Native American writers] which, by their humor, work to unmask

and disarm history, to expose the hidden agendas of historiography and thereby, remove it from the grasp of the political panderers and return it to the realm of story. . . . [Through] play and intellectual bantering they force a reconsideration of the processes and powers of historical reckoning and thus, essentially, liberate the reader from preconceived notions and incite an imaginative reevaluation of history. ("New Frontier" 39)

One can argue that King forces just such a reconsideration in *Medicine River*. He liberates the viewer through the humor that reconstitutes the power dynamic between Indian and non-Indian. Having control of the camera, as it were, the Indigenous photographer (or writer) reshapes or reconstitutes history and thus reality, and he thereby takes political control and achieves a form of visual sovereignty.

The opening sequence of *Medicine River* has yet another important function: it provides the story behind the portraits of the general, insisting that portraits do indeed include stories. Meanwhile, the officer burns the "action" photos, the photos Will is on assignment to take; the film allows and narrates the destruction of these photographs, photographs that would actually contain story. Yet the film never allows the viewer to see them. The portraits Will takes throughout the film, in contrast, allow the viewer to come to know the stories they contain. The stories are an inherent part of the portraits' very existence, an integral a part of representation of the tribal elders.

Unlike *The Exiles*, which uses nondiegetic photographs both as a part of the historical context and as a bridge into contemporary Los Angeles, *Medicine River* makes repeated diegetic use of photographs. Will's portraits are an essential component of the narrative itself, available to both the viewer and the characters. Thomas King and director Stuart Margolin do run the risk with such photographs, however, of reinscribing the same limiting stereotypes evident in ethnographic photography. Will's photographs of the elders for the calendar are meant to capture images before the people themselves have died, for example, and indeed the first photograph in the series is of Will's own mother, taken just before her death. Furthermore, Will's portraits are, for the most part, staged. George poses on the fence railing during the shoot, for example, and Martha Old Crow asks whether or not her buckskin dress is appropriate: "This okay?" she asks just before Will begins to photograph her. "The dress? I want to match this chair" (*Medicine*). There is a reversal here, however, in that Martha Old Crow, not the photographer, has chosen how to dress and where to sit.

The filmmaker's decision to occasionally offer the viewer a shot of these stills further complicates the danger inherent in challenging the stereotypical artificial renditions by contributing to them. In several scenes the viewer sees a very carefully contrived black-and-white version of each portrait as soon as Will shoots it. Such images forcefully recall the type of ethnographic photographs that virtually every viewer of the film will have been aware of and will, on some level, recognize. The plot element of photographing the elders thus raises a series of questions. How do Will's photographs differ both in physical characteristics and in context from ethnographic photographs by non-Indian photographers? Or, one might ask, how do King and Margolin challenge and disrupt the traditional use of photographs as limiting and stereotyping? Does the film merely recreate what early twentieth-century photographers and earlier painters had done? Or do they reverse the ethnographic trend previous photographers and Hollywood itself have so famously and firmly established?

To respond to such questions one need only consider a few specific moments in *Medicine River* and ask how the film does indeed offer something different. One such moment involves the photographing of Lionel James (Jimmy Herman), an elder who supposedly never comes to town. Will's young assistant, Clyde Whiteman (Bryon Chief Moon), just out of jail for robbing a camera store, absconds with all the equipment, taking it to the home of Lionel, who happens to be his grandfather. Not knowing better, Will believes that Clyde has stolen the cameras and tripods and about everything else in the studio, so he and Harlan follow this suspect to the reserve and Lionel's homestead, where they find Clyde innocently setting up the equipment in order to photograph his grandfather, the elder. While Will and Harlan are there, Lionel tells a humorous story about a trickster figure:

> It was on a night like this that old Coyote got on a plane to go to Ottawa to see the Prime Minister.
> "Boy, are we happy to see you," said the Prime Minister. "Maybe you can help us with our 'Indian problem.'"
> "Sure," said Coyote. "What's the problem?" [Laughter]. (*Medicine*)

During the telling of this story, the viewer sees a long shot of four figures silhouetted against a visually stunning orange sky at sunset as the men walk along a ridge above Lionel's home. Although they are "Indians," the film gives no indication that they have any of the problems the prime minister might be referring to. They have just eaten, they enjoy an evening stroll, and they joke and laugh together. Any portrait of the elder Lionel is thus inextricably intertwined with the stories of the taking of them, stories of the day the four men spend together. The photographs are imbued with the humor of the Coyote story, with Will's mistrust of Clyde, with Will's being introduced to Lionel, with the meal the men have just eaten, and with the hike they take in the evening light. Margolin and King provide all this context for the portrait, yet the viewer never actually sees any photographs of Lionel. His presence in the calendar as far as the viewer knows and as far as the film allows is in the stories exclusively, not in any visual image or still photograph. That verbal presence constitutes a reversal.

The sequence at Lionel's home is significant in the film on several levels. Perhaps most obviously, it is humorous in that there is a good joke at the center of it. As Kilpatrick writes, "to a Euro-American audience [Lionel's story] might be entertaining, but to the problematic Indians in question, it would be hilarious" (202). The sequence also makes overt reference to the trickster Coyote, calling attention to the many other trickster figures in the film: Harlan is certainly one of them, as is Martha Old Crow; indeed, the whole community plays the role of trickster (Harlan, Bertha, Clyde, Martha, and others) in its schemes to keep Will from leaving Medicine River and going back to Toronto. Another part of the humor in the sequence as a whole is that Clyde has not actually stolen the equipment. The joke is clearly at Will's expense, and Harlan gets a good laugh out of it, but the joke is also on the viewer because the film lets the audience think that Clyde might indeed have stolen the equipment. This joke suggests the viewer's complicity in a general mistrust, and by extension the viewer becomes aware of stolen photographs.

The sequence is structured around the fact that the four men are together in the first place because the former thief Clyde Whiteman has borrowed the camera equipment in order to take shots of his grandfather. Clyde's earlier crime was robbing a camera store, and thus his crime inevitably suggests some connection with stolen photographs. Clyde's robbery, which happens before the action of the film, disrupts whatever role a studio such as Wild Rose Photography might play in making available photographs of Indians, and at the same time that robbery enables Clyde to take control of the hardware involved in producing such photographs. He controls the master's tools, as it were. He challenges the mainstream by co-opting both the means and the results of traditional portrait photography. Like Will, he takes control of both the camera and the image, both inside and outside the limits of white legal and moral restrictions. *Medicine River* works in this way to reverse the ethnographic standard, as it were. The portraits that Will and Clyde take offer a reversal based on two fundamental principles: it is important who holds the camera, and every photograph contains a story.

Another element in the process of reversing the mainstream standard is Will's oft-repeated insistence that he does not do portraits. His insistence further separates him from a non-Indigenous outsider who does portraits ethnographically. Twice in the film Will states emphatically that he is not a portrait photographer. The first time, as we have seen, is in Malawi. The next time he says the same to Harlan and Bertha when they first suggest he do the calendar:

> WILL: I'm not a portrait photographer. What you need is a portrait photographer.
>
> BERTHA: A photographer who doesn't take pictures of people?
>
> WILL: I take pictures of wars and disasters, that sort of thing. (*Medicine*)

Will's boss and sometime partner Ellen also reminds the viewer that Will claims not to be a portrait photographer. On her surprise visit to the studio in Medicine River, she sees some of the photographs Will has taken and exclaims that "These are incredible, Will. And all this time you've been telling me 'I don't do portraits'" (*Medicine*). She reminds the viewer that whatever it is Will is doing, it is not taking portraits. That is, one way of reading the film's repeated insistence that Will does not do portraits is to maintain that what he does do—even once he gets to the reserve and begins taking photographs of the elders—is something other than portraiture. Even though the photographs he takes could appear to be portraits, they are more than this or something other than this; they are visual narratives. As the film unfolds, the viewer witnesses that much of the plot consists of the stories of taking the photographs, as evident in the adventure at Lionel's described above. Portraiture becomes secondary to the story being told.

The portrait of George (Malvin Yellowhorn) at the fairgrounds includes the story of Will as a boy on his father's lap. As Will snaps the photos, George tells the story of the photographer's father falling in fresh horse manure and then driving home. Will, as a boy, doesn't mind, and sits on his father's lap in the car, as George tells it, "pretending to bring us home." The viewer can thus not see any of the photographs of George without knowing the story of how, when, and where it was taken as well as recalling George's association with Will's family.

> GEORGE: I used to rodeo with your father. I used to stay with your mother and father in Calgary before you were born. Well, there was a bronco riding event; your father comes out of this chute on this big chestnut. . . . That horse turned hard; Howard went flying into a big pile of horseshit. . . . He only had the one shirt. We all had to drive home with him smelling like a horse. That was Howard. He said he'd smelled worse. And you Will, you sat in his lap all the way, never minding that shirt, turning the wheel, pretending you were bringing us home. (*Medicine*)

This scene, as George tells the story of Will's coming home, includes deep focus shots of that home: in the middle ground, George and Harlan are perched on the fence; in the near background behind them are the horses, a corral, and a group of other people; further still in the background are the trees; and finally the mountains are in the far distant background. This great depth of field shooting reinforces George's story about coming home, but as George is talking, Will walks away from the two perched on the fence. He moves into the foreground, facing the motion-picture camera, but with his back to the others and the community. As Will becomes more and more associated with community during the course of the film, however, the attitude of metaphorical distance depicted in this scene changes. Just as George finishes the story, Will finishes the shoot; he snaps the last photograph at the moment George says the word "home." Turning from George and Harlan, Will says, "Yeah, I know the story," and he walks away (*Medicine*). At this moment too, the film's nondiegetic leitmotif music begins, cueing the viewer to associate George's story and thus the photographing of George with Will's coming home.

The portrait of Martha Old Crow involves the story of Will and Harlan's negotiating the difficulties of getting to her home and the actual visit itself. They get lost, they tumble down a cliff, and they "swim" across the river. During the shoot, Martha Old Crow adopts Will, tells stories of his family, and gives him a rattle for Louise's baby. In a sense then, one could argue that the viewer of the film *Medicine River* does not distinguish, or is not cued to distinguish, between the product and the means of production, the mechanical equipment and the photographs that result. The entire adventure to Martha Old Crow's place is embodied for the viewer in the photograph itself; yet, in the case of Martha Old Crow as of Lionel James, the story is *all* that the viewer gets. That is, the viewer never sees any of the photographs that Will takes of Martha. The portraits of Martha Old Crow exist exclusively of the story: of Harlan and Will's getting lost, tumbling down the hill, and wading across the river to get to her place, but also the story of Martha's adopting Will and giving him a rattle. The act of taking the photographs of Martha Old Crow also looks forward to the final scene at the picnic when Will and Louise (Sheila Tousey) realize that Martha is a trickster of sorts. She has given them identical rattles. Instead of black-and-white portraits, which would be reminiscent of ethnographic photography, the film presents only the actual Martha Old Crow and the stories surrounding the photographing of her. In this way *Medicine River* undercuts the very value it seems to place on the photographs in the first place. The images that would be portraits of an elder exist for the viewer solely as story.

In addition to the portraits of the elders, only a few of which the viewer ever sees, the film offers several photographs that Will has not taken. These images provide background to and motivation for the plot, and thematically they parallel the photographs for the calendar. Will picks up two framed photos when he first arrives at his mother's house in Medicine River, for example, one presumably of his mother (who, as the viewer knows, has just died) and one presumably of himself and his brother, James, as children. Will is looking at these framed snapshots when he falls asleep in the chair, and he is still holding them when he wakes in the morning. Early on, the film thus locates the past as something contained in photographs and implies that as such they can offer Will a means to settle in and even perhaps reconcile himself to his mother's death. As his directions to the taxi driver suggest, he might not know how to find his mother's house, but he is able to locate himself, past and present, by studying the two snapshots.

In another instance suggesting the role photographs play in one's past and in one's sense of place and identity, Will digs through a box of pictures to find one in particular just after hearing George's story about coming home. The camera zooms to a snapshot of three men in cowboy hats, and given the context of Will's search, two of those pictured are presumably his father, Howard, and George, but the subjects are otherwise unidentified. The viewer must infer from the context that George's story has inspired Will to find this particular photograph, almost as if for Will the photographer, finding and seeing the photograph is the corroboration he needs to verify the truthfulness of George's verbal account, a verification necessary even though Will has told George that he knows the story. The film thus cues the viewer to assume that, in addition to the contexts of their being taken in the first place, Will's photographs of the elders will be bound up in and provide equally important stories and contexts.

Another photograph that the film marks as very important is one of Will's mother. This portrait, taken by the brother, James, is essentially what convinces Will to delay his return to the city and to agree to participate in the calendar project. The film prepares the viewer for this scene in different ways. As noted above, Will has already studied one picture of his mother, and when the camera zooms to a close-up of James's photograph, the viewer is able to recognize the subject as Will's mother. At the instant Will takes the print from Harlan, nondiegetic music begins and continues as Will walks the photograph to the window to study it more closely in natural light. Thematically, the scene is important because it implies that it is specifically the portrait of his mother that convinces him to help out with the calendar project. The film cues the viewer to appreciate the importance of this photograph at this moment in part because of story: the viewer already knows that Will has been away during his mother's illness and death, that he has missed her funeral, and that he is unable to locate his brother, the one who took the photograph. These narrative elements combine to insist that the value of such a photograph is in its story.

In the context of Will's deciding to stay in Medicine River and assist with the calendar project as the photographer, it is worthwhile to glance at one interesting instance of a choice the filmmakers made in adapting King's novel to film. In the novel Will returns to Medicine River because he has run out of options in Toronto. He has "become unemployed," as he says, and he has discovered that Susan, the woman he thought was his girlfriend and with whom he has fallen in love, turns out to be married (King 96; see 113–14). In the adaptation, in stark contrast, Will puts his successful, high-profile, professional, and artistic photojournalist career on hold, and essentially breaks off his relationship with his lover and boss, Ellen Lesly (Janet-Laine Green), to remain in Medicine River. At the same time, he begins a relationship with Louise Heavyman (Sheilia Tousey); he joins the basketball team; and he becomes friends with Harlan and some of the others in town. Whereas he initially tells Ellen back in Toronto that "there's nothing for me here" (*Medicine*), he soon finds excuses not to return to the city. He turns down his boss personally when she visits in Medicine River and professionally, as it were, when he finally refuses an important assignment in South Africa. Whatever the personal-political ramifications of his coming home, Will in the film is actually prepared to sacrifice his professional life and his personal relationship to stay in Medicine River. These sacrifices emphasize the radical and momentous importance of his homecoming. To the film thematically, one could argue, it is important that a photographer be a photographer and be in Medicine River by choice rather than by default. Will seems to decide relatively quickly to stay in Medicine River to do the calendar project, but throughout the entire film he is also always on the verge of returning to Toronto, the place where his job and his lover wait.

In the film, it is unequivocally the death of Will's mother that brings the son home, and thus, as do several other Indigenous North American films, *Medicine River* begins with the death of an elder. The mother dies before the action of the film, but her presence is felt throughout the film, and her presence undercuts and refutes the notion that she is representative of a dying culture. To drive the point home, the film offers several instances of the dead mother's continued presence. The first sequence after the credits includes a phone message from James informing Will of their mother's death. Will's first act once he gets to Medicine River is to enter his mother's house and look at a photograph of her. Another photograph of her inspires Will to remain in the town, and several characters, including Martha Old Crow and Louise, tell Will that they knew his mother. He misses her funeral, and Bertha reminds him that he missed it, but the film misses the funeral as well. That is, in that her death and funeral actually precede the action of the film and in that the film depicts neither, there is an implicit denial of her death. Where the film does admit her death, it at the same time always also insists on her presence. She is never far from any given character's consciousness, and she continues to motivate the plot from beyond the grave, as it were.

To further undercut any misguided mainstream notion of a vanishing race, the film emphasizes throughout the importance of Louise's pregnancy, leading up to the birth of her daughter. Not only is the birth of South Wing what ultimately keeps Will from leaving town, the baby takes center stage in the film's final sequence when Louise holds her in her lap during the photo shoot of the community group, a group that, as mentioned in the epigraph above, "refused to stay in place" (King 214). Metaphorically, of course, this idea from the novel is picked up in the adaptation in that the people themselves refuse stasis. As a people they are in constant flux. Individuals might die, but others are busy being born, and others still are negotiating how to carry on in a complex contemporary world.

The film contrasts Will's homecoming and photography with his brother's globetrotting and postcards in a playful but thematically relevant instance highlighting the importance of Indigenous photography. In this regard, the film uses picture postcards as unreliable locaters, specifically to (mis)inform Harlan and Will, as well as the viewer, of James's whereabouts. The viewer never actually sees Will's brother, and the film keeps track of him only vaguely by the postcards he sends first to Harlan and then finally to Will. He is in Vancouver, or traveling the west coast of the United States, or ultimately in New Zealand or Australia. The unreliability of the postcards is made manifest when Harlan gets the news from Will, who has gotten a postcard, that James is not where he last informed Harlan via postcard he would be.

> WILL: Hey, did I tell you I got a postcard from James? He's in Australia.
> HARLAN: Australia? . . . He told me New Zealand. Australia? (*Medicine*)

In the face of this information, Harlan can only shake his head and walk off muttering to himself. The scene seems to suggest that picture-postcard information is unreliable, or at least mystifying, and that it flies in the face of what was held to be true. In contrast, the viewer knows that the stories Will's photographs tell are true and reliable because the film allows the audience opportunity to witness those stories firsthand.

The entire photographic project results from a trickster act, which is a story in itself. Underlying the many instances of photography throughout the film is the fact that the entire project is made possible because of the community's grant proposal to do a "Photographic Study of Wildlife Migration Patterns in Southern Alberta," wildlife shots that enable the Community Center to get the grant that enables the calendar project. These photographs are proposed, trickster fashion, but no one actually ever takes them. The scam recalls Harold's pinch-bean proposal in *Harold of Orange*, in which Harold and the others have duped the granting agency as part of their ongoing mythic revolution at the bend in the river. Similarly, Harlan and the others in *Medicine River* have reappropriated government money to satisfy their own needs, providing a wonderfully circuitous argument to explain acquiring the means to pursue the calendar project:

> WILL: So, you got a loan on the cameras that you got from the government to buy a van, and then you got a loan from the council to pay for the calendar but you bought basketball uniforms instead.
> HARLAN: Bingo, that's right.

BIG JOHN YELLOW RABBIT: We use the cameras to do the calendar. We sell the calendar and pay back the band council. Because we have nice uniforms we win the championship, which has a five thousand dollar first prize, and we pay back the loan on the cameras.

WILL: And I get to take pictures of moose and elk. (*Medicine*)

One of the several ironies here, however, is that as far as *Medicine River* the film is concerned, neither Will nor anyone else ever photographs wildlife. Such pictures are of no interest to the film.

The many instances that stress the importance of visual representation force a comparison between Will's photographs and the film *Medicine River* itself. Such a call for comparison is especially evident in the film's final scene, in which Will photographs the entire community as a group. The scene subtly subverts and calls attention to notions of photography as mediator and emphasizes the underlying artifice of film. The film breaks its own illusion, to some extent, and it certainly calls the viewer's attention one last time to the artifice of the filming. In this way, the film anticipates the use to which Masayesva puts his camera in *Imagining Indians*. As the dental patient in that film begins scratching the lens, the fiction is broken and the viewer becomes fully aware of the artifice of film. Although the metanarrative is subtler in *Medicine River*, here too the viewer is invited to acknowledge that someone unseen controls the camera. In the case of *Medicine River*, that someone, Will, becomes visible, and as a member of the community he photographs, he has the power to direct the viewer's gaze at the same time he includes himself as part of the observed subject.

The final scene begins with a medium close-up of Will's back as he looks through his camera's viewfinder before the filmmaker racks back to a long shot of the entire group, the subject of Will's photo. Behind the group in this deep focus shot are the trees, and behind them stand the mountains. Both visually and thematically, the moment of the film's final scene recalls the earlier scene in which Will photographs George as he sits on a corral fence with mountains in the background and tells the story about Will as a little boy pretending to be driving his father's car bringing everyone home. The viewer is further prepared for this final scene in which Will includes himself in the photo early in the film. That is, early on, as part of his attempt to trick Will into doing the calendar in the first place, Harlan begins asking questions about the camera and other photographic equipment. Though only reluctantly, Will does respond to Harlan's questions, informing both Harlan and the viewer and foreshadowing the film's final sequence:

HARLAN: What's this button?

WILL: It's a time delay. Harlan, there's a little more to it than just knowing the camera parts.

Group portrait. *Medicine River*. Courtesy of Barbara Allinson.

HARLAN: What's it do?
WILL: [sighs.] Well, say you wanted to take a picture that you wanted to be in too. You set the time delay, press the shutter release, and you have about ten seconds.
. . .
HARLAN: You mean I could take a picture and be in it too? (*Medicine*)

As Harlan asks this last question, he sets the camera on the table, walks quickly a few steps away, and sits down, as if posing for his own photo. Between his pressing the button and the actual shutter release a few seconds elapse, and in these seconds there is time for action. That is, there is narrative time between the pressing of the button and the snap of the shutter. In this sense, in a motion picture, the event or action can be seen to imbue the actual photograph with story.

Most immediately this time-delay function enables Will to include himself in the photograph in the film's finale. Literally, he is able to be in the photograph; figuratively, he is able to join the community. There is the narrative of what happens between Will's pushing the button and the snap of the shutter. Again literally, in this case, he runs from the camera to the lawn chair, turns and sits in time for the snap of the shutter. But figuratively, the time-delay mechanism, as Harlan's questions infer early in the film, has great potential for narrative. The final scene includes humor as well as a metafictional element in that it takes Will several attempts to finally get into his own picture.

These humorous attempts call attention to the artifice of film. They insist that the photographer gets to choose what is on the film as well as choosing if, how, and when any such photograph might be viewed.

The idea of a self-timer is also important in the context of self-representation. As Harlan discovers early on, and as the final scene implies figuratively, thanks to the time-delay button, Indigenous peoples can take and be in their own photographs. They can represent themselves. The notion of a time-delay button also suggests that at long last the subject can control the camera, can take control of both sides of the lens and thus control history. In the final shot of the film, Will's camera stands in the foreground on a tri-pod, and Will has run to turn and face that camera. This shot of the entire community, including Lionel James, who supposedly never comes to town but who does evidently attend community picnics, also includes Will, who, true to his character throughout, is at first reluctant to join the group. The still over which the final credits begin to roll includes Will's camera on a tri-pod, the group in the photo, Will himself, and the trees and mountains in the background. The still and the motion picture, that is the photograph and the film, merge at this point. They are one and the same, and both include the Indigenous photographer.

Such a shot has the potential to subvert the genre of portraiture of Indigenous peoples through its multiple reversals, and as a film *Medicine River* actually reverses the colonial gaze in that it enables the viewer to see the photographer photographed on the screen, and that photographer is an Indigenous man. This final photograph, accompanied by the film's nondiegetic theme music, completes the reversal. The photographer is part of the very community he photographs, and one can argue that visual sovereignty exists when "the community and the requirement of a method of portraying that community with respect become one and the same" (Stuart Murray 17). As an insider, finally, Will has taken a photograph in which he sits beside Louise and South Wing, surrounded by the other members of the community: elders, their children, and their children's children.

SIX

Keep Your Pony Out of My Garden

Powwow Highway and "Being Cheyenne"

PHILBERT: In the old days, how long did a take a warrior to gather
   medicine?
HARRIET: What'd you do, find a token in a Cracker Jacks box?
PHILBERT: I had a sign. The time has come for me to gather medicine.
[Harriet cackles.]
PHILBERT: I already have a pony. What did the old ones say about . . .
HARRIET: [interrupting] I get sick of being asked for good old Indian
   wisdom. I ain't got none. So get the hell outta here.
[Philbert starts to leave.]
HARRIET: Hey Fat Philbert, come! Here's a quote from Dull Knife. He
   once told my Great Uncle Benny Looks Twice, he said: "Keep your
   pony out of my garden." —*Powwow Highway*

The exchange between Philbert (Gary Farmer) and his Aunt Harriet (Maria
Antoinette Rogers) early in the film *Powwow Highway* suggests that Jonathan
Wacks's film adaptation of David Seals's 1979 novel, *The Powwow Highway*,
combines a man's search for identity with both sarcasm and humor. As an
early indication of Philbert's quest for a sense of self and an understanding of his Cheyenne heritage, the exchange also implies that along with that
humor the film raises serious questions about appropriation as well as about
genuine cultural and spiritual renewal. Aunt Harriet's reference to Dull Knife
foreshadows the film's emphasis on historical awareness and connectedness
versus the Hollywood trope of the vanishing Indian, and it also anticipates
the several intertextual references to *Cheyenne Autumn*, John Ford's 1964 historical fiction film that traces Dull Knife and Little Wolf as they flee the U.S.
Calvary in their attempt to reach their homeland. Intertextuality allows *Powwow Highway* to talk back to Hollywood by challenging the stock version
of history with its limited point of view and thereby overturn long-standing
filmic attitudes. The film takes control of history and provides a vehicle for
Indigenous self-representation.

    Powwow Highway is a narrative fiction film set in the twentieth century
and based on a novel by Huron writer David Seals. Though directed by non-
Native Jonathan Wacks, the film has a largely Indigenous cast, with Cayuga

actor Gary Farmer as Philbert, Apache/Cheyenne actor Joanelle Nadine Romero as Bonnie, and Cherokee actor Wes Studi as Buff, for example. It is not clear that A Martinez, the actor who plays Buddy Red Bow (Red Bird in the novel), has any Native American ancestry. Kilpatrick assumes that he is non-Native, writing that "since Buddy Red Bow is the lead character in a film that consciously deals with appropriation of identity, a Native American actor would have been a better choice" (119). Rodney Simard agrees, and suggests that "in terms of ethnicity" the casting of Martinez to play Buddy is "problematic" (20). In his discussion of the issue of non-Indians playing Indian roles in Westerns, Eric Anderson makes no mention whatsoever of Martinez's heritage. This silence is perhaps appropriate, for on at least one website Martinez self-identifies as tribal: "My mother was part Blackfoot Indian and they were from the Dakotas" (Martinez), and a Santa Fe newspaper identifies him as "part Blackfoot" (*Santa Fe Reporter*). Interestingly, in the context of tribal affiliation, it is Martinez's character who is quite ambivalent about his tribal past and heritage.

Briefly recounted, *Powwow Highway* tells the story of two Cheyenne men, Philbert Bono and Buddy Red Bow, who leave Lame Deer on the Northern Cheyenne Reservation in southeastern Montana and drive to Santa Fe in a beat-up wreck, a 1964 Buick that Philbert names Protector the War Pony. Their mission is to rescue Buddy's long-lost sister, Bonnie Red Bow (Joanelle Nadine Romero), who has been wrongly imprisoned. The mining interests in Montana, with the help of the Santa Fe police and the FBI, have arrested Bonnie in order to get the politically active and tribally influential Buddy away from his center of power immediately before an important vote concerning the renewal of a mining operation on the reservation, a mining operation he opposes and evidently has the political power to get defeated. Philbert has a two-fold purpose in taking the trip to Santa Fe with Buddy. He too wants to rescue Bonnie, but he also wants to continue his quest to gather medicine. En route he takes an excursion to the sacred site of Sweet Butte, South Dakota, attends a powwow at Pine Ridge, and stops off at Fort Robinson, Nebraska. As a part of his quest he prays in a stream, climbs Sweet Butte, and during the journey as a whole finds several tokens that signify his progress toward becoming a warrior. The two Cheyenne men get to Santa Fe, team up with Bonnie's friend Rabbit, and rescue Bonnie and her children. Having successfully eluded police pursuit, Bonnie, the children, Philbert, Buddy, and Rabbit are finally safe and ready to drive home together with tribal chairman Chief Joseph (Sam Vlahos), who has come to Santa Fe on his own.

Critics and reviewers have classified the film as a road movie and a buddy film, in which the two heroes travel together for over a thousand miles, share their very different perspectives of the world, come to appreciate each other, and finally rescue the wronged and innocent Indian woman Bonnie. Douglas

Heil argues that the "filmmakers harness [Buddy and Philbert] together through their shared objective," and "imprison them within the same Buick" (35). The film can also be classified as action-adventure, a comedy, a Western, or even a cult film. As Eric Anderson writes, "to some extent, the makers of *Powwow Highway* rework and refute the stereotypical image of the Hollywood Indian simply by taking advantage of multiple film genres and conventions" (137). In addition to refuting stereotypes, the film offers a reversal of the typical Hollywood Western. Ellen Arnold suggests that it "can be read as an appropriation of the typical Western format to serve Indian purposes" (351), and Marshall Toman and Carole Gerster suggest more specifically that the film is a "direct reversal of the old [rescue] plot (epitomized in John Ford's *The Searchers*)" (34). *Powwow Highway* counters the standard Western plot in which a non-Native cowboy or soldier defeats the Native Americans in order to establish order, enact revenge, or rescue a kidnapped or endangered white woman, as is the case in *The Searchers*. More pointedly and specifically, *Powwow Highway* can be seen as a response to another Ford film, *Cheyenne Autumn*. Jonathan Wacks offers references to *Cheyenne Autumn* specifically, such as when Philbert stops at a historical marker commemorating the escape of Dull Knife's band of Cheyennes from Fort Robinson in 1879. At this moment, Wacks's depiction of Philbert and Buddy as they journey southward echoes and mirrors the historical northward march of the Cheyennes a century earlier as depicted in Ford's film. Fort Robinson is the literal point of intersection.

Even before Philbert crosses paths with his ancestors at Fort Robinson, however, *Powwow Highway* makes an intertextual reference to *Cheyenne Autumn*. Buddy asks his long-time acquaintance (they can hardly be called friends at this point in the film) whether or not he is willing to drive to Santa Fe to rescue Bonnie: "So what do you say? Can I count on you or what?" Philbert acknowledges his willingness by stating, first in Cheyenne and then in English: "*Natahe Omesehese*. We are Cheyenne." Buddy understands immediately that Philbert's statement constitutes a "yes." Philbert makes this statement a total of three times in the film, and he makes each statement in the context of freeing Bonnie. In the first instance, "We are Cheyenne," means "yes, of course I will drive to Santa Fe with you to rescue Bonnie." The second occurrence comes just after Buddy has been thrown from the car and has broken his gun as a result of his wanting to kill a spider. Philbert tosses off Buddy's question about how they are going to free Bonnie without the gun with the same statement: "We are Cheyenne." He implies that acknowledging and accepting their Cheyenne heritage will somehow guide them. The third iteration comes as Philbert drives through the streets of Santa Fe with Bonnie's two children, Jane and Sky. He says "We are Cheyenne" as he is reassuring the children that they will indeed succeed in their attempt to break their mother out of jail (*Powwow*). Philbert uses this invocation at three crucial moments in the rescue plot. The film thus weaves Philbert's quest to gather medicine, acquire tokens, and discover what it means to be Cheyenne with the plot devoted to rescuing Bonnie.

Philbert's repeated assertion, "We are Cheyenne," echoes a very specific similar moment in Ford's *Cheyenne Autumn*. A white schoolteacher, Deborah Wright (Carroll Baker), hears that the Cheyennes are preparing to escape the reservation, and she immediately drives her buckboard to the camp to express her concern for the children's safety. In response the Cheyenne character Spanish Woman (Delores Del Rio) explains that the children will indeed be safe and able to undertake the journey:

DEBORAH WRIGHT: What about the children?
SPANISH WOMAN: They are Cheyenne.
DEBORAH WRIGHT: But who will care for them?
SPANISH WOMAN: We will do what we can. They are Cheyenne. (*Cheyenne*)

In both films the exchanges are shot straight on with medium close-ups, a camera angle and distance that forces the viewer to focus on the characters as it emphasizes what they are saying. The statements are made with great earnestness in both films, suggesting the speaker's confidence and seriousness. As a Cheyenne man, Buddy understands immediately what Philbert's statement means; as a white woman, Deborah has to ask a second time, but Spanish Woman expects the statement to be clarification enough; she simply repeats it. The speakers in both films imply that the statement of heritage and identity is loaded, and if it alone does not guarantee the success of the undertaking in question, it certainly does carry many layers of meaning beyond a mere statement of the obvious fact that they are Cheyenne.

John Ford takes great liberties with history in his film *Cheyenne Autumn*, but he does rely on the source material as represented in Mari Sandoz's 1953 book by the same title. After witnessing broken promises on the reservation in Oklahoma, the Cheyennes begin the journey for their homeland by fleeing northward toward present-day Montana, Yellowstone country, a march of about fifteen hundred miles. A century later, Buddy and Philbert trek southward, on a quest of their own, and the two parties, and the two films, cross paths at Fort Robinson, Nebraska.

Philbert stops the car at the historical marker in a blizzard and gets out, leaving his companions Wolf Tooth, Imogene, and Buddy complaining in vain, calling for him to come back. He stands in the wind and snow to contemplate the message on the commemorative marker. In Seals's novel these characters actually understand and respect his wish to visit the spot, and they remain silent: "It was a place of supreme peace now, because it had once been a place of utter anguish. . . . Philbert turned off his engine and got

A token from the old ones. *Powwow Highway*. Screen Capture. Handmade Films.

out quickly and closed the door. The others were surprised but did nothing" (183). In the film Philbert wipes the snow from the marker as if clearing away the fog of history, and reads of the Cheyenne Outbreak of 1879. Although the text in the film differs from that on the actual marker, the basic information conveyed is similar, and the film allows the viewer to read along with Philbert:

FORT ROBINSON

THE CHEYENNE OUTBREAK

On September 9, 1878, some 300 Northern Cheyenne, under the leadership of Dull Knife, began a trek from Oklahoma to their homeland in the North. One hundred forty-nine survived and were imprisoned at Fort Robinson. (*Powwow*)

As Philbert contemplates the marker, he apparently envisions the Cheyennes a hundred years earlier and sees them making their way on foot through the same snowstorm. The viewer gets an extreme close-up of Philbert's face, and this close-up of long duration, almost four seconds, allows the viewer to enter Philbert's head, as it were. The film cuts to the people in his vision, weary and travel-worn, moving toward the camera. During this scene the viewer hears only a slow, low nondiegetic drumbeat interrupted by a diegetic horse's whinny, diegetic in so far as the horse is part of what Philbert and the viewer see. The scene is filmed in a bluish light, evoking the deep blue cold of the snowstorm and suggesting its otherworldliness. The lighting also suggests what in the novel David Seals maintains is the sacredness of the ground these people walk on. Although Philbert's vision as related in the novel is of an episode that takes place two years earlier, the sentiment expressed applies here: "No more evil could ever penetrate into this hallowed ground, for evil had purged itself from here with its own foul breath" (183).

The parallel scene in Ford's *Cheyenne Autumn* is of a group crossing a wide valley. As they trudge through snow in Ford's film, Dull Knife's and Little Wolf's bands separate. Dull Knife (played by Mexican-born actor Gilbert Roland) has decided to travel toward and seek refuge at Fort Robinson. With a long shot, Ford depicts the people trekking through the snow angling away from one another in two single-file lines. The wide-angle, long shot allows the viewer to see the people separate and also see the sky covered with low, gray clouds and the vast snow-covered plain between mountains in the distance. As in *Powwow Highway*, the scene in *Cheyenne Autumn* is shot as if with a blue filter, emphasizing the eerie coldness. With the long shot, the viewer has the advantage of seeing the two groups move apart. The camera zooms closer as a young woman breaks from one group to join the other. *Powwow Highway* includes a subtle filmic hint of the split. As the travelers approach the camera in Philbert's vision, one on horseback leaves the frame to the right, as if heading in a different direction, then another remains in the background, as if not accompanying those on foot. The scene consists of cuts back and forth between the people in the vision and Philbert's own face, marked with sadness as he watches or envisions.

It is at this point that Philbert finds the second of his tokens. He reaches into the snow for what is perhaps a small piece of ice or an ice-covered pebble: "A token from the old ones," he says to himself, and he thereby incorporates this moment and this place in history into his own efforts to understand himself as a Cheyenne man. The specific past, the specific Cheyenne history, is thus very much a part of his present. If this moment in the film serves to link past and present, there is a similar theme present in the novel, even if in a different context: "Past hopes, past excuses, past regrets lay thickly upon his soul. . . . Memory was always a thing of the present to an Indian. All he had to do was walk past a piece of dirt and he would be reminded of the sorrows of Little Wolf. The cries of the past could never die in a man who dwelt on the soil where his ancestors were buried. They became the cries of these his children today" (Seals 7). The sequence at Fort Robinson in *Powwow Highway* marks one of the several ways that history and tradition are important to Philbert's quest and to the film as a whole. It signals that the film takes the quest earnestly. The scene also indicates one of the ways in which *Powwow Highway* makes a point about survival.

Historically, as intimated in the film, one band of fleeing Cheyennes remained with Dull Knife and another took a different route, under the leadership of Little Wolf, whose band made it eventually to the homeland in present-day Montana. The other band was not so fortunate. Although the sign the viewer sees in the film makes no mention of it, the actual marker, just west of Fort Robinson on Highway 20 in northwestern Nebraska, does commemorate the result of the midwinter escape attempt of Dull Knife's band: "Unable to find horses, the Cheyenne eluded pursuing troops for 12 days by heading northwest through the rough terrain of the Pine Ridge. Soldiers discovered their hiding place on Antelope Creek January 22, but the Indians refused to surrender. During the outbreak, 64 Cheyenne and 11 soldiers were killed. More than 70 were recaptured and several escaped. The number of casualties made the Cheyenne Outbreak one of the major conflicts of the Indian Wars" (Nebraska Historical Marker). As Mari Sandoz tells it, just after the Cheyennes crossed the North Platte River there is a confrontation between Dull Knife and Little Wolf that almost comes to a fight: "Warriors of both sides moved against each other, knives out, guns up, tempers taut as dry bowstrings worn by the long flight." At this point Little Wolf, who argues against division of the group by insisting steadfastly that they must continue northward, moves apart, saying "'Let those who would go on to the north follow'" (117). According to historian Alan Boye, "somewhere south of the Platte the Cheyennes spilt into two groups. It was a parting of consequences, for the two bands would never rejoin. . . . [J]ust as the exact location will forever remain a mystery, the reasons for the separation will remain honored by silence" (214). Boye goes on to note, however, that "Grinnell claims that Little Wolf wanted to keep moving northward with caution, but Dull Knife believed that because they were in the north again nothing bad could happen. Grinnell also maintains that the split did not happen all at once, but that small groups of Dull Knife's band split off over the course of several days and then regrouped north of the Platte" (Boye 344; see Grinnell 409–10).

John Ford labored to tell, as he put it, "the Indian side. . . . They are a very dignified people" (qtd. in Friar and Friar 170). Film scholars debate the degree to which Ford's film does indeed offer a sympathetic view of the Cheyennes' trek from Oklahoma and their attempted escape in Nebraska. One reviewer writes, for example, that "Warners doubtless anticipated another 'great Western in the classic Ford tradition.' Ford delivered a film designed to question that tradition and to destroy the legend which, of all people, he himself has been most instrumental in creating" (Perkins 153). Michael Hilger's praise of Ford for promulgating a sympathetic view is somewhat tempered when he admits that Ford's "noble Native American characters are more symbols of white exploitation than believable characters in themselves" (*From Savage* 153). Jacquelyn Kilpatrick echoes this point of view, writing that in Ford's hands the Cheyenne people become "symbols for the oppressed, but the film was also Ford's attempt to correct some of the stereotypes he had helped to create" (67). As John O'Connor writes, the producer of *Cheyenne Autumn* "bent over backwards to sympathize with the Indians' plight, but they did nothing to correct Hollywood's characteristic carelessness in portraying historical events and the complexity of Native American cultures" (37).

For all its sympathy, Ford's film did very little to change Hollywood's insistence on casting non-Indians to play any significant Indian roles. In *Cheyenne Autumn* non-Indians continue to take the Native Americans' speaking parts: Dull Knife (Gilbert Roland), Spanish Woman (Dolores del Rio), Red Shirt (Sal Mineo), and Little Wolf (Ricardo Montalban), for example. In the *Only Good Indian*, Ralph Friar and Natasha Friar consider non-Indian acting as an indicator that the film is not particularly sympathetic: "*Cheyenne Autumn* was long and unbelievable, especially the Indian caricatures played by whites. . . . The film proved to be nothing but a vehicle for an all-star cast" (168). Such casting is certainly typical of Hollywood, but it is also a clear indication that however sincere Ford might have been in his desire to portray the *historical* Cheyennes sympathetically, he did not extend that sense of sympathy to any recognition of American Indians as his actual contemporaries in Hollywood, as people who could have portrayed the significant Indian characters in his film.

Regardless of questions about how Ford does or does not exhibit sympathy toward Native Americans and the history of their interactions with non-Indian settlers, it is important to note and understand that his films had, and in ways still have, an important impact on contemporary (mis)understandings and (mis)representations of nineteenth-century American Indian histories and cultures, whether Mohawk, Apache, or Cheyenne, (mis)representations that Indigenous films such as *Powwow Highway* are hard pressed to correct. As Ken Nolley argues, Ford's films tend to conflate history and myth, and with this conflation his films "function as if they were historical texts, constructing a sense of Native American life on the frontier, participating in the social and political debates of the era in which they were produced, and helping to construct much of what still stands for popular historical knowledge of Native American life" (47). Ford's representations in this regard deserve to be challenged not only through scholarship, but on screen as well. In the face of films like *Cheyenne Autumn*, that is, it is vitally important that the viewer see a contemporary Cheyenne character, such as Philbert, who acknowledges the past even as depicted by Ford, and who is willing to acknowledge and accept that past at the same time he has the capacity, ability, and willingness to move beyond it.

Immediately preceding the scene in which Philbert pauses at Fort Robinson is a scene in which Bonnie's two children, Jane and Sky, make their own escape from the detention center in Santa Fe, where they are being held while their mother is in jail. The juxtaposition ties together the two different lines of action; it implies a temporal simultaneity and emphasizes a thematic parallel. That is, at essentially the same time that Philbert considers the historical marker commemorating a Cheyenne escape, two twentieth-century Cheyenne children slip away from their place of detention; both scenes concern breakouts; and both look forward to Bonnie's escape later in the film. The other kids are oblivious to the escape because as Jane and Sky make their way out a window, they are watching a *Robotech* cartoon—a syndicated daily that ran from March 1985 through September 1988. The particular installment of the cartoon series on screen depicts an episode in the Macross Saga called "Countdown," part of an epic battle of the good earthlings against the invading evil aliens. The young girl Minmei is caught in a crossfire and needs help. The young boy Rick sits at the controls inside what is called a Battloid, a giant robot that can convert itself into a jet airplane. It is otherwise not unlike and is very much in anticipation of the manned, headless hominid robots in the final battle sequence in *Avatar* (2009). From inside the contraption the boy Rick operates a huge mechanical hand toward the girl in order to rescue her. The viewer of *Powwow Highway* does not necessarily know all this, but does know from the television clip itself that amid the sound of gunfire Minmei calls for help and that a male voice responds:

> ROY: Take it easy honey, you're okay. We'll protect you. Take care of the girl, Rick; I'll hold them off.
> RICK: You can't handle them alone.
> ROY: Don't argue with me! I'll try to fire while you get her out of here.
> RICK [to Minmei, from inside the robot]: Stay right there. I'll pick you up. [at which point the viewer sees on the television screen the giant robotic hand cradle Minmei.] (*Robotech*)

Ellen Arnold argues that this interlude in *Powwow Highway* continues the "rescue of the princess" motif, already well established in the film and continued with Rabbit's giving herself and her rescue mission over to Buddy (see Arnold 352). Beyond the film's failure to allow women to break through male-defined stereotypes, the intertextuality here plays an important role in that the cartoon offers important and significant parallels. In the television series, earthlings—including children—are battling an armada of alien interstellar invaders, and most immediately two young men must rescue a young girl. In *Powwow Highway* the FBI and the Santa Fe police have combined forces, and hence two men engage in a rescue attempt of a young mother. "I thought you were an amateur," the viewer of *Powwow Highway* hears the television voice of Minmei say to Rick just as Bonnie's daughter Jane helps her brother escape through the window. "Trust me, I can do this," replies Rick from inside the robot (*Powwow*). In the cartoon's "New Generation" series, evoked by this clip from an earlier episode, the Robotech Expeditionary Force, allied with the so-called Earth rebels, undertakes the challenge of retaking their ancestral homeland, robbed from them by the alien invaders. It is clearly no arbitrary decision to include a glimpse of this particular cartoon on television just as Jane and Sky make their own escape. The two children are, in a sense, beginning their own quest to regain a homeland as well as an identity, and their quest can perhaps be said to continue just after their escape. Sky asks Rabbit about his ancestry over the phone: "Rabbit, what tribe are me and Jane?" (*Powwow*). With Sky's question is an immediate crosscut to the old Buick on a snowy highway just before Philbert stops at the historical marker where he has his vision. Through this crosscutting, the film answers Sky's question: he shares the same ancestry as Philbert: they are descendants of the people trekking through the snow. They are Cheyenne. Philbert's vision in the snow at Fort Robinson demonstrates for the viewer some of what that identity means.

Back on the highway, immediately following the interlude at the Fort Robinson historical marker, Philbert and the other travelers stop for gas at a convenience store where Philbert gets a glimpse of a William S. Hart Western playing on the television. In the few seconds he watches, he sees Hart's character tie a rope to a jailhouse window and pull the window out. This moment inspires Philbert; it gives him the idea ultimately of how to free Bonnie. In the novel, in contrast, it is Sky who has seen a television program, *Hopalong Cassidy*, and has the idea of how to work the break out (Seals 173). As these two television clips make clear, the intertextuality apparent in *Powwow Highway* is not limited to echoes of the film *Cheyenne Autumn*. One effect of such a multiplicity of references and allusions is that they demonstrate that Cheyennes of the late 1980s are living and clearly integrated into the wider society and culture. This multiplicity of intertextual references also suggests another manner in which Wacks's film manages to challenge the single-mindedness of Hollywood stereotypes of American Indians. The film suggests that Philbert, as a Cheyenne man on an identity quest, fuses and makes use of elements from many different modern-day cultures and genres; it reveals explicitly, as evidenced from his vision at Fort Robinson, that the past is an important part of his present. His original inspiration to acquire a war pony (an automobile) and begin his quest to gather medicine comes, after all, from an automobile advertisement he sees on television.

Philbert's travel companion Buddy Red Bow, in contrast, seems to feel no need to seek, establish, or question his identity. He seems to feel no compulsion to reconnect in any way with his tribal past. As he tells Philbert early on, "I'm the Tribal Purchasing Agent, god-damn-it" (*Powwow*), and that sense of self and that unreflective self-confidence appear to remain with him throughout the journey. The extreme example of Buddy's swagger is at the moment he attacks a pursuing police car after the jailbreak. Unlike Philbert's visions in which Philbert can be seen to receive lessons from his ancestors, Buddy shape-shifts into a pre-twentieth-century warrior. In this scene he stands on the Santa Fe street holding one of the Buick windows at one moment, and at the next moment the film cuts to a shot of him instantaneously appareled in full buckskin, befeathered, face painted. He leaps through the air, and the car window transforms itself into a tomahawk that he sends slicing through the air, causing the pursuing patrol car to crash. On one level the scene clearly disrupts whatever realism remains in the film. In contrast to Buddy's transformation, the film clearly marks Philbert's visions as visions. The shot of Buddy perhaps suggests that he has finally learned something from Philbert, and this possibility is especially evident if one compares it with Buddy's other battle scene. In the Hi-Fi Hut in Sheridan, Wyoming, Buddy goes berserk because of a misunderstanding, destroys the shop, and ends up getting shot at. But in both cases, Buddy clearly sees himself as a warrior whose method is brute force.

In addition to the issue of Buddy's mystical transformation into a nineteenth-century warrior, some critics find fault with another plot twist, the introduction of the non-Indian character Rabbit Layton (Amanda Wyss). Disregarding the fact that Rabbit is also a character in Seals's novel, Kilpatrick is disappointed and writes, "unfortunately, someone must have felt that the film needed a little sex thrown in, so [Rabbit] wears jeans that are amazingly tight and pursues Buddy in no uncertain terms. It is as if she sees him as the exotic Cheyenne warrior, and the ghosts of all those Hollywood Indians come back to haunt us" (120). Arnold is similarly disappointed and writes that Rabbit "succumbs to Buddy's macho display in his bar scene attack on Sandy Youngblood. . . . 'I know what I want,' she says passionately to Buddy, and signs on as his dutiful helpmate" (352). But who are those ghosts and what does it mean to sign on as a helpmate? Another way of looking at the plot twist Rabbit's appearance introduces is precisely what Arnold and Kilpatrick find objectionable: it intimates a future, suggests the possibility of an ongoing relationship between Buddy and Rabbit. Such a relationship can be seen as important to this film and to American Indian film in general because it has the potential to reverse the long-standing Hollywood taboo against interracial relationships and marriages.

A taboo against miscegenation is almost as old as the Hollywood film industry itself. As Philip Deloria writes, many very early films (of the silent era) "meditated . . . seriously on the problems of postconquest social relations," one of which is of course interracial marriage. However, continues Deloria, although Indians "could lead whites to the primitivist wellsprings of nature and virtue, they did so with full knowledge that white men and white women belonged together, creating a future in which there was no room for Indians" (87). Since as early as 1925, with the silent film *The Vanishing American* (in which Richard Dix plays Nophaie, a Navajo man who falls in love with a white woman), Hollywood has disallowed interracial relationships to survive the end of the film. Nophaie dies in his white lover's arms, and any potential they might have had as a couple dies with him. In *Laughing Boy* (1934) the

Navajo title character kills his Navajo wife when he finds her with her white lover, ending any possibility of any interracial relationship. In *The Searchers*, one sister dies after being sexually assaulted by her Indian captors, and Debbie (Natalie Wood), who has been kidnapped and has lived with Scar (Henry Brandon) must be separated from her lover and brought back to civilization, although the John Wayne character wants to kill her outright for her having been with an Indian man.

In 1928 there was a proposed constitutional amendment that would have federally banned interracial marriage, and it wasn't until as late as 1967 that the Supreme Court declared state miscegenation laws to be unconstitutional (*Loving v. Virginia*). But the high court's ruling did not change Hollywood's attitude. Just three years later, in *A Man Called Horse* the white hero's Indian wife Running Deer (Greek actor Corinna Tsopei) dies when she falls from the horse of a Shoshone would-be abductor. In *Little Big Man*, the same year, the Dustin Hoffman character watches his Sioux wife and children slaughtered by the U.S. Cavalry just after he himself has opted to save the old man Old Lodge Skins (Chief Dan George) rather than his wife and children. Even as late as 1990 in *Dances with Wolves*, true to the long-standing taboo against interracial relationships in film, Hollywood avoids the issue of an interracial marriage when Dunbar's lover Stands with a Fist (Mary McDonnell) turns out to be a white woman, adopted into the tribe as a child. Not even in *House Made of Dawn* can the relationship between Abel and Milly succeed. "Go home Abel," Milly tells Abel. "There's nothing for you here" (*House*). In *Powwow Highway*, however, Jonathan Wacks is willing to reverse that trend, as is Seals in his novel, at least by implication. The film encourages the viewer to believe Buddy and Rabbit might end up together, in that they are both fugitives from the law and they walk off together at the film's end. The open-endedness of the relationship is certainly significant as a reversal of the tropes common to the Hollywood Western.

In "Culture Isn't Buckskin Shoes: A Conversation around *Powwow Highway*," Toby Langen and Kathryn Shanley comment that at the end of the film there is "catharsis . . . [but politically] you're no better off for having seen that film" (26). Ellen Arnold makes a similar point, more emphatically, when she argues that after the chase-scene finale, "all the real issues the film raises have been dropped": the mining deal, the violent regime at Pine Ridge, the film's concerns with capitalism and exploitation and racism, for example; all disappear after the chase scene. According to Arnold, for "Native American audiences, the film carries the disturbing message that political activism and resistance are less effective . . . than lawless revenge" (353). The ending of the film is especially disturbing in Arnold's view, in that the heroes "must now 'vanish' back to the reservation, never to leave again on pain of arrest" (353). Corinn Columpar argues similarly that "the only point of reference that the film has for its vision of the ideal home is the hypothetical past[,] . . . a time when the reservation was not in the clutches of corporations and people had access to the 'good old Indian wisdom' at which Philbert's Aunt Harriet scoffs" (125).

These readings of the film, which can apply equally well to the novel, focus on Buddy and his political role in the film. Buddy is the one who seems to have the power to thwart the mining deal; he inevitably resorts to brute force both early and late in the film. Buddy has the connection to the American Indian Movement and Pine Ridge, whose problems are left unresolved. Buddy tears up the Hi-Fi Hut in a fit of rage about the assumed poor quality of the merchandise and against the racism and condescension exhibited by the salesman. Those aspects of the film are indeed Buddy's. But as Toman and Gerster assert, by the end of the film "political activism and ritual tradition have become meaningful counterparts" (36). Buddy's story is necessarily linked to Philbert's.

Some readings of the film tend to ignore Philbert, who plays a crucial if sometimes critically overlooked role in the film. Indeed, his role arguably stands as one of the most important innovations of the film and the novel. One can read the film as one that portrays Philbert's coming to terms with his Cheyenne identity. As one reviewer puts it, "Buddy is given all the p.c. lines . . . But Philbert has the movie's soul" (Hoberman 57). Another reviewer submits that it is Philbert "who is finally able to defuse some of Buddy's rage" (Maslin CII). Eric Anderson maintains that Philbert is the "comic hero, the protagonist," and that "the movie is as much Philbert Bono's story as Buddy Red Bow's" (138, 140).

If one allows that the film tells Philbert's story right alongside Buddy's, it is possible to see the resolution in a different light. The viewer remembers that however absurd the finale, it is Philbert, not Buddy, who rescues Bonnie. It is Philbert who recoups the monies that Buddy misappropriated and that Rabbit put up as bail. It is Philbert who retrieves the children and effects everyone's escape from the Santa Fe police pursuit. The film thus cues the viewer to recognize that Philbert's quest results in effective action every time and everywhere it is needed. Philbert, not Buddy, is the one who does the work of the contemporary Cheyenne warrior.

Philbert carries a final token as he climbs the hill from the burning Buick at the end of the film, saying "my pony threw me" (*Powwow*). Both the novel and the film make the point explicitly. In the novel Philbert climbs the hill from the burning car with his third token, a cigarette lighter, and to Bonnie he says, "'Will you make me a pouch for my medicine bundle? Make it out of the cloth of your prison dress, maybe?'" She agrees, and "Philbert smiles. It would be the fourth token for his medicine power. He would be complete now" (293). In the film it is Sky who relays the same message: when he thinks Philbert has died in the burning car, he says, "He was almost a warrior," and a moment later when he sees his new friend climbing the hill carrying the Buick's door handle, he runs to him and shouts, "The third token" (*Powwow*).

One especially important indication of Philbert's character, his development, and his thematic importance in the plot is contained in the trickster story he tells of the plums, rendered almost verbatim from the novel. In the film, Philbert tells the story just after the midpoint of the journey, almost as if it is a centerpiece. In the scene following the visit to Fort Robinson, set at a fueling break along Interstate 25 with power-plant smoke stacks pictured in the background, Philbert comes out of the convenience store with food and coffee. He has just glimpsed the jailbreak scene in the William F. Hart film on television, and so he also comes out of the store with a mental image of the way to get Bonnie out of jail. In this layered context, then, he begins his monologue about the trickster and the plums:

> One day he saw some plums floating on the creek. Now, Wihio loves to eat. So, he reached for those plums but they disappeared, and he fell into the creek. He crawled out, all soaking wet. Saw them plums again shimmering in the water. He kept diving, and they kept disappearing. Three days later his wife found him still splashing around. "Woman," cried Wihio, "during the day juicy plums float in this magical spot, but at night they go away." His wife screamed at him: "Stupid dog of a dog. The plums are still on the tree. You worthless fool of a husband, chasing shadows when the truth hangs over your head." (*Powwow*)

The scene is shot first with a medium long shot of Philbert and his travel companions at the table with the power plant in the background. As he tells the story, a low-angle shot emphasizes that his auditors in the film are looking up to him, literally because he stands while they sit, and also perhaps figuratively because he is the storyteller. The dialogue that follows the telling of the story is shot with medium close-ups of both Philbert and Buddy.

Buddy growls to Philbert that such stories don't have any meaning, and Philbert contradicts him. The storyteller insists that the stories are more than mere fairy tales, they are "the stories of our ancestors; how the old ones dealt with problems; often the problems never change; nor the people" (*Powwow*). They have a power. They embody and make manifest Trickster. White America will not take the coal and oil and uranium from Indian land, insists Philbert, because "Trickster won't let them." The thematic suggestion here is that, ironically, it is Buddy who is looking at a reflection rather than at reality. In this sense he is the one chasing mirages or mere images. Rather than the root causes of the problems, he is hacking at some of the more obvious manifestations. He goes berserk in the electronics shop; he gets in a fight with Sandy Youngblood (Geoffrey Rivas) in a Santa Fe bar; he carries a pistol he cannot use. Even his bravado in the jailhouse is ineffectual. Despite all his fury, he accomplishes nothing. In his attitude and approach in general, meta-phorically, he is looking at the reflection of the plums, charging windmills, while Philbert suggests that the real plums are hanging heavy on branches just above his head. All he needs to do is look up. Philbert is the one who looks up.

The intertextual references to Hollywood in *Powwow Highway* demon-strate for the viewer that Philbert comes to recognize that he is a living de-scendant of the very people who are depicted in *Cheyenne Autumn*. His pres-ence a century later indicates that their trek, so grimly depicted in Ford's film, was ultimately successful. *Powwow Highway* thus moves well beyond the earlier film and challenges its limited and limiting viewpoints. An Indian actor plays an Indian character, and unlike the myriad Indians in Westerns before him, this character develops, changes, and survives the end of the film. He gains wisdom, and he also takes initiative in ways he never has before. De-fying the stereotype of the stoic warrior, this Cheyenne man cries on screen. He seeks knowledge of the past and of his ancestors, yet he is not stuck in that past. He accepts change; he lets Buddy buy him new clothes, he reads the manual for the tape player, and he comes to realize that the television series *Bonanza* is not the place to get knowledge of American Indian history. He takes what he wants and can use from television and Hollywood and leaves the rest. The man who early in the film is acted upon by his Aunt Harriett and by Buddy takes control and takes responsibility, as he tells Buddy, "Nobody grabs me no more" (*Powwow*). Perhaps most important, he rescues Bonnie's children; he teaches them, and includes them in the rescue of their mother. In short, he helps them become Cheyenne, and he thus ensures a future. These elements—a focus on upending Hollywood tropes, on Philbert's reclaiming and asserting his Cheyenne identity, on his learning and appreciating tribal history, on privileging oral tradition and traditional stories, on mentoring the children—all work within the film to empower Philbert and to advocate an Indigenous point of view. There are inherent components of Indigenous sov-ereignty, political and cultural sovereignty, and through the medium of film, visual sovereignty. All this works together to insist on the survival into the future of these Cheyenne people.

SEVEN

Feeling Extra Magical
The Art of Disappearing in *Smoke Signals*

Happy Independence Day, Victor. Are you feeling independent? I'm
feeling independent. I'm feeling extra magical today like I could make
anything disappear. Houdini with braids. . . . I'm so good I could make
myself disappear. Poof. I'm gone. —*Smoke Signals*

Smoke Signals is unique among the Indigenous films examined in this study
in that it is one of the very few to have been widely released and to actually
become a moneymaker, grossing between six and seven million dollars. By
Hollywood standards the gross is miniscule, of course, but the film did indeed pay for itself and did reach audiences in mall movie houses throughout
the United States in ways that few other Indigenous films have done.

Chris Eyre's *Smoke Signals* marks a pivotal moment in the history of
American Indian film as the first American Indian film to achieve this relatively wide acclaim, and reviewers and scholars readily commend the film
in this context. Ward Churchill identifies the release of the film as "a vitally
important event," pointing out that it is directed by an American Indian,
and "the screenplay was also written by an Indian, adapted from a book of
his short stories, and virtually the entire cast is composed of Indians. To top
things off, the director, Chris Eyre, an Arapaho, teamed up with the script-
writer, Spokane author Sherman Alexie, to co-produce the venture. *Smoke
Signals* was thus, from top to bottom, an American Indian production,
and that made it historically unprecedented" (Churchill, "*Smoke Signals*"
n. pag.). In *Wiping the War Paint off the Lens*, Beverley Singer points out
that several all-Indian productions actually did precede Chris Eyre's and that
"these films, all by Native Americans, set the stage for Eyre's film and [they]
represent the struggle by Native Americans to overcome the visual genocide
and to reimagine and revisualize what it means to be an Indian" (62). At the
same time, however, she does maintain that the "production of *Smoke Signals*
demonstrated that American Indians can make a good commercial product
while telling a good story with Indians as the central characters" (61). Filmmaker Barry Barclay lists *Smoke Signals* as one of the very few Indigenous
"dramatic feature films" in the world (7), and Ernest Stromberg argues that

despite some limitations, "*Smoke Signals* represents a significant evolution in the cinematic representation of American Indians," especially in that the film undoes "the ideological assumptions that seem to burden the tradition of cinematic representations of Indians" (39). Jhon Gilroy concludes his 2001 essay on the film by noting that it "signals the paradigm shift that Alexie sees as necessary for opening a new era of filmic self-representation" ("Another" 38). According to Gordon Slethaug, writing in 2003, *Smoke Signals* can be recognized as the first American Indian film to enjoy "the popular support that would lead to increased production possibilities for Native American films [and] might significantly alter public opinion on Indians in American society or their role in the Arts" (131). Corinn Columpar calls it a "landmark film," in part because of its "integration of a conventional story and unconventional protagonists" (126).

As is evident from these comments and commensurate with its being identified as a pivotal film, *Smoke Signals* has received much scholarly attention. In addition to discussions of the film as groundbreaking, investigations have explored many of the film's thematic issues. Kilpatrick argues that "the specters of alcoholism, injustice, and loneliness form the skeleton upon which this film hangs, and the fact that it is also very funny doesn't keep it from showing a Native present that is devoid of much hope for the future. In significant ways, it falls into the clichéd stereotypes of mainstream Hollywood films" (230). Gilroy, in contrast, describes the important subversive characteristics of the film, and he details "how the film departs from the classical Hollywood buddy/road movie tropes in its efforts to subvert these stereotypes" ("Another" 31). John Mihelich agrees, writing about ways in which the film breaks stereotypes through its reaching out to the masses and its "humanizing efforts." Furthermore, according to Mihelich, the film "appeals to a mainstream audience because it addresses familiar human conditions" (132). Echoing Mihelich, Corinn Columpar argues that the film is interested in "familial experiences that are common to a variety of cultural communities" (127).

These several scholars point out that *Smoke Signals* humanizes the characters and contextualizes their lives, and my argument here is that it also contextualizes death and disappearance. It begins this contextualizing as early as the opening sequence. As part of a voice-over accompanying the opening credits, the character Thomas Builds-the-Fire (Evan Adams) recalls the 1976 house fire in which his own parents perish and from which Arnold Joseph (Gary Farmer) saves him as an infant. Thomas concludes this voice-over by commenting that for years after that fire, Arnold "threatened to vanish; he practiced vanishing, until one day he jumped into his yellow pickup and did vanish" (*Smoke*). After this opening sequence, the viewer learns through a series of flashbacks from the film's present, 1998, that Arnold leaves his wife, Arlene (Tantoo Cardinal), and son, Victor (Adam Beach), on the Coeur d'Alene Reservation in Idaho and eventually settles in Phoenix, Arizona, where he dies. At the news of his death, which comes early in the film, his son, Victor, and Victor's friend Thomas decide to travel together by bus to get and bring home Arnold's ashes. The film tells the story of that trip.

Two scenes in which Victor's mother, Arlene, in the film's present gets a telephone call informing her of her husband Arnold's death serve to frame an important scene set ten years earlier, a scene in which Arnold figures prominently. This flashback depicts the twelve-year-old Victor (Cody Lightning) and his father as they ride home from the store on Independence Day. The film cuts from the phone call to the flashback of Arnold driving his pickup truck. Arnold's appearance immediately after his wife and the viewer get the news of his death allows the film to insist that he does not disappear. Arnold declares to his son in this scene that he is feeling extra magical on this anniversary of America's declaring its independence, so magical that he could make himself simply disappear. A major irony in the film, however, is that although Arnold does leave the reservation, and although his death early in the film does motivate the plot, the film itself does not, in a figurative sense, let him die. His presence is pictured and felt throughout—from the opening moments when he saves Thomas from the fire until his ashes are thrown into the Spokane River in the film's finale. The implication of the ubiquitous presence of the dead father is that the film is interested in contextualizing his death as a means of talking back to and refuting the Hollywood trope of the vanishing Indian. Arnold Joseph dies, but he does not vanish, and his son survives the end of the film.

The voice-over during the opening sequence sets up the context for Arnold's ultimately leaving the reservation, and it also plays an important role in setting up the narrative voice of the film as a whole. That narrative voice insists on Arnold's presence throughout. As Gilroy points out, "While Thomas is providing the voiceover narration, the visual imagery is not necessarily from his point of view" ("Another" 32). Indeed, on occasion, what the viewer sees during the voice-overs is not from Thomas's perspective at all; he even admits to not remembering being saved by Arnold. He is not yet a year old when he is thrown from the window of the burning house, and his narration, according to Gilroy, "articulates the cultural necessity of 'knowing the stories'" (33). Thomas tells a version of the story or stories that he has heard, presumably from his grandmother, from Arnold himself perhaps, and from others in the community who witnessed or who know about the fire and subsequent events. The important detail in the story of the burning house, in addition to Thomas's being able to fly, is that it was Arnold who saved him. In the course of the film, however, Thomas's account is called into question, and so from the film's outset, the viewer is exposed to some of the ambiguities inherent in storytelling. Later in the film, for instance, the viewer encounters contradictory versions of how Arnold also saved Victor from the fire. At the very end of the film, the viewer is cued to suspect that Thomas knows, and has known all along, what Victor finds out from Suzy near the film's end: Arnold is the one who accidentally set the fire that killed Thomas's parents. Thomas knows and has apparently known this a long time, but interestingly, it is a true story about Arnold that, as far as the viewer knows, Thomas chooses never to tell.

The film takes care to keep the focus on Arnold from the opening moment on, most apparently through interspersed flashbacks from different characters' points of view. The viewer sees Arnold literally save Thomas and lament the burning of the house, sees him drive home with the young Victor, sees him get drunk at a neighbor's party, sees him slap his wife and drive away in his truck, sees him come across Thomas on the bridge, sees him befriend Suzy Song in Arizona, sees him tell the story of a basketball game with Victor against two Jesuits, sees him rush back toward the burning house supposedly to save Victor, and finally sees him reach out his hand to help Victor to his feet. In addition to offering these visual instances, the film provides Thomas several opportunities to narrate stories in which Arnold is the protagonist. In one story he is the perfect hippie and war protester; in another he is the greatest basketball player ever; in yet another he takes Thomas to breakfast; he is said to look like Charles Bronson; and on one occasion he is reputed to have eaten fifteen pieces of fry bread. In short, though dead, he is never not present in the film.

Smoke Signals insists on the omnipresence of Hollywood and mainstream culture in the lives of these Coeur d'Alene characters at the same time that it asserts Arnold's presence throughout its entirety. It has an intertextual richness that can be seen to underscore and contextualize its own self-conscious response to mainstream American mass culture. It references and mocks different elements of mainstream media culture. Given the film's status and popularity, these numerous intertextual references take on added significance. If on one level the film seeks to refute Hollywood by presenting complex characters and exposing a century's worth of (mis)representations, on another level it challenges the viewer to contemplate the (im)possibility of honest or truthful representation in any medium. That is, in the midst of demonstrating the unreliability of its own narrator and the ambiguity about the historical past of its account of the Coeur d'Alene characters, it offers repeated intertextual references to Hollywood's (mis)representations of history and character. In this way the film both undercuts the mainstream media and complicates any easy reading of a truer or more honest representation. The film does this in part by intricately interspersing allusions to mainstream culture into the story of Arnold, while at the same time refusing to offer any one reliable version of its own stories. Perhaps most immediately apparent is the pronounced difference between Thomas's extolling what he sees as the virtues of the man Arnold versus Victor's recollections, which are much less laudatory. Thomas sees and tells stories about the man as savior of the flying baby, as an American Indian activist and hero, and as one who buys a boy a memorable breakfast at a restaurant. Victor remembers a man who is an abusive drunk, a man who abandons his wife and son, and a man who accidentally burns down a house, killing Thomas's parents. The ubiquitous presence of Arnold and the ambiguity of his character combine to suggest the extreme difficulty of any completely truthful representation.

In addition to mainstream Hollywood, *Smoke Signals* can be seen to make intertextual reference to Jonathan Wack's film *Powwow Highway*. Alexie, screenwriter and coproducer of *Smoke Signals*, speaks of his early fondness for that film in an interview with Dennis West and Joan West: "When it came out, I loved it, and saw it three times." He says that he only saw it again after working with Chris Eyre on their own film: after "seeing what we could do, *Powwow Highway* now seems so stereotypical. The performances are fine, but it trades in so many stereotypes, from standing in a river singing, to going up on a mountain-top to get a vision, and the generic AIM political activism. Every stereotypical touchstone of a contemporary Indian art film is there" (West and West 29). Corinn Columpar echoes Alexie, commenting that "*Smoke Signals* succeeds where *Powwow Highway* falters. . . . Whereas the uneven *Powwow Highway* occasionally compromises its re-vision of Indigenous subjectivity . . . *Smoke Signals* is characterized by a much greater degree of consistency" (126).

Alexie and Eyre do owe a debt to *Powwow Highway*, however, even if only in reaction against the earlier film. There are certainly noteworthy intertextual connections between the two films; most obvious perhaps is the buddy road trip itself. In each film two emotionally, physically, and politically very different young men of the same tribe (acquaintances but certainly not friends before beginning their trip) set off on a mission of rescue. Thomas and Philbert are the two films' respective storytellers, and as Jacqueline Kirkpatrick points out, both look to a more "traditional" sense of who they are as Native Americans (see 231–32). Buddy and Victor, in contrast, are the bolder, more experienced, more unsettled men, and both are less interested in an identity based on their tribal history or culture. Both pairs travel from their respective reservations in the north to points in the southwest. En route they come to better understandings of themselves and of what they mean to each other. In both films their missions are successful: Buddy and Philbert rescue Bonnie, while Victor and Thomas retrieve Arnold's ashes and his truck. *Smoke Signals* does not have the same overt and obvious specific references to nineteenth-century tribal history that *Powwow Highway* has, but it does insist that Thomas has a certain unspecified role as tribal storyteller and historian.

These several parallels suggest that the correspondences between the two films run deeper than mere coincidence of genre, but *Smoke Signals* makes no overt reference to *Powwow Highway*. References to other films and genres are more obvious. The names of two friends, Velma and Lucy, recall the buddy road film *Thelma and Louise* (1991). *Smoke Signals* alludes to and mocks *Little Big Man* when it playfully perverts the battle cry "It's a good day to die" with "It's a good day to be Indigenous," or "It's a good day to have breakfast" (*Smoke*). Victor scoffs at how many times Thomas has seen *Dances with Wolves*, and even as a child Thomas can list "Last of" titles, including the film *The Last of the Mohicans* and a short story called "The Last of the Winnebagos." Thomas also mentions Charles Bronson's *Death Wish* series. Victor and Thomas evoke the genre of the classic Western most specifically with their conversation and song about John Wayne, and the young Victor's response to a question about his favorite Indian recalls Jim Jarmusch's *Dead Man* (1995), in which Gary Farmer (who plays the boy's father in *Smoke Signals*) plays an Indigenous man named Nobody.

In her essay "John Wayne's Teeth," Joanna Hearne refers to Stuart Hall as she outlines "several ways that indigenous filmmakers engage in 'passionate research' by re-contextualizing earlier images, texts, oral narratives, and songs" (190). Hearne points out the intertextual reference or allusion to *Dead Man* and Gary Farmer's character called Nobody. Hearne argues that the reference is important in the context of disappearing and absence; it is an "intertextual joke associated with Indian vanishing" (194). This reference is actually extremely complex and multilayered. One night at a party, when Arnold in *Smoke Signals* is, according to the direction note in the screenplay, "too drunk to tell the difference" between anger and celebration (49), he asks his young son who his favorite Indian is. Victor replies "Nobody," a response Arnold the father is not particularly happy with:

> ARNOLD: Hey Victor, who's your favorite Indian, huh? Who's your favorite?
> ARLENE: It's your momma, huh? Tell him it's your momma.
> YOUNG VICTOR: Nobody.
> ARNOLD: What did you say, Victor? Speak up, boy. Who's your favorite Indian?
> YOUNG VICTOR: Nobody.
> ARNOLD: Nobody, huh? Nobody! Did you say nobody?
> ARLENE: He didn't mean it. Come on, tell him, Victor. Tell your daddy you didn't mean it.
> YOUNG VICTOR: Nobody. Nobody. Nobody. (*Smoke*)

Arnold walks off, alone, repeating to himself: "Nobody! Nobody! Nobody!" This scene recalls the moment in *Dead Man* when William Blake (Johnny Depp) asks the character played by Gary Farmer his name: Farmer's character responds by saying "Nobody." Blake does not understand and asks for an explanation, to which Nobody responds that his name is "He-Who-Talks-Loud-Saying-Nothing," but, he says, he "prefer[s] to be called Nobody" (*Dead Man*). One of the ways in which this reference to Jarmusch's film works to reverse the tradition of the vanishing Indian is its subtle implication that in *Dead Man*, it is the white man who is dead and Nobody, the Indigenous hero and possessor of knowledge, survives the end of the film. Thus, when the young Victor offers the possibility that this man is his favorite Indian, he is not only dismissing his father, he is repudiating a pervasive Hollywood trope. He chooses the intelligent, well-read, survivalist Indigenous man as his favorite, and by implication, if not his own father, Arnold, at least the man and actor Gary Farmer, who is able to play both roles.

As this evocation of the film *Dead Man* suggests, *Smoke Signals* intricately layers the intertextual meanings. On the one hand, Victor simply tells his drunken father that he does not like Indians; he has no favorites. No one is his favorite because, he implies, he does not like any of them, not even, or perhaps especially not his drunk of a father. Hearne makes the point that the young Victor's repetition, "Nobody. Nobody. Nobody," refers "at once to the triad of himself, and his mother and father" ("John" 194). But on another level, in that it is Gary Farmer in the roles of both Arnold (Victor's father) in *Smoke Signals* and the Indigenous character Nobody in *Dead Man*, Victor is actually acknowledging that on some level he does indeed have a favorite Indian. By this means the intertextuality takes the viewer outside the film itself in order to make a point about the complexity of Victor's feelings for his father, emphasizing that his is a love-hate relationship. The implication of the importance of one's "favorite Indian" takes on thematic importance because, as it turns out, his father's leaving is extremely difficult for the young Victor, and he remembers it and is angry about it as a twenty-two-year-old adult in the film's present. Indeed, it is the search for the father, albeit a dead one, and the urge to get and/or offer forgiveness that motivate Victor's trip to Phoenix. The search serves as motivation for the plot of the entire film.

The naming of Nobody in this scene is important in another context as well. *Smoke Signals* evokes and makes a point of noting the importance of revealing one's name in an early scene, just after the Fourth of July fire. Thomas's grandmother, who has just become sole guardian of the baby Thomas talks about the name *Victor*:

GRANDMA: (to Arlene): Arlene, your son? His name is Victor, enit?
ARLENE: Yes it is.
GRANDMA: A good name. It means he's going to win, enit? (*Smoke*)

The exchange between Arlene and Thomas's grandmother implies to the viewer that Victor will ultimately succeed. And indeed, he does finally retrieve the ashes, return them to his mother, and come to terms with his own relationship to his father. In this sense, the very complex and multilayered allusion to the Hollywood trope of the vanishing Indian is intricately intertwined with the story of Arnold and of Victor's relationship with him.

Another important and more extended allusion to Hollywood comes in the film in a sequence immediately following a flashback in which Victor remembers his father's leaving and his fight with the young Thomas (Simon Baker), who asks innocently why his father left. The sequence begins in the film's present with Thomas's question: "What do you remember about your dad?" (*Smoke*). The question inspires Victor to take Thomas to task about his appearing to be some sort of medicine man, always telling pointless stories. This exchange leads in turn to Victor's instructing Thomas in how to be a real Indian, how to dress and how to wear his hair. And perhaps most important, insists Victor, "You got to look like a warrior" (*Smoke*). These instructions and Thomas's apparent transformation are followed by a scene in which the two young men are displaced by two cowboys, who take their seats on the bus.

A cowboy wearing a "This is my gun cleaning hat" tells Victor and "super injun there," referring to Thomas and his newfound Indian appearance, to find somewhere else to sit. Victor is helpless in the face of this blatant racism, so the two grab their belongings and move toward the back of the bus. As potentially grim as this scene is, Eyre and Alexie are able to lighten it. First Thomas ribs Victor by telling him that his warrior look doesn't work all the time. The viewer knows this to be a joke by the way the camera catches and pauses on Thomas's smile just after he makes the wry statement. The joke lightens the mood, and the film then turns to more humor, beginning with a reference to Hollywood cowboy heroes.

THOMAS: Man, the cowboys always win.
VICTOR: The cowboys don't always win.
THOMAS: Yeah they do. The cowboys always win. Look at Tom Mix. What about John Wayne? Man, he was about the toughest cowboy of them all, enit?
VICTOR: You know, in all those movies you never saw John Wayne's teeth. Not once. I think there's something wrong when you don't see a guy's teeth. (*Smoke*)

Following their brief discussion about how the cowboys always win, Victor and Thomas begin tapping out and then singing an impromptu song about John Wayne's teeth.

Joanna Hearne is particularly interested in the film's use of this and another song, the Irish song "Garry Owen" that plays nondiegetically in the bus when Victor and Thomas are initially displaced. The "John Wayne's Teeth" song that Victor taps out and sings is diegetic until the camera cuts to a long-shot view from outside the bus; at this moment the Eaglebear singers take over the song. In writing about the scene, Hearne points out that the "diegetic sound becomes nondiegetic sound as the shots of the interior of the bus cut to long shots of the bus moving through the Western desert landscape" ("John" 198). The shift from diegetic to nondiegetic sound occurs at the moment of the cut to the shot of the outside of the bus so that only the viewer hears the Eaglebear singers' version of the song, and only the viewer, not the characters, sees the bus rolling through the landscape. Such blending of sound and scene, such movement between diegetic and nondiegetic sound, can only happen in film, especially when the music is juxtaposed with the visual of the bus moving through what is supposed to be north-central Arizona, that is, John Ford country. Eyre did the actual filming on location in eastern Washington State, but the extreme long shot from the exterior of bus moving from right to left, then cut to left to right on a two-lane highway through the red cliffs that loom in the background—coupled with the overt reference to John Wayne as "the toughest cowboy of them all," as Thomas calls him—certainly recalls the red buttes and rock formations of Monument Valley where Ford filmed several of his classics starring John Wayne, including *Stagecoach*, *Fort Apache* (1948), *The Searchers*, and *She Wore a Yellow Ribbon* (1949). Thus, both the song lyrics about John Wayne and the fact that the bus is somewhere north of Phoenix, as if traveling through Monument Valley, cue the viewer to connect the modern-day Evergreen Stage (the bus) with the stagecoach of yesteryear. In this version, however, rather than as antagonists, the American Indians traveling through this desert are the film's heroes; they are the ones traveling inside the stage. Later, our heroes have an interview with a reasonable and sympathetic police chief (Tom Skerritt), a contemporary incarnation of Sheriff Wilcox (George Bancroft) in *Stagecoach*. The irony here depends to a large extent on the subtle reference to the typical lawman of the Western. After the interview with the police Thomas offers a concession: "I guess your warrior look does work sometimes." The humor here, however, is at Victor's expense in that the viewer knows full well that the warrior look has nothing at all to do with the lawman's not charging them with assault. Rather, this lawman is simply able to see the case without the anticipated racist blinders.

These varied instances of intertextuality throughout *Smoke Signals* complicate any easy reading of representation, and correspondingly the film challenges any easy reading of simple explanation of truth within its own narrative structure. It becomes most immediately clear, as mentioned above, that Thomas is the quintessential or paradigmatic unreliable narrator as he tells his stories, and this unreliability is an integral aspect of the way the film refuses to settle on any one version of the truth. The viewer simply cannot know to what extent Thomas's stories are faithful representations of the past, especially because Victor so often contradicts him and because on occasion Thomas seems to contradict himself or at least render himself of questionable authority as a historian. At one point, for example, Thomas tells his grandmother that Victor "wasn't always mean" to him. He makes this assertion, yet from every indication the viewer has, Victor is indeed and always has been mean to Thomas. He is mean to Thomas in the gym; he lies to his fellow basketball players about the foul; he is mean to Thomas as a kid, he says mean things about the deaths of Thomas's parents, and he fights with Thomas, giving him a bloody nose. Victor even mocks Thomas in the market when he offers to help him get to Phoenix. Every bit of filmic evidence argues against Thomas's assertion that Victor has not always been mean to him. Another instance suggesting Thomas's unreliability occurs just before the crash scene, when Victor and Thomas get into their fiercest argument. Thomas accuses Victor of abandoning his own mother even though he lives in the same house as she does, and he says to Victor: "You make your mom cry" (*Smoke*). Again, every bit of filmic evidence belies this statement. Victor treats his mother with nothing but concern and respect, in complete contrast to the way he treats Thomas. The most visible and obvious instance of his kindness to his mother is when the viewer sees him rubbing her hands as she complains of arthritis pain. That is hardly the action of a son who has abandoned his mother as Thomas claims. These examples make it difficult to know to what extent the viewer can rely on Thomas to give a true account of Arnold or of anything else.

The viewer simply cannot know whether or not Thomas's stories are fair representations of an actual past. According to Victor, Thomas as a storyteller is "full of shit." Victor maintains that his father was not the Vietnam-era resistance hero whom Thomas describes. Nor did he look like Charles Bronson in *Death Wish V* (1994), as Thomas tells it. When Thomas asks Suzy Song (Irene Bedard) to tell a story, there is again the filmic suggestion that Thomas is unreliable, that he is not necessarily interested in distinguishing between truth and lies, reality and fiction:

THOMAS: So I told you a story, now it's your turn.
SUZY: What, you want lies, or do you want the truth?
THOMAS: I want both. (*Smoke*)

Another instance in which the film refuses to clarify the truth is during the film's climax in the context of Victor's getting to know his father. Suzy Song tells the story of how Arnold saved him from the fire when he was a baby: "Your dad ran back into that burning house looking for you. He did one good thing. He came back for you," she explains (*Smoke*). Victor has trouble believing her and denies this account at first. This is also the first time the viewer hears this version of the fire. Suzy's version, which she could only have gotten from Arnold himself, differs substantially from Thomas's initial voice-over account. Arnold saves the Thomas in Thomas's account, but there is no mention of Arnold's having saved Victor. Nor does the film itself offer any visual support for Arnold's running back into the house for Victor or for anyone else. The camera depicts the scene from Arnold's perspective: through the hair that has fallen into his eyes Arnold sees the burning house. He goes toward it but, as far as the viewer sees, not into it, and he is still outside when Thomas is tossed from the upstairs window, presumably by one of his parents, both of whom, Thomas tells us in the voice-over, die in the fire that Arnold accidentally sets.

There is no way for the viewer to know whether Suzy is any more reliable as a narrator than Thomas. But visually the film certainly does not corroborate her account of Arnold's trying to save Victor. In the visual that accompanies Suzy's retelling of what Arnold told her, the viewer sees Arnold set the fire and sees Arnold make a diving catch of the baby bundle that is Thomas, but even as Suzy narrates, there is no filmic evidence to corroborate her account that Arnold saves Victor. According to Victor, his mother saved him. Even after he hears Suzy's version of that fatal night, he insists to Thomas that Arnold never saved him. In a later scene, just before they crash the truck, in a few lines that are not part of the written screenplay, Victor screams at Thomas: "He saved your dumb ass in that fire. He didn't save me. He never saved me" (*Smoke*). It is significant that this statement comes after Victor's conversation with Suzy and after his reconciliation with his dead father. Clearly, he still denies that his father saved him.

Suzy's version of the history thus contradicts Thomas's voice-over account, the film's visual evidence, and Victor's own statement. This discrepancy creates an interesting gap in the narrative concerning the line between fact and fiction, storytelling and relating history. It is thus no surprise that Victor distrusts Thomas's stories about his father: "I don't know if half of them are true. Why is that Thomas?" (*Smoke*). Though Thomas does not have an answer at the moment, one possible response to Victor's question might simply be that no one can know what is true: stories are inherently both fact and fiction. The past, *Smoke Signals* suggests, can only exist in the ways people remember it and carry it forward. The film suggests that perhaps there is no external independent fact or truth. Such a version of the place of the past in Victor's life, or in anyone's life, is represented filmically in one of the film's match cuts. A shot of the young Victor running after his father cuts a shot of the adult Victor on the bus, watching his younger self running along the highway. This match cut parallels or emphasizes the film's thematics in that Victor is still in search of his father, is still running both toward and away from him. Even as an adult riding on the bus, he is pursuing his absent father.

Suzy's version of the basketball game, as narrated by Arnold to make Victor into a twelve-year-old hero, suggests another gap in the historical continuity and a potential reason for the viewer to mistrust Arnold and thus doubt any stories of his that Suzy relates. Suzy begins her narrative by stating that

Basketball magic. *Smoke Signals*. The Kobal Collection at Art Resource, N.Y. Miramax.

Arnold was always talking about playing basketball with his son; the shot cuts from Victor's face as he listens to a shot of Arnold holding a ball as he stands next to an outdoor basketball hoop and backboard in the evening half-light. He tells Suzy, presumably, about a basketball game in which he and his son take on two Jesuits. As Arnold tells it, Victor "took it to the hoop. He flew man; he flew right over that Jesuit. Twelve years old and he was like some kind of indigenous angel. . . . My boy, he was the man that day. He took that shot, and he won that game. It was the Indians versus the Christians that day and for as least one day, the Indians won" (*Smoke*). At the end of the scene, Arnold throws the ball into the air, and it rolls to Victor, who picks it up in the film's present.

This match cut is much different from the others in that the ball as a physical object rolls from one scene, from one temporal moment, into the next. Arnold has been holding the basketball during his account of the game against the Jesuits before it comes rolling toward Victor and Suzy at the end of Arnold's story. It rolls across space and time: across the yard from the basketball hoop to Victor and across the moment of Arnold's telling the story to Victor's hearing it from Suzy. Such a cut suggests a sort of magical or counterreality moment. In the "Scene Notes" at the end of the *Smoke Signals: A Screenplay*, Alexie writes that "the movie needed more magic and I kept trying to think of ways to create it" (164). Suzy Song's recapitulation of Arnold's story about the basketball game gives Alexie this opportunity. Alexie also writes in the notes that "when Suzy tells Victor that Arnold was like a father to her, he drops the basketball into the dirt. The dust that rises appears to be a ghost floating across the screen" (164). That image does not make it into the film, but such ideas could help bring some magic to the film and augment the suggestion in Arnold's story that the spiritual is indeed at work.

With the match cut back to the present action, Victor accepts the ball, as it were, but he still denies the accuracy of Arnold's account of the game as Suzy relates it.

VICTOR: So, he told you I made that shot?
SUZY: Yeah.
VICTOR: Yeah, well, I missed the shot. I lost the game.
SUZY: You mean your dad lied to me?
VICTOR: Yeah, a lie that made me look good.
SUZY: He was a magician, you know?
VICTOR: I know. (*Smoke*)

It does not seem to matter to Victor, at least not initially, that his father evidently lied to make his son look good or that the man abandoned wife and child not because of the family but because of guilt he felt over the accidental killing of Thomas's parents. Emotionally distraught and confused, Victor goes into his father's trailer, finds a photo of father, mother, and son with "Home" written on the back, and then he cuts his hair in mourning, as Arnold had cut his twenty some years earlier. But for all this opportunity to learn and reconcile, Victor is little changed. He leaves at dawn without saying good-bye to Suzy, and Thomas makes a note of the inappropriateness and selfishness of such an abrupt departure in a voice-over: "We left Phoenix without telling Suzy good-bye. I thought we were leaving in a bad way, but Victor didn't seem to care a bit" (*Smoke*).

Victor's change in attitude and his maturity come finally during his long run to get help after he crashes the truck. During that run, Victor flashes back to the house fire and to Suzy's words: "Your dad talked about that fire every day. He cried about it. He wished he could have changed it. He wished he hadn't run away. But you have to remember one thing Victor. He ran back into that burning house looking for you. He did one good thing." Interestingly, this version in Victor's memory is different from the version Suzy has just told him. She finishes by repeating, "He went back for you"; Victor changes that by remembering Suzy's including a different final sentence: "He did one good thing." In both instances, the viewer sees Suzy as she recounts what is supposed to have happened. The moment thus recalls an exchange just before, in which Victor has challenged Suzy: "You're telling me all these stories about my father, and I don't even know if they're true" (*Smoke*). Nor does the viewer know what is true. Did Arnold do more than one good thing? Did he also save Victor?

It becomes clear as he runs for help that Victor has finally created his own version of the story and of his father's history and significance. It is through Thomas's eyes at the same time, however, that Victor finally sees his father. He collapses during his run for help, and lying on the roadside he hallucinates: he sees his father on the bridge, as the viewer has seen him through Thomas's eyes in an earlier story. Arnold extends his hand to him just as he had reached to Thomas. Although very different from the basketball match cut in an earlier scene, this moment does recall the magic in that the physical hand from Victor's hallucination does reach through the shot to help him to his feet. It is thus indeed his own father who helps him up. As Gilroy comments, "This is *exactly* the same shot from a previous flashback focalized by Thomas. . . . When Thomas relates this story, Victor tells him 'I've heard this story a thousand times' . . . but he obviously never truly listened. His obsession with the 'Truth' as he conceived of it always blinded him to the other possible truths contained within Thomas's stories" ("Another" 38). Victor's last flashback before he collapses is indicated by a shot of his father holding a basketball next to that outdoor hoop and exclaiming, "Everything in the world can fit inside this ball. It's all about magic, man; it's about faith" (*Smoke*). This is Victor's recollection of the story Suzy told, yet neither this particular shot nor these particular lines are part of Suzy's narrative. The flashback can thus be considered not so much a memory as Victor's own vision, his own version of the story, and thus a new and different facet of Arnold's history. Whether or not these events as Victor recalls them ever took place, they exist because Victor visualizes them. The film does not necessarily pause to distinguish between fact and fiction here anymore than it pauses elsewhere to make such distinctions.

That Alexie and Eyre choose to use Victor's run as the climactic moment in the film recalls the use the run is put to in the 1972 *House Made of Dawn* film. As Abel runs at the end of that film, he falls but gets up again, with the inspirational help of his dead grandfather. He continues running and morphs into perhaps a vision he has of himself as a traditional Pueblo man, or in the language of the novel, a longhair as his grandfather would have been; as Abel runs, the viewer hears the grandfather's voice over: "Those who run are the life of the people" (*House*). Just as the earlier film calls on the Pueblo grandfather, the Navajo Ben, the Kiowa preacher, and the non-Indian Milly to get Abel home and running, *Smoke Signals*, in a sense, suggests that it takes an entire community to help Victor back to the reservation: his mother's telling him, "I don't do it alone"; Thomas's repeated and positive stories about Arnold; Suzy's eye-opening account of his father; even Victor's being needed by others at the car crash to protect them from a drunk and abusive man. These moments all contribute to Victor's being able to identify the tin can of ashes as his father: "Let me hold onto Dad," he is finally able to say to Thomas

(*Smoke*). Such moments enable him to apologize to Thomas about the fight before the wreck and to thank him at the end of the film.

Victor tells Thomas that spreading his father's ashes in the Spokane River will be like cleaning out the attic, throwing away what one no longer has any use for. The film's final moments belie this assertion, however. Victor shares some of the ashes with Thomas, and when he throws the ashes, he screams as if in pain, relief, agony, but certainly not in indifference. Meanwhile, a voice-over reading of an adaptation of Dick Lourie's poem "Forgiving Our Fathers" reminds the viewer that Arnold is still very present to the film as it asks repeatedly, how do we forgive our fathers? Whether or not it is through magic, memory, or story, Arnold is ultimately able to offer his son, Victor, and his son's friend Thomas a legacy that will serve them well. Arnold does not vanish.

EIGHT

Making His Own Music

Death and Life in *The Business of Fancydancing*

MOUSE: He took my life, man. . . . It's like I'm not even alive. It's like
I'm dead. Hey Ari, I'm dead.
ARI: You ain't dead, man. —*The Business of Fancydancing*

Sherman Alexie's film *The Business of Fancydancing* tells the story of Seymour Polatkin, a Coeur d'Alene man, played by Coast Salish actor Evan
Adams, who leaves the reservation to attend a university in Seattle. Through
a series of flashbacks and flashforwards, the viewer learns that Seymour
acknowledges and comes to terms with his homosexuality while still a stu-
dent, and that he achieves a successful career as a poet. Ten years after leaving the reservation, he returns only once and only briefly for the funeral of
his long-time, former friend Mouse. A major theme driving the film considers the problems inherent in the decision Seymour faces as he retains ambivalent feelings throughout about staying away from the reservation. He
continues in the city to finish college even though his friend Aristotle, Ari
(Gene Tagabon), asks him to quit and return with him to the reservation.
Immediately after Mouse's funeral service at the end of the film, Seymour
returns to the city to rejoin his partner. Even though he has achieved international acclaim as a writer, the urban Indian poet remains divided, held
by his reservation past. He pursues a career as an urban poet although he
cannot shake the reservation from his poetry. As the film's unnamed interviewer (Rebecca Carroll) reminds him, despite his literary success and his
worldwide travels, "ninety-five percent of [his] poems . . . are about [his]
reservation" (*Business*).

One can thus argue that *The Business of Fancydancing* is Seymour's film.
Alternatively one can argue, as I do here, that the story of the character of
Mouse is actually absolutely crucial and central, and one can understand
the film as a vehicle for telling Mouse's story. Seen this way, the film has a
somewhat different emphasis, and a plot summary would read as follows: in
the opening sequence Mouse (Swil Kanim), a high school dropout and accomplished violinist, uses his video camera to film his two friends as they
celebrate their high school graduation. He remains on the reservation after

they leave for college in Seattle, and there he meets and becomes involved with Teresa (Cynthia Geary), a non-Indian woman; he plays violin, and he continues to imbibe alcohol and drugs of all sorts. His friend Ari, who had been in Seattle with Seymour, joins him on the reservation after quitting college, and the two of them experiment with different methods of getting high, including huffing gas and eating bathroom cleaner sandwiches. On one occasion, without provocation, they beat up a lost white guy. Mouse dies evidently from a drug overdose of some sort, though the film does not make the precise cause of his death clear; it could perhaps have been suicide by taking pills. Mouse's death occurs relatively early in the film and motivates the plot, and much of the film offers flashbacks after his death as a means of focusing on his life. Perhaps the most important indicator of Mouse's centrality to the film is that at the same time he ridicules Seymour's poetry he insists that the poems actually describe his own life, not the poet's. "He took my life," Mouse tells Ari at one point as they read from Seymour's book (*Business*). Seen in this way, 95 percent of what Seymour has to say is about Mouse, and thus *The Business of Fancydancing* is actually a film that tells Mouse's story.

This emphasis on the character of Mouse, who dies early on but whose presence is absolutely crucial and is felt throughout the entire film, suggests that the film has much in common with several other American Indian films examined in this study. Relatively early in its plotline the film presents and portrays the death of a major character, and although he is dead, the film nevertheless deals in significant detail and depth with that character's life. The film insists that the character is critical to the film's plot and its major thematic elements. In this way *The Business of Fancydancing* can be seen to evoke the Hollywood cliché of the dead or vanishing Indian while it also repudiates it. The film actually insists on the life of precisely that specific character, and like others this film also privileges and centers the contemporary characters who are deeply affected by that death but who survive the end. Blake Hausman writes that "Alexie gives us one dead character at the beginning (Mouse) and a whole tribe of survivors at the end. Thus, *Fancydancing* inverts the generally expected tragic Indian story, concluding with several characters who are alive to continue their respective journeys" (89).

The emphasis on Mouse and the survivors as survivors enables Alexie to talk back to Hollywood. This talking back is multiform, however, and can be seen from different angles. Most immediately, perhaps, the film privileges Mouse as the one who motivates the plot and in a sense survives his literal death. Alexie develops another important angle with what we can term self-reflexivity. That is, many scenes in the film are of Mouse doing the filming with his own handheld camera, and other scenes, like the pseudo-documentary scenes of Seymour being interviewed, call deliberate attention to the camera. This self-reflexivity exposes the artifice of film at the same time it insists that it is the Indigenous people, not mainstream directors and producers, who are in control of the camera and thus in control of the story.

Scholars considering *The Business of Fancydancing* tend to focus on Seymour, one of the survivors. His relationships with and his alienation from the people on the reservation are of special interest in many studies. Scholars typically refer to the character of Mouse only in passing. Lisa Tatonetti, Quentin Youngberg, and Gabriel Estrada all offer insightful readings of Seymour's homosexuality in the context of American Indian film, and Blake Hausman investigates how Alexie's film interpenetrates the Shakespearean sphere, with special attention paid to Seymour. Hausman argues that Alexie aligns Seymour with both Shakespeare and the character Hamlet, in that Seymour is the actor throughout. The results of his actions, like Hamlet's in the death of Polonius, for example, are sometimes somewhat unintentional (see Hausman 90–91). The comparison with Hamlet's killing Polonius raises the question of whether or not Seymour through his poetry (unintentionally) kills Mouse. This chapter offers to build upon these scholarly responses to the film by arguing that it is Mouse and his life that do indeed give shape and meaning to Seymour and his poetry and thus to the film as a whole. This is especially important in that Mouse—like Victor's father Arnold in *Smoke Signals*, Abel's grandfather in *House Made of Dawn*, and Will's mother Rose in *Medicine River*, for example—can be seen to transcend a literal death and retain significance beyond it.

Mouse confides to Ari at one point, somewhat hyperbolically, that he senses that he is dead because Seymour has coopted his stories and reconstituted them as poems. His accusation is valid in part because every poem is to some extent about Mouse as much as it is about Seymour the poet. The viewer becomes well acquainted with Mouse through these poems and from several other sources within the film. Mouse offers his own account, made available to the viewer through flashback, and other characters offer their insights into his character as well. He makes a filmic record of much of his own life with his handheld camera. Seymour, the film's ostensible main character, offers accounts of Mouse's life through poetry. Mouse's friend Teresa offers a long, multifaceted narrative about him at his funeral, and the film makes Mouse's presence palpable throughout her narrative with cuts to a living Mouse. The viewer sees Mouse as he lies in bed with her, playing violin. She describes the first time she ever sees him, so that the viewer sees Mouse walking a wooded road playing his violin. Teresa stands in front of a photograph of Mouse as she speaks at his funeral, and the living Mouse, dressed as in that photograph of him beside his coffin, actually speaks some of the lines that Teresa quotes. The final shot of Teresa's speech at the funeral is of Mouse again as he lies in bed with her, playing violin. By such means the film manages to insist that Mouse has a continuing, living presence even though he has literally died. In scene after scene the film refuses to let the viewer forget that he is in many ways still very present in the minds and lives of the characters who knew him, and these characters bring him alive for the viewer of the film. They remember him; they quote him. The film offers flashbacks to his life; and he even appears to Seymour on occasion as if he were a ghost.

In addition to his other roles in the film, Mouse plays the critical and thematically important role of cameraman. His filming of his own life on the reservation includes several scenes, all from his point of view. The viewer sees Mouse and Ari ridicule Seymour's book of poetry, sees Mouse filming Ari as he demonstrates "how to huff-gas," witnesses the arrival of Agnes Roth (Michelle St. John) as she looks for the schoolhouse, observes the playing of a game of freeze tag, and is present with Mouse and Ari as they beat up the "lost white guy." These are all life-on-the-reservation episodes as selected by Mouse, and they contribute to the story about his own life there.

This camera-within-a-camera, which recalls the "Mousetrap" play-within-a-play in *Hamlet*, constitutes, as noted above, a form of self-reflexivity. Hausman's observations in this regard are again helpful: "Within Alexie's narrative structure, the Mouse character is both still alive and already dead. Mouse's presence as both speaker and documenter signifies his presence as 'coauthor' of Seymour's poetry, for he speaks both to Seymour, by filming Seymour and Aristotle, and to the audience itself, by turning the lens upon himself, creating a camera-within-a-camera" (91). Use of the handheld camera invites the viewer onto the reservation as it projects a representation of exactly what Mouse, who is already also on the reservation, sees and finds worthy of recording. In this sense the viewer is an invitee and is actually brought onto the reservation as an initiate, and as such that viewer becomes an eyewitness to the events that Mouse films. A handheld camera gives the illusion of the viewer's being in close proximity to the action insofar as the viewer sees only what the character doing the filming sees, as if there is no editing, no filter between what Mouse films and what the viewer sees. This is not the case, of course, but the technique can nevertheless be said to heighten suspense and to suggest that the viewer is seeing events as they actually occur. In a sense it removes one filter or degree of distance between the viewer and the characters and action of the film. On the filmic level the technique of the handheld camera has the effect of creating a feeling of intimacy between the viewer and the characters themselves, of bringing the viewer close to the action, almost to involve the viewer in that action. One can argue that "the handheld point of view involves the audience more immediately and concretely in the action" (Corrigan and White 117). Seeing through the lens of a handheld camera, the viewer can be said more nearly to have the feeling of experiencing what the characters experience.

The film hints at the documentary genre and that particular style of de-picting reservation life as Mouse makes a filmic record of his life there. The camera-within-a-camera, one of which is handheld, thus recalls anthropo-logical filmic studies, studies that have made efforts to document life on In-dian reservations for as long as there has been a film technology. "Ethno-graphic film offers an impression of authenticity," writes Bill Nichols, and it leaves the viewer with the important "impression that the ethnographer was there and that his or her representation is, therefore, to be trusted" (221). Of critical importance here, however, is that it is Mouse rather than a non-Indian outsider or anthropologist who does the recording. Mouse is in charge and in control of what gets filmed. In Barry Barclay's terms (7–11), Mouse is the Indigenous filmmaker ashore, and he is filming Indigenous peoples from an Indigenous perspective. The handheld camera serves both to insist on the realism as it evokes the ethnographic or anthropological documentary, and at the same time it continually calls attention to the artifice of what the viewer witnesses. Paradoxically, the sense of realism and inclusion coincides with a heightened awareness of artifice. *The Business of Fancydancing* is a narrative fiction film, after all. Nichols argues that especially in ethnographic film an "alliance of science and documentary . . . within the discourses of sobriety suggests that the highly problematic representations of the Other in fiction will be overcome" (201). They are not overcome, of course, as Nichols dem-onstrates, but the underlying assumption remains. Because of the tenacity of this assumption, the filmic technique allows Alexie a potent means of talking back to dominant discourses and mainstream depictions. Mouse continually reminds the viewer that the filmmaker, if not the character himself, is per-petually turning the tables by taking complete control of what that viewer sees. Mouse selects and omits at will. With the use of Mouse's handheld cam-era, Alexie creates a situation in which the viewers are immediately asked to become hyperaware of the artifice of film: they witness a film of a filming, and at the same time they actually serve as participants in that filming, mak-ing what the camera sees all the more real.

Film theorist Christian Metz points out that viewers typically tend to iden-tify with the camera itself and therefore, like the camera, they gain a sense of being all-seeing and thus even omnipotent; that is, seeing without being seen gives them a sense of power: "the spectator can do no other than iden-tify with the camera . . . which has looked before him at what he is now look-ing at" (174–75). As is well known, traditional Hollywood tends to hide the camera's activity and all that goes on behind the scenes. The viewers become uniquely aware of the camera perhaps only as the camera itself becomes a visible part of the fabric of the film. Viewers who have subconsciously identi-fied with the camera anyway become especially aware as the camera itself becomes part of the conscious viewing experience. They simultaneously lose that sense of power, privilege, and distance because they see who does indeed control the lens. In this sense, then, by seeing the character Mouse in the film as he holds a camera, sometimes even turning it on himself, the viewers are made conscious not only of the camera they otherwise would not see or be conscious of, but they also become aware of their complicity in the action and production of the film. The viewers are no longer invisible in the same way. And it is the character Mouse who has the power to make this consciousness or self-awareness possible. Mouse as cameraman is yet another indication of how his overall role in the film is so central. He becomes the link between the story and the audience for that story. Whereas Seymour performs his reservation poetry in front of an audience within the fiction of the film, Mouse creates the story with his camera in the first place. But he does not create the audience. For Mouse, by virtue of his camera, it is as if the audience exists outside the fiction of the film. Mouse involves the film's viewer as he meta-filmically creates both Seymour the poet and that poet's auditors and fans.

The viewer sees Mouse's camera off and on throughout the entire film, whereas the camera itself, even in documentary, tends to be hidden from the viewer, handheld or not. Documentary as documentary actually rarely calls attention the camera because that camera typically remains unseen. When Alexie puts it into a character's hands and films that camera, the idea of the fact of filming becomes all the more apparent. On one level it has the effect, suggested above, of bringing the viewer closer to the action, almost to the point of including the viewer in that action. On another level, however, almost paradoxically, the filming of filming serves to distance the viewer. The implication is that at certain moments Mouse's camera thus stands for or stands in for the unseen camera since it is through that *seen* camera that the viewer sometimes *sees* the action of the film. Even though the viewer sees only one of the cameras, Mouse's, that viewer has to be aware that there are indeed two cameras, one seen, one unseen, and this awareness draws attention to the artifice, thereby excluding the viewer from any reality or realism as such. In this way, Alexie is able to both evoke the idea of documentary and at the same time expose its artifice and represent it as the construct it is.

That Mouse holds the camera signifies that he is the one in control. He is sovereign. He makes the choices. As camera operator, he decides what to film and what not to film. He constructs and tells the story. The film's opening sequence serves immediately to demonstrate this effect. The viewer does not initially see Mouse's camera but rather what the camera sees: Seymour and Aristotle, the two graduates, as they frolic in celebration of their past successes and in anticipation of their leaving for college in Seattle. Distortions both visual and aural make immediately clear that the viewer is witnessing this action through a handheld camera. Mouse turns the camera on himself, an action that provides a close-up both visually and verbally. He makes a grim joke, telling the camera and thus the viewer that whereas the other two, Seymour and Aristotle, are on their way to college, he is going to work in the uranium mine. The joke offers a ghastly foreshadowing of his actual death a few scenes later. There is of course no indication in the film that Mouse either actually does go to work in a mine or that his death is a result of his having worked in a mine, but the joke does nevertheless foreshadow his untimely death.

This technique is also vividly apparent in a scene in which Mouse and Ari read from Seymour's book of poetry *All My Relations*. The cuts are between what Mouse films and Alexie's shots of Mouse as he films. This contrast crosscutting calls special attention to and thus emphasizes the existence of two different cameras. The series of crosscuts bounce the viewer back and forth between seeing both the book through Mouse's handheld camera and seeing both Mouse and the book through the unseen camera. The one shows Mouse as he films with his own camera; the other shows what he films. The viewer sees the book itself and even a book-cover photograph of Seymour, but sees that book and cover through Mouse's lens. In this scene, as in others, both the verbal and the visual texts reinforce the centrality of Mouse. A somewhat detailed description of the sequence makes this point: as Agnes and Ari are spreading a blanket over Mouse's casket in the film's present, the viewer hears what begins as a nondiegetic voice-over in Mouse's voice. He recites one of Seymour's poems, a poem called "Memorial Day 1972." That Mouse speaks in the first person cues the viewer to understand the experience Mouse describes as Mouse's own experience. This identification is especially so in that it recalls the idea of the uranium mines to which Mouse refers in the opening scene. In the voice-over Mouse recites as follows:

> I was too young to clean graves
> so I waded into the uranium river
> with a cat that later gave birth
> to six headless kittens. (*Business*)

At the completion of these voice-over lines, there is a cut from the casket to a medium close-up flashback of Mouse himself, alive and dressed in the dark jacket and tie that the viewer will recognize as that which he wears in the photograph displayed on the coffin; in person, as it were, he finishes his reading of the poem: "Oh Lord remember, do remember me." The shot of Mouse is followed by a flashback shot of him with Ari as they look at Seymour's book. Mouse reads from the book, repeating the lines he has just spoken to the camera: "Oh Lord remember, do remember me." The shot of Mouse's holding of and reading from Seymour's book makes clear for the first time that the lines are not Mouse's after all but Seymour's. But even in this specific context when the film finally but clearly identifies the lines as Seymour's, Mouse still insists that the experiences those lines describe are his own: "It's all lies Ari; those are my kittens. He took my life, man. . . . It's like I'm not even alive. It's like I'm dead" (*Business*). The scene as a whole provides a microcosm of the film: like the film in general, that is, the scene depicts Seymour, the ostensible protagonist, as the one who tells the story, but tells a story that is not his own. He tells Mouse's story, and Mouse, literally dead, continues to live through and as a result of *his* stories. Ultimately it is Mouse who provides Seymour with a voice.

The one obvious exception to Mouse as the one who holds and controls the camera is a late scene in which Seymour's non-Indian partner Steven (Kevin Phillip) films the poet in the bathtub. As in the other such scenes, the filming invites the viewer in, and in a sense this time to an especially private moment: Seymour is naked in his own bathroom and is reciting a somewhat erotic ad-lib poem to and for Steven, who is doing the filming. On the one hand, perhaps, the moment suggests that Seymour's partner is taking over Mouse's role as chronicler of Seymour's life, echoing his earlier insistence that he has replaced Mouse and the others on the reservation, insisting, as he says in a voice-over, "They aren't your tribe anymore. I'm your tribe now" (*Business*). But on the other hand, in a sense, the scene serves to call attention to Seymour's actual distance from his reservation home. Seymour's urban love poems do not make it into his book. This scene comes late in the film, but it depicts an event that takes place before Mouse's death and Seymour's trip back to the reservation. This inverted chronology further suggests that what Steven films is not an integral part of the history, but rather an exception.

In addition to his use of the handheld camera, Alexie chooses an additional method of calling attention to the camera in filming. That is, there are several scenes in which an unnamed interviewer talks with either Seymour or Ari, and during the interviews a mobile frame and a circling camera echo the handheld camera used in other scenes. Each interview, by virtue of its being an interview, has the effect of a documentary and inherits a documentary's pretense of representing reality authentically. Alexie simultaneously undercuts the pretense of veracity by using the circling camera during the interview scenes. This circling certainly calls attention to the camera itself and exposes the artifice. As with Mouse's handheld camera, the circling technique severs the fiction of the documentary, a genre that would otherwise ask the viewer to believe in a poet and interviewer who exist outside the film or documentary itself. The camerawork forcefully reminds the viewer that there is a camera, but it is not the camera one typically expects. That is, the camera remains unseen in this instance, even though the situation would seem to call for a camera as part of a videotaped interview session. Alexie defies expectations, but at the same time he draws attention to the fact of a camera filming an American Indian poet being interviewed about his poetry.

The Business of Fancydancing calls the viewer's attention to American Indians on film in this self-reflexive way, and it thus inevitably offers an evocation of Hollywood. But in this film there are not necessarily any overt references that so often find their way into such films. *Smoke Signals*, for example, as we have seen, makes numerous overt references as if it is involved in a conscious effort to acknowledge and yet distance itself from Hollywood. Victor actually names *Dances with Wolves* in one reference, and Thomas calls attention to a Western on a television screen in the background of the action in another. Alexie's film does, however, offer several implicit references. With the title of her 2002 review of the film, "Giving Hollywood the Business," Sarah Phelman makes a note of the distance between *Fancydancing* and Hollywood. She writes that "in Alexie's work, Indians are depicted as complex and flawed. It's a universe light years away from the myth of Indians as a bunch of war-paint-wearing, shape-shifting noble savages" (Phelman). This very straightforward account of a major difference between Alexie's film and standard Hollywood fare is instructive in that it suggests some of the ways in which Alexie's film breaks new ground in presenting a different caliber of Native character.

Mouse is indeed a flawed but complex character, and several scenes offer intriguing glimpses of this complexity. The viewer is cued to sympathize with him, for example, when as noted above he complains that Seymour has taken his stories and thus his life. And the film cues the viewer to appreciate and respect him for his abilities as a violinist. But if the film sometimes asks the viewer to sympathize with and appreciate the dead Mouse, it offers cues on other occasions that compel that viewer to keep him at a distance. Especially troubling is Mouse's own filmed account of how he and Ari brutally attack and beat an unsuspecting non-Indian who has asked for their help as he stands alone beside his car, which has evidently run out of gas. After this unprovoked attack, Ari and Mouse simply drive away, leaving the man lying on the roadside, severely beaten. Mouse records on his own camera much of this attack, rendering it all the more realistic and thus all the more difficult to forgive. Perhaps above all, this attack serves as an example of how the film refuses to allow the viewer to see Mouse as either noble or ignoble. It is instead an example of his complexity.

Mouse's girlfriend, Teresa, offers a funeral oration in which she presents Mouse as a complex character. He is perhaps sometimes mean, but he is not without redemptive qualities. She describes him as bitter, almost racist, in his attitude toward her on occasion yet also as sometimes loving and giving. She points out that he was extremely talented as a violinist, and the viewer knows that at the same time he has such talent he also abuses his body and mind with ridiculous excesses in his efforts to get high.

That Mouse. He was never all that nice to me. But, jeez, he could play the violin, and he'd play for me. He could play almost anything. He'd never complain about taking requests. But every time after he was done he'd, he'd give me that Mouse evil eye and he'd say "Hey, what the hell you doing here, Suyapi, and when are you leaving?" I'm telling you, I'm, I'm really gonna miss that mean bastard. I'm gonna miss the way the river changed when Mouse was making his music. (*Business*)

Presenting complex Indian characters is but one means of refuting Hollywood stereotypes and talking back to mainstream (mis)understandings and (mis)representations of Indigenous peoples. Even when it is not implicitly talking back specifically to Hollywood, *The Business of Fancydancing* reverberates throughout with mainstream combinations and allusions. As Blake Hausman demonstrates, for example, the film is full of references and allusions to *Hamlet*—a centerpiece in the Western literary tradition. According to Hausman, "Alexie's work consciously opens itself up to a dialogue with the center of the Eurowestern canon" (102). In this context it is certainly not a stretch to suggest that Alexie's film is talking back to mainstream tradition even if not specifically to Hollywood Westerns as a genre.

Another example of this western European reverberation is an early scene in which Agnes prepares Mouse's body for the funeral, one of the longest scenes in the film. She covers him with a blanket, smudges with smoke, and then offers a Jewish prayer. The moment is analogous to an early scene in *House Made of Dawn* when Abel is preparing his grandfather after he has died. Abel takes the turquoise necklace from its peg on the wall and places it on his grandfather's breast. In the midst of this Pueblo ritual, however, the camera lingers on the grandfather's cross, which Abel has left hanging on the wall. Like the grandfather's, Mouse's ceremony offers a combination of traditions. Agnes and Ari dress a mannequin with a fancydance outfit as a part of the setting for the funeral, yet the ceremony itself can be described as very Western, with the casket and eulogies. The ceremony includes Agnes singing of both "Amazing Grace" and "Osinilshatin," a song in Salish.

Mouse contends that Seymour coopts his stories, as noted above, and as a living Mouse makes this statement to Ari, the film cuts to the funeral and a memorial song. The cut and juxtaposition of Mouse's statement and funeral underscore the validity of Mouse's contention: "It's like I'm not even alive" (*Business*). There is an irony in the contention that Seymour kills Mouse when he steals his stories to make and publish poems. The effect of this contention, that is, puts Seymour, the urban poet, at a distance as it alienates him from the people on the reservation. This alienation implies a connection between what the poet is doing and what Hollywood has been doing since the beginnings of the industry: stealing Indigenous stories and thereby causing

Eulogy for Mouse. *The Business of Fancydancing*. Screen Capture. A FallsApart Production.

American Indians to vanish both literally and figuratively. As Mouse insists on telling his own story, on reclaiming his history, so too Alexie insists on telling his own Indigenous story as a counter to any version the West might tell. Hausman argues that Alexie's film refers indirectly to Hollywood, particularly with Seymour's reading of the poem "How to Write the Great American Indian Novel": "This poem partially explains Seymour's success—Americans love tragic stories about Indians, and Seymour delivers. It also parodies the expectations of Seymour's audiences who have been schooled in the 'traditional' doctrines of Manifest Destiny, right away holding the mirror up to Hollywood" (92). Alexie wrote this poem before the making of the film, of course, and published it in the collection *The Summer of Black Widows*. Within the fiction of the film, however, the sentiment that the poem expresses can certainly be seen to apply to Mouse. Seymour reads the poem, but like the other poems in the film, it tells Mouse's story. Mouse's lover Teresa is a "white woman," for example, and she maintains that her relationship with this man was rough in part because Mouse could be unpredictable, stormy. According to the poem,

> Indian men, of course, are storms. They should destroy the lives
>
> of any white women who choose to love them. All white women love Indian men. That is always the case. White women feign disgust
>
> at the savage in blue jeans and T-shirt, but secretly lust after him. (94–95)

The poem applies to Mouse in another way as well. Mouse appears throughout the film after he has died and after Agnes has laid him out. He sits at one of Seymour's poetry readings, he plays violin in the backseat of Seymour's car, and he recites poetry after his own death. In this sense, he takes on characteristics of a ghost, as described in that same poem.

> In the Great American Indian novel, when it is finally written,
> all of the white people will be Indians and all of the Indians will be ghosts.
> (94–95)

To whatever extent one can see parallels between the poem and Mouse's life and death, they are inevitably a better match than anyone can draw between the poet Seymour himself and his poem.

In his efforts to write the great American Indian poem, Seymour thus borrows or steals his material from the reservation and tells stories that Mouse claims as his own, yet when the interviewer challenges the poet by reminding him that almost all his poetry is reservation based, he gets extremely defensive. He describes how his sister's life was ruined on the reservation and how his mother gave him a dictionary as his means of escape. He demands that the interviewer not tell him what he can and cannot write: "Don't tell me what I can write, and don't tell me what I can remember. . . . I'll be a hard-ass whore if I want to be" (*Business*). The exchange between the interviewer and Seymour constitutes the film's final dialogue. The rest is music.

Mouse provides Seymour with a voice throughout the entire film. In addition to his being filmed, written, and talked about, Mouse speaks, he reads, he films, he plays music. Seymour in contrast ultimately loses his ability to speak; he becomes mute. This poet, this man of many words, stands beside Mouse's coffin in front of the other mourners and is unable to utter a single word. For the first time, now that he stands in front of Mouse's coffin, Seymour has nothing to say. The film renders him mute, and from that moment until the end of the film, he remains speechless. The film thus insists, even if only implicitly, that without Mouse to borrow from or to take words and stories from, Seymour is without voice. Steven declares that "they aren't your tribe anymore. I'm your tribe now" (*Business*), and his assertion echoes and takes on added meaning once the viewer sees Seymour standing wordless among former friends. Alexie achieves this disconnect filmically through the doubling of Seymour's character.

In one version of himself, a version that he imagines, Seymour screams and cries as he stands in front of the coffin. In contrast, in the version of himself that his former friends actually witness, he has no voice, no words; he makes no sound at all. After standing speechless in front of the coffin, he walks away, out of the house and toward his car. As he leaves, Agnes stands and begins to sing "Osinilshatin." Seymour walks to the sound of Agnes's singing. The film cuts to a shot of Seymour's double, already sitting in the car, and as that version of Seymour drives away, the other version stands stock still in the driveway. Meanwhile Agnes's diegetic song becomes nondiegetic as one of the Seymours drives out of earshot. Another cut returns the viewer to Seymour removing his fancydance accoutrements: armbands, vest, bone necklace, and beaded moccasins. His disrobing is juxtaposed with a shot of Ari, seen as if in the rearview mirror. Ari takes a few fancydance steps. A crosscut back to Agnes follows, which is in turn followed by a cut to Seymour, back in Seattle, as he climbs into bed with Steven, at which point the screen goes dark. Meanwhile, Agnes continues singing in Salish and is joined by another female voice. Credits begin to roll.

These shots and cuts imply rather forcefully that without Mouse there is no poet. The film thus seems to insist that if Seymour's poetry cannot escape the reservation, then without the reservation, without Mouse in particular, there is no poetry. Even though he is dead, however, Mouse, in stark contrast to Seymour, retains his voice throughout the film. Literally, verbally he has his voice, and figuratively he continues to speak through his music. That is, just because Seymour becomes mute, Mouse does not. His voice and camerawork provide the film's opening sequence; he plays music and appears in numerous scenes in various capacities; and he is making ironic music, for example, with a rendition of "The Star-Spangled Banner" when he first meets Teresa. He plays violin in other contexts as well. After his death, he, or his ghost, even plays during one of Seymour's readings, and he finishes the piece from the backseat of Seymour's car as the poet drives out of Seattle toward the reservation and the funeral. Ultimately, he plays the music accompanying the final credits: Mouse's violin rendition of "Ten Little Indians." If not the film's final words, Mouse does have the final say. His music plays on after the end of the film and so continues to speak to the viewer. In this sense he survives both his own death and the end of the film. And he speaks not through Seymour, the urban poet, but through his music and for himself.

Mouse can be said to survive the end of the film only figuratively, of course, but the other characters survive literally, and except for Seymour they all remain on the reservation. In this way the film clearly privileges them and their lives. One telling instance of how the film demonstrates the communal vibrancy of those left living is in the depiction of Ari dancing. A shot depicts him as he takes a few fancydance steps behind the car as Seymour is leaving the reservation, driving back to the city. Not only does Ari remain at home, as it were, his lively dance steps are contrasted through juxtaposition with the immediately preceding crosscut shot of Seymour as he dejectedly removes much of his dance outfit. More telling still, perhaps, is another aspect of the final sequence, the scene in which Seymour walks away from the funeral and the house. The film's final sequence consists of several short scenes, beginning with the shot mentioned above of Seymour, wearing a fancydance outfit lacking the bustles, as he falls to the ground. As he falls, nondiegetic singing begins: Agnes's rendition of "Amazing Grace." Such shots and juxtapositions suggest the power of those who remain on the reservation, all connected by Mouse, and this detailed recounting of the final sequence demonstrates just how filmically significant the surviving characters are. Even Seymour, who returns to Seattle in the film's final moments, clearly leaves a part of himself, his double, perhaps the emotional, vibrant part of himself, on the reservation. Ari remains and dances. Agnes remains and sings. The film depicts these Indian men and women as survivors and contrasts them with the Indian man who dies early but who continues after his death to motivate the plot and influence the living. He refuses to vanish; he keeps coming back again and again. And without exception *The Business of Fancydancing* insists that the other characters continue to live, continue to thrive—in part as a result of the death of one of their relations.

NINE

Sharing the Kitchen

Naturally Native and Women in American Indian Film

VICKI: Courtney, these are your great grandparents.
COURTNEY: Wow! I didn't even know I had any. —*Naturally Native*

Following a title that reads "1972," in the opening shot of Valerie Red-Horse's *Naturally Native*, the camera zooms to a folder containing adoption papers and to a black-and-white snapshot of two girls holding a baby. A male voice-over informs the viewer that in 1972 the children are up for adoption. From the voice-over, the viewer learns that the "real mother" has died: "It was the alcohol that killed her" (*Naturally*). Like *The Business of Fancydancing* and *House Made of Dawn*, among others, *Naturally Native* takes as its point of departure the death of Indian characters who will nevertheless have significant roles throughout the film.

The opening scene at the adoption agency is merely the first instance of how *Naturally Native* makes explicit, self-conscious use of photography to challenge the legacy of Native Americans in photographs as objects without context rather than fully contextualized as subjects. The black-and-white still represents "living" Indians and makes explicit that although the mother has died, the children survive. Moments after this introductory sequence, the viewer discovers that the photograph is of the film's three adult leads, taken when they were children some twenty-six years before the film's present action. The film's use of the photograph to anticipate its subsequent focus on the adult presence of these three women is thus similar to the use of photographs in *The Exiles* and *Medicine River*, for example. Such use of a photograph provides the Native filmmaker one method of talking back to a history of visual (mis)representation and appropriation. The opening anticipates the film's final scene when Charlie (Charlie Hill), the Viejas museum curator, shows the sisters a photograph of their grandparents. Vickie's daughter Courtney also looks on:

VICKIE: Courtney, these are your great-grandparents.
COURTNEY: Wow! I didn't even know I had any. (*Naturally Native*)

That is, she had not known of them because her mother Vickie herself had not had access to knowing them until this moment. The curator has the film's final words as the group stands looking at the photo album, words spoken to Courtney (Courtney Red-Horse Mohl): "Welcome home," he says. In this way the film comes full circle, beginning and ending with snapshots. In the beginning, before the film's present action, they are young girls forced to leave their reservation home, and by the end of the film the community brings the adult women back into its fold. They are home.

Naturally Native tells the story of the three women as they attempt to start their own business producing and selling health and beauty products based on tribal recipes. The eldest, Vickie (Valerie Red-Horse, also writer, codirector, and coproducer), is married with two children and is living in the suburban house she and her sisters have inherited from their non-Indian adoptive parents. The other two sisters, Karen and Tanya, are single. Karen (Kimberly Norris Guerrero) has just finished her MBA and is looking for a job; Tanya (Irene Bedard) has had a short career as a model and actress. Both are living with Vickie, her husband, and their two children. The plot consists of a series of the women's encounters with various potential moneylenders as they seek funding to start up their business. After three dead ends, they return to their roots on the reservation, where they and their parents are remembered and where they receive a loan from the Viejas tribal council.

The film follows the brief 1972 backstory of the opening sequence with another title "PRESENT" and a scene throughout which Vickie's husband, Steve Bighawk (Pato Hoffman), walks through a crowd with his video camera, filming a poolside party in celebration of Karen's earning her degree. The film immediately puts a video camera in an Indian character's hands, and as in *The Business of Fancydancing*, such a move makes explicit from the outset that Native people are in control of the filming and the telling of the story. There is an immediate acknowledgment of the existence and importance of visual sovereignty. At the same time that it demonstrates who is in control of the camera, the scene calls immediate attention to the artifice of film. That is, the technique calls attention to the fact of filming itself in that the viewer sees a camera and sees some of what that camera sees. Paralleling the use of still photos as a framing device, so too Red-Horse uses Steve Bighawk's filming with his own video camera in both first and last present-action sequences.

As the plot summary and recounting of the opening and closing scenes suggest, the film weaves an intricate web of motifs, linking the dead ancestors, the current and future generations, and the place of photography in the lives of the characters. The role that women play throughout the film arches over these several motifs. In this chapter I argue that the film's self-reflexive use of both still and video photography provides a means of talking back to

Hollywood concerning the typically limited and stereotypical roles of women in depictions of American Indians on screen and the stereotypical, superficial representation of Indians as inevitably dead and vanished by the end of those Hollywood films.

The film's opening can certainly be seen to have thematic significance, but the initial filming at the pool party is also simply what enables the film-maker to provide introductions. Steve introduces the principal characters as he films them, and thus the viewer learns that Steve has a wife, two kids, and two sisters-in-law. The viewer also learns immediately that the Bighawk's extended family resides in a large suburban house with space enough for at least two aunts and that it has a large patio with a pool. The viewer realizes from the outset that these people are middle to upper-middle class, educated bourgeois suburbanites. An implicit question that the opening sequence thus raises and that this chapter will address is this: do the family members accept the social norms that are typically inherent in such a bourgeois setting?

Early in the film, as she lies in bed beside her husband, Vickie Lewis Big-hawk asks her husband for permission to share the kitchen where he and his male friends will be playing poker the following evening. She trails off mid-sentence, realizing her husband has once again fallen asleep in the midst of a conversation. In this particular scene and in the film in general, Valerie Red-Horse as director establishes herself and her two entrepreneurial sisters as the central characters and the prime movers in a film that puts women front and center in an American Indian film.

Naturally Native is indeed groundbreaking in its presentation and representation of American Indian women. This is especially evident when one considers that its release coincides with the release the same year of the very male-centered and much more widely distributed film *Smoke Signals*. For all its innovation in this regard, however, *Naturally Native* did not and does not receive nearly the press or critical attention that *Smoke Signals* did and does, and thus Red-Horse's film has not gained the cachet of Eyre's film. Scholarly response to the two films has been equally unbalanced. *Smoke Signals* receives the lion's share of scholarly attention, while scholars tend to over-look *Naturally Native*. Red-Horse's film is nevertheless deserving of recognition as the groundbreaking film it is in several ways: it introduces female leads to feature-length Native American film; it casts American Indian actors, and its writer, codirector, and funding are all Indigenous as well. In an interview, Randy Redroad comments that when "*Smoke Signals* came out, it was a very historic thing, but there was something just as historic that happened with two other movies—*Tushka* (1996) and *Naturally Native*. The Pequot tribe was the executive producer of *Naturally Native*. They put in the money. . . . It's like you had [films] written, directed, and produced by Chris [Eyre] and Valerie [Red-Horse], with Valerie's film funded by Indians"

(Svenson). *Naturally Native* is definitely a significant and welcome innovation that allows American Indian women a central place in Indian film and has the potential to open the way for new directions in Indigenous film.

The roles of Indian women in both Hollywood Westerns and in American Indian films have, for the most part, been extremely limited. *Smoke Signals* is very much a film about men, male friendship, and father-son relationships. The three leads are male: Victor, Thomas, and Arnold. Angelica Lawson argues that the women in the film "act as catalysts for both narrative and character development," implicitly acknowledging that despite offering counters to Hollywood depictions of Native women, they ultimately play second fiddle to the male characters (95). Jhon Gilroy points out that although "the female characters in *Smoke Signals* no doubt contribute important aspects to the narrative, their role is ultimately subordinated to the simultaneously overarching and underlying theme of the relationships between fathers and sons" ("Another" 32). A similar argument can be made about *The Business of Fancydancing*. Whether one sees Mouse or Seymour as the main focus, the film is unquestionably male centered and offers male perspectives. This said, it must be noted, however, that actor Michelle St. John does an excellent job in the role of Agnes, and that her character provides a center and touchstone around which the male characters Mouse, Seymour, and Ari orbit. But her role remains subordinate to those of the male characters. Another interesting film in this context is director John Hazlett's *In a World Created by a Drunken God* (2008), based on Ojibwa writer Drew Hayden Taylor's play by the same title. There are no women; the only two characters are two men, half brothers who meet as adults for the first time.

Ubiquitous emphasis on Indian men rather than women in film predates films by Alexie and Eyre by roughly a century. From the silent era onward, males constitute the vast majority of celluloid Indians, and even in those few films with strong female Indian supporting actors, the perspective remains male. The films are male centered, male oriented, male dominated, and inevitably told from a male perspective. Of the films through 1998, when *Naturally Native* was released, there is little or nothing that might be seen as a precedent. Angela Aleiss points out that from 1985 to 2003, "the number of male Indian actors has remained nearly three times that of females" (148). In the preface to her study of female Indian roles in film, *Killing the Indian Maiden*, Elise Marubbio argues that for a century Native American women, with few exceptions, have been confined almost exclusively to sacrificial roles. Hollywood cinema, Marubbio writes, "depicts a young Native American woman who enables, helps, loves, or aligns herself with a white European American colonizer and dies as a result of that choice" (ix).

A few examples from the long list of Hollywood Westerns should suffice to demonstrate how minor and demeaning the role of Indian women has been. In the landmark John Ford film *The Searchers*, for example, the one Indian woman with any presence, the character Look, or Wild Goose Flying in the Night Sky (Beulah Archuletta), is portrayed as one who devotes herself wholly and fully through marriage to Martin Pawley (Jeffrey Hunter), because he has unwittingly traded for her. Martin mistreats her verbally, and he physically abuses and then abandons her. The film then kills her off; she is found dead in a village after a cavalry attack. Indian women fare no better in later, so-called anti-Westerns. The roles for Indian women in *Little Big Man* could hardly be more problematic in this context. The protagonist's Cheyenne wife Sunshine (Amy Eccles, born in Hong Kong) dies in a massacre as he looks on. Custer and his 7th Calvary slaughter her, her three sisters, and her newborn child, along with most of the rest of the people in the village in a dawn attack. Sunshine's death (along with the death of her newborn child) enables the film to disallow the continuance of any interracial marriage and offspring for its protagonist. At the beginning of the attack, Jack Crabb, as Little Big Man (Dustin Hoffman), makes the very deliberate choice to save his adoptive father Old Lodge Skins (Chief Dan George) rather than make any attempt to save his wife and children. In this way, the film *Little Big Man* sends a very powerful misogynistic message, if only subliminally, to its viewers. Even though the film is arguably an anti-Western, heralded as sympathetic to American Indians, it nevertheless embraces all the limitations of Hollywood Westerns in general. It continues and perpetuates stock images and patterns viewers have by 1970 become accustomed to: a non-Indian woman plays a leading Indian woman's part; as one partner in an interracial marriage, she necessarily dies; a plot set in the nineteenth century serves to write twentieth- and twenty-first-century Indians out of existence; and the film delivers an ultimate final message that guarantees the demise of Native Americans. As Old Lodge Skins says in the film's final sequence: "We won today; we won't win tomorrow" (*Little*). In *A Man Called Horse* there are indeed important female Indians with speaking parts, actually two with speaking parts and a third who wails. While they are alive, they are all definitely subordinate to the male principals Yellow Hand (Manu Tupou), Horse himself (Richard Harris), and Batise (Jean Gascon). Horse in fact names his wife Little Freedom because he sees her almost exclusively as his means of escaping the prison of the camp in which he has been held captive. None of the three women survives the end of the film.

Especially unfortunate in the context of portrayals of American Indian women and their place in films that include Indian characters, plots, and issues is *Dances with Wolves*. In this much-acclaimed and hugely successful film, the "Indian" woman, Stands with a Fist (Mary McDonnell), turns out to be non-Indian. Her European American ancestry is her pass, even though she was raised by the Lakotas, to survival; that heritage allows her to survive the end of the film and to be able to ride off with the non-Indian man Dunbar (Kevin Costner). There are no Indian women to speak of in *Last of the Mohicans*; the women around whom the plot of Cooper's 1826 novel and the 1993 film revolve, and the choices for Uncas, that last Mohican, are the white daughters of the English colonel Edmund Munro. Michael Apted's sympathetic film *Thunderheart* is also very much a man's movie: male FBI agents, with the help of a male tribal policeman (Graham Greene), pursue male suspects, and a male elder offers up his wisdom. The one important female role is limited to begin with, and she ends up dead as well. As Marubbio points out, Maggie (Sheila Tousey) is the "only primary Native woman character," and "she is depicted as a love interest for the white hero." She "betrays her own people by aiding Ray, and is metonymically connected to the landscape, all of which invoke memories of the Princess figures" (*Killing* 205). Marubbio argues that "the use of the Celluloid Maiden figure in the film weakens the film's political agenda and positions age-old stereotypes on contemporary images of Native American women" (*Killing* 206). Her place in the film is also intertextually connected with the minor position afforded Indian woman in film in general, in both Indian and non-Indian films. If one looks to some of the recent, contemporary "Westerns" with Indian characters and issues at their centers, one discovers a similar lacuna. In Ryszard Bugajski's *Clearcut*, starring Graham Greene, no Indian woman of any thematic or narrative importance appears. With the exception of a Makah woman as a one-time sexual partner, there are also no Indian women of thematic importance to speak of in Jim Jarmusch's *Dead Man*, starring Johnny Depp and Gary Farmer as Nobody.

Unfortunately, if not surprisingly, American Indian women fare little better in independent American Indian film. There are no Indian women in Momaday and Mackenzie's *House Made of Dawn*; of the few Indian women from the novel (Porcingula, who in the present-day portions of the novel has become an old witch, and Josie, who laughs and farts), none makes it into the film. Nor in Vizenor's *Harold of Orange* does any Indian woman make an appearance. Men exclusively populate the community center at the bend in the river. *Powwow Highway* introduces the viewer to Bonnie Red Bow (Joannelle Nadine Romero), but the film reduces her from her dynamic character in the novel to a helpless Indian princess in the film. Sandra Baringer writes that Bonnie in the novel is "the quintessential but self-conscious 'Indian princess,' incorruptible by cigarettes, sex, alcohol, and innumerable other drugs" (50). In the film, however, submits Baringer, the subplot involving Bonnie is "significantly sanitized and oversimplified," so that the character "is an innocent decoy used by the FBI to set up her brother" (51). Even later films are relatively weak when it comes to their presentations of female characters. As we will see in the next chapter, for example, there are no Indian women with significant roles in Chris Eyre's film *Skins*. Randy Redroad's *The Doe Boy* does include Maggie (Jeri Arredondo), as wife and mother, and Geri (Judy Herrera), who befriends the male protagonist and becomes a love interest. They are present, but they remain secondary to the film's main action. They mostly facilitate the film's almost exclusive interest in the father-son and grandfather-grandson relationships and the son's coming of age story.

In the midst of all these films lacking any significant female Indian presence, *Medicine River* offers one of the few exceptions. Louise Heavyman (Sheila Tousey) is a self-motivated and self-sufficient First Nations woman. She is a self-employed career woman professionally, and personally she demonstrates her independence by choosing to have and raise a child on her own. She reminds the film's protagonist Will and thus the viewer any number of times of her independence. "We're going to have to talk," she says to him, and that often repeated statement is her shorthand method of telling him that she does not want a husband or a live-in boyfriend. About raising her baby she says, "I want to do this on my own" (*Medicine*). The film also introduces Bertha Morely (Tina Louise Bomberry), the woman who works at the Friendship Center, as well as the delightful trickster Martha Old Crow (Maggie Blackkettle). But despite its promising female supporting actors, even *Medicine River* ultimately remains focused on a man as it essentially tells story about Will reconciling himself to his coming home, connecting with his familial past, and learning to appreciate his heritage. Another notable exception to the general rule of films without significant Indian women characters is Greg Sarris's made-for-television film *Grand Avenue* (1996). Directed by non-Native Daniel Sackheim and based on Sarris's 1994 novel by the same title, this HBO film is almost exclusively about and acted by women. Other exceptions include Shane Belcourt's *Tkaronto* (2007) and Sterlin Harjo's films, which will be discussed in subsequent chapters.

This overview of Indian women's roles in Native and non-Native films demonstrates just how groundbreaking Red-Horse's *Naturally Native* actually is. In the context of women in feature-length Indian film, then, the film takes a clearly refreshing and promising direction: it is a film in which Indian women play central and prominent roles; they not only survive the films ending, they thrive throughout. It is undeniably their film. It is also significant that the three sisters procure the financing that enables the establishment of their own business. At the same time, the film is in this way refreshingly progressive; however, in its social-sexual politics, it seems quite conservative. What Valerie Red-Horse achieves by putting women front and center in the context of a very male-dominated film industry is actually analogous to what Alexie seems to achieve with his presentation of a homosexual Indian man in *The Business of Fancydancing*. As Lisa Tatonetti argues, for example, Alexie's film "means to privilege a dominant version of sexuality that precludes intersectional understandings of sexuality and indigeneity. In doing so, *The Business of Fancydancing* relies on a set of settler colonialist logics" (170). In *Naturally Native*, Red-Horse breaks new and important ground with her female leads, but at the same time her film seems to privilege the understandings of sexual mores, the social interaction, and even the religion of mainstream colonist culture. In this regard, the film embraces a sort of benevolent multiculturalism and ultimately becomes assimilationist. The film pulls the viewer in two directions: it provides important, central filmic roles for women, giving them and Native Americans the opportunity for self-representation as it challenges Hollywood stereotypes in one direction. And in another direction, it provides Red-Horse an arena in which she can essentially reinscribe traditional mores of mainstream American settler culture, especially concerning the centrality of the nuclear family, gender roles, attitudes toward sex, and religious practice.

One method Red-Horse uses to achieve a sense of benevolent multiculturalism is to educate the viewer concerning "Indian" practices or worldviews. Her tactics in this regard are much different from Alexie's in *The Business of Fancydancing*, for example. In an interview with John Purdy, Alexie explains how he intentionally creates subtexts exclusively and specifically for Indian viewers: "I load my books with the stuff, just load 'em up. I call them 'Indian trapdoors.' You know, Indians fall in, White people just walk right over them" (145). According to Quentin Youngberg, "Alexie's 'trapdoors' serve to make the literature familiar to the Indian reader in such a way that maintains the boundary between the outside and the inside, yet without completely alienating other audiences to the text" (61). Red-Horse is more generous. Rather than exclude and alienate the non-Indian viewer, she closes off such potential trapdoors almost completely and actually welcomes the opportunity to educate and thus include that viewer. The most obvious instance of the tactic of inclusion is perhaps that her film presents a quintessentially mainstream, middle-class family, and within that construction she offers several educational moments. The first comes early in the film when Karen explains to her non-Indian friend Craig what a dream catcher is:

CRAIG: What is that? I saw a bunch of them hanging in the house.
KAREN: Yeah, that's my sister Vickie. She has one in every single room. It's called
    a dream catcher and they say they that if you hang one over your bed that
    all the bad dreams will get caught in the web and the good dreams will pass
    through the hole and to you.
CRAIG: Do you believe it?
KAREN: I believe in dreams. (*Naturally*)

Not only does the unschooled Craig thus get an educational lesson, so does the viewer. And further catering to the non-Indian worldview concerning such (pop) cultural manifestations as dream catchers, Karen implicitly agrees to meet the very western-oriented Craig halfway by refusing a direct answer to his question about her own personal beliefs.

In scenes concerning problems of Indian drinking, the film again reaches out to educate the viewer, although by doing so it runs the risk of relying on stereotypes of Indians as biologically prone to alcoholism. Several times throughout the film Vickie considers having a glass of wine, but her husband, Steve, a teetotaler, repeatedly dissuades her. Their discussions about drinking inevitably turn into arguments whose subtext is the inevitability of Indian alcoholism. As the viewer remembers from the opening sequence, Vickie's mother is presumed to have died as a result of her heavy drinking. This early reference to the mother's cause of death runs the risk of reinscribing a stereotype, of course, as it might be said to reflect a perspective the mainstream viewer of American Indians in film expects.

VICKIE: I have a right to a glass of wine now and then.
STEVE: And your real mom, did she have the right to drink herself to death?
. . .
VICKIE: You know something, if I were Caucasian nobody would think twice about it. But because I'm Indian, "Oh no, you better not." (*Naturally*)

Only when the house is empty of husband, children, and sisters, does Vickie finally open that bottle of wine, and inevitably she proceeds to get drunk enough to pass out on the bed. Her inability to drink in moderation, one could argue, is lesson enough in this regard. Red-Horse's message here seems to be that all Indian people should avoid drinking alcohol. At the same time that Vickie is getting drunk by herself and in the privacy of her own home, her sister Tanya, on an internet date, is also drinking wine. Tanya's date assaults her after that dinner. Although the attack is not a result of Tanya's having drunk wine, the juxtaposition of drinking and assault makes the implicit suggestion that dire consequences somehow accompany any alcohol consumption. After all, Tanya ends up in a hospital bed the evening her sister passes out on her own bed at home. In this sense, the film seems to subscribe to a specific attitude toward Indians and drinking.

In another example of the plot's accommodating the film's desire to educate the viewer and bring two different worldviews closer together, Vickie explains to her son, Derek (Lowell Raven), and thus to the viewer why the "Fighting Indians" mascot on his little-league team jersey is inappropriate. The boy's sister, Courtney, offers the explanation that "there's a pro sports team with a logo just like it." The father gets angry: "You are not playing ball in that, young man." Then his mother explains to Derek why the mascot is so inappropriate: "Honey, what you have on your shirt is a cartoon picture of an Indian person. It makes us look less than human. Look at him. He's got a beet-red face and big buck teeth. We don't look like that, do we? It hurts us. It hurts your mommy and your daddy and all of us" (*Naturally*). In this way, Red-Horse is able to introduce the issue to the viewer and at the same time offer a specific political comment about the ongoing controversy over the inappropriateness of certain sports teams' mascots. In *American Indian Stereotypes in the World of Children* Cornel Pewewardy comments that children need to be aware that "these trappings and seasonal insults offend tens of thousands of other Americans" (189). Red-Horse makes the controversy much less confrontational than it might otherwise be by couching the discussion as a domestic incident between family members and by making it at the same time a teaching moment.

As a part of its apparent assimilationist philosophy, the film offers the viewer glimpses of the place of mainstream religion in this Native family, insisting that Sioux and Christian religious practices can coexist perfectly comfortably, and in fact can thrive side by side. The role of religion is emphasized in that several times in the course of the film Vickie and the others find a need to pray. The role of religion in the film serves to educate the viewer about an Indian tradition (burning sage, smudging, and praying to the Great Spirit) and about Native peoples at the same time accepting Christianity. "We're Presbyterians," Tanya tells one of the potential financiers in all innocence. There are several scenes in the film when Steve's Lakota beliefs are shown not to conflict with Vickie's more Christian beliefs. They both seem to participate in both systems as they pray over Tanya in the hospital bed, for example. Implicit here is the suggestion that the filmmaker deems it important that the movie demonstrate that Indians can be Christian and maintain "traditional" or non-Christian practices at the same time.

As the film can be said to embrace a multicultural approach to religion, it seems less open to anything but marital, heterosexual sex. The women's roles rely on standard stereotypes that severely limit the female characters. In one exchange between homemaker Vickie and her younger sister Tanya, for instance, the film seems to accept unquestioningly mainstream notions of the central place of marriage, heterosexual love, and raising a family. A conversation about clothing turns to body types:

TANYA: God gave you the better boobs . . .
VICKIE: Hey, breastfeed two kids; your boobs will get bigger too.
TANYA: You gotta have a husband first. (*Naturally*)

Emphasizing this fact, in one scene Tanya wears a T-shirt with words emblazoned across the front: "They're real." Despite this apparent disparaging of the culturally sanctioned practice of breast implants, however, Tanya does seem to privilege larger breasts, and her statement suggests that she has adopted, apparently unreflectively, the notion that to have children one must be married.

As a part of its educational enterprise, *Naturally Native* depicts graphically the potentially very serious risks involved in dating and casual sex, and it contrasts these dangers with another extreme, the character Karen who is a virgin at age thirty. The film juxtaposes and contrasts the two unmarried sisters' situations relating to their sex lives with Vickie and Steve's marital bliss. In a two-and-a-half-minute sequence in which Karen and Craig amble through his Edenic acreage looking for medicinal plants, there are crosscuts to Tanya with her dinner date at a restaurant and Vickie at home drinking. These two scenes are followed in rapid succession by a series of short takes, and they are linked by nondiegetic music, a song by Joanne Shenandoah, "In Love." A listing of the cuts demonstrates how the themes are interconnected and intertwined:

Vickie takes the bottle of wine out of the cupboard,
Steve sits on a hilltop,
Karen and Craig dance out on the land,
Vickie opens the bottle of wine,
Steve sits on a hilltop,
Tanya and her date drink wine at the restaurant,
Vickie drinks wine as she tries on a black dress,
Karen and Craig laugh and hold hands on the land,
Vickie tries on make-up and continues to drink,
Tanya and her date leave the restaurant,
Vickie passes out on her bed.

As the bridging music fades, Tanya walks from the restaurant into the parking lot where her date assaults her.

Although both of her sisters warn her not to, Tanya goes on a date with someone she has corresponded with on the internet but not yet met in person. The date ends in a vicious physical assault. This sequence of a dinner date and the brutal attack by the white male predator of the Indian princess or his "little Pocahontas" as he calls her is juxtaposed with the scenes of sister Karen's having a serious talk with Craig about how she has made the choice to remain a virgin. Karen's implication, though never stated outright, is virgin until marriage. At least that is how Craig understands her decision, exclaiming: "That's great." He then articulates his idea of the obvious resolution: "I think the solution is simple. I'll just have to marry you" (*Naturally*). The film implies that he can prove his worth, virtue, and merit by waiting. If he can wait, the exchange implies, he will definitely deserve the true virginal Indian princess.

The film presents Karen professionally as a successful business school graduate who can put together an excellent business proposal, but it depicts her personal life somewhat stereotypically. In real life she may be unique, as she maintains; but as a character in film she certainly fits a clichéd notion of the Indian princess. As she herself says, "You're looking at probably the only thirty-year-old virgin in the state" (*Naturally*). Her would-be white lover, the man who plays John Rolfe (or John Smith?) to her Pocahontas, is all the more enthralled. He offers his solution, interestingly, even though Karen has said nothing about waiting until marriage; this assumption clearly underlies his thinking, and perhaps underlies the philosophical tenet of the film as well.

The exchange between these two potential lovers takes place on a parcel of undeveloped land that Craig owns. At this point there is no particular or overt emphasis on the irony inherent in this non-Indian being the landowner, but later in the film the tribal museum curator Charlie does refer to ownership of land by non-Indians. His comment reverberates and harks back to the fact of Craig's owning the land that he and Karen find medicinal flowers on. Charlie shows the sisters a museum display of a ledger book showing, as he describes it, "a rancher's accounting of how many Indians they killed when they stole the land here" (*Naturally*). The implicit accusation is that Craig's ancestors stole the land and may well have been headhunters across the very land upon which Karen and Craig gather flowers and dance in the film's present. The film might seem to gloss over this irony, but the details of land ownership are especially poignant when one reflects that whereas the white man Craig owns countless acres outside of town, Vickie and her sisters must do their gardening on a small plot of ground, borrowed from a white woman neighbor.

In contrast to the virginal Karen, Tanya, the youngest of the three sisters, might be said to fit the role of the loose woman and thus complete the virgin/whore dichotomy between the two unmarried women. According to Karen's description at one point, Tanya "flirt[s] with every guy in the Western world" (*Naturally*). Throughout the film, however, Tanya behaves like a spoiled princess. And predictably, the white man she does go out with propositions her. She refuses his advances, and he assaults her, first verbally, then physically. According to her sisters' attitudes toward internet dating, Tanya somewhat foolishly gets herself into the situation in the first place. She is reformed, however, and will ultimately realize that Steve's Lakota cousin Mark is indeed the man for her. The two drastically different sequences—one of a verbal and physical assault in a parking lot and another of an enlightening conversation and then a dance in the garden—contrast significantly with the film's only sex scene, a scene that takes place in a bathtub and involves the married couple, Steve and Vickie. After the scene, the two children, who are afraid that the man who assaulted Aunt Tanya will find them, come to get in bed with the parents.

A third place in a typical paradigm of roles for women is the homemaker, and that one is nicely filled by Vickie, the film's lone wife and mother. When

Vickie herself starts to denigrate the relative value of a stay-at-home mom, Tanya upbraids her:

> VICKIE: If you're a failure, what am I, huh?
> TANYA: You have a family, a husband, people who need you everyday . . . Is it wrong that I want that too?
> VICKIE: No Tanya, you're not wrong to want that. Why don't you just give the Creator a chance? (*Naturally*)

There is an implicit irony here in that this conversation takes place on the large patio beside the swimming pool, as if to ask, "Who would not want that too?" Vickie says of herself to her sisters at another point, "Look guys, I'm resigning from the business. . . . I'm just a mom. I don't have an education; I react from my gut" (*Naturally*). And perhaps because she is willing to devalue her role as housewife, she tells Steve that she has made the decision to go back to work to help with the household bills.

> VICKIE: Hey, I'm going to start work tomorrow. The restaurant took me back.
> STEVE: What about the kids?
> VICKIE: I'm just going to do breakfast and lunch. I'll be home by three. Let me do this for a while. I know we can make it work. Please. (*Naturally*)

Despite her insistence and her husband's apparent acquiescence, however, the viewer never sees her actually return to work. The next morning Vickie is still in her own kitchen, watering a plant, rather than doing breakfast at a restaurant, and her sisters join her in that space.

The film does allow these three characters to grow and to break out of the limiting stereotypical roles to which both Hollywood and Red-Horse herself seem to have proscribed them, however. As a result of her being assaulted, Tanya changes. She is the one who refuses to trash the business proposal; she takes the initiative to call the people on the reservation to set up a business-loan appointment; and she decides she can indeed date an Indian man, something she has resisted up to that point. Karen does not grow or change as significantly, perhaps, but she does agree to a date with Craig, something she earlier avoided. And the rebellious Vickie promises her husband that she is done with drinking, and she later dresses in the back garters he has suggested would please him, something she had earlier resisted doing.

The major plotline follows the women as they continue to pursue their dream of establishing their own product line, and in this regard the film seems much more interested in issues of Indian identity than in sexual politics or sexual identity. In their first interview, the sisters fail to get the loan they seek because they are not enrolled members of a federally recognized tribe. They have no numbers, so they are not Indian enough. The second encounter is with a non-Indian woman exploiting sacred artifacts and rituals to make money, something the sisters will have no part of, even though they are perfectly willing meanwhile to commodify other aspects of their culture in order to market their naturally Native product. In their third attempt, they are turned down, ironically enough, because they *are* Indian, and the potential lender opposes Indian gaming. In this context, a closing credit argues the benefits of Indian gaming, clarifying that a decade after the 1988 Indian Gaming Regulatory Act, "the number of American Indian families on public assistance has been decreased dramatically" (*Naturally*). As is clearly evident in each of these encounters with potential money lenders, the difficulties in procuring the loan and starting a business of their own are never about their being women. The difficulties are in every instance wholly, in one way or another, about Indigenous identity. And when they do get the loan finally, they get it because they have a tribal, not a sexual or gendered, affiliation.

As the film sublimates any overt issues of gender politics it also seems to undercut any feminist statement it might otherwise make by relying on an extremely conventional setting. Whatever their Native cultures and traditions may have designated as separate but equal realms, these Indian women have entered mainstream America, fully assimilated, having coopted Western, European American worldviews and lifestyles: housekeeping, college degrees, modeling careers.

The film makes the thoroughness of their assimilation all the more evident in the spheres for action that it offers them. Many of the scenes in the film concern the trials and tribulations the sisters encounter: their discussions about the product, about men and marriage, about finances, about naming the product, and about their own futures. These discussions all take place either in the kitchen or in a bedroom, the two traditional spaces open to women in their own homes. Although the film presents a housewife, a single, recent MBA graduate, and a not-quite-successful, single actress and model, it still in a sense relegates these women to the home space, and to the most domestic spaces within that home at that, while it simultaneously depicts the sisters' entrepreneurship and their initiative. The first time the viewer sees Vickie, in fact, she is off to the kitchen. She has something in the oven. There are numerous scenes of Vickie in that kitchen. She is often wearing yellow rubber kitchen gloves. She is depicted carrying a laundry basket and in the children's bedroom, reading stories. To be fair, it should be noted that Steve also helps with the children. He reports that he has put them to bed, but the viewer does not see that. Instead the viewer sees him come into the kitchen, where his wife is busy. The women are in the kitchen while the men play poker. Much of the business conversations and work go on in the kitchen or at the nearby breakfast table.

In addition to the kitchen, the film depicts Vickie in bed several times with her husband, a spouse who falls asleep in the midst of Vickie's attempts at conversation with him. Or she is on her son's bed reading. Once there is a shot of her as she lies across her own bed, passed out from having drunk too much wine. Tanya, the youngest of the three, is closely associated with the bedroom and her bed. Early in the film, she runs to her bed and her stuffed animals to have a cry. It is in her bed that she immediately gets comfort from her sisters, who sit with her on that bed. In managing to stay out of the bed of her internet date, she ends up in a hospital bed. Here again she is comforted by the sisters and stuffed animals. The sister most spatially liberated is Karen, in that she is twice in the garden shop and once on Craig's land, but in those excursions Craig is always beside her. Much of the work she does on her laptop is done at the breakfast table, in the midst of all the goings-on around the house. These women clearly do not have any space of their own outside the bedroom.

There are of course also those scenes in which the film depicts the sisters in boardrooms asking for their loan and at the tribal offices. Ultimately, one can certainly argue, the film allows these women to break free of some of the societal constraints imposed by the dominant culture and imbibed by the characters. They do get the business loan they need through perseverance and ingenuity. They do make a connection with their heritage and even some distant relatives on the reservation. They do set up an office space for the business, and they do take control of that business.

The sisters' publicity photo shoot. *Naturally Native*. Red-Horse Native Productions.

If one framing device is Steve's working the crowd with his video camera in the opening and closing sequences, another framing device, as mentioned above, is use of photographs of the three sisters. Paralleling the opening shot of the sisters as children up for adoption is the sequence late in the film of the three sisters trying to find just the right publicity photo for their product line. They try one shooting dressed in buckskin and wearing bone chokers and feathers with their hair braided. Tanya wants nothing to do with such a pre-twentieth-century Indian-princess look, so she walks off the shoot. She has resisted such a connection with her tribal past throughout the entire film, and as is consistent with her character, she demonstrates her unwillingness through grimaces and gestures even before she walks off altogether. They next try a shooting in which they stand in a sort of green, leafy jungle, but Karen, who has been associated with the garden all along, seems to be allergic to the plants, so they scrap that shoot as well. Finally, they find the look they prefer, mainstream Western. They don floor-length satiny evening dresses, and they wear their long dark hair loose. Having found just the right look and just the right product name, they exclaim, "That's it!" At this moment the viewer sees that publicity photograph.

In the midst of the sisters' hunt for financial backing and an image is their identity search. As they tell more than one potential funding agent, they don't have tribal numbers or papers that would demonstrate emphatically their tribal affiliation. They do not know their tribal connections or relatives, because they were adopted as children, but their dead parents' influence and importance is stressed throughout the film. As noted above, because of the mother's death from alcoholism, Vickie is not allowed to drink for fear of becoming alcoholic herself. And it is the sisters' father from whom Vickie has gotten the recipes that will become the new "Naturally Native" product. In this sense the film is framed by allusion to the elders, parents, grandparents, and great-grandparents. Further, the film stresses the lives of the children and grandchildren. It insists that the future lies in the hands of these children, all of whom survive the end of the film, and who have successfully entered mainstream settler culture.

TEN

In the Form of a Spider

The Interplay of Narrative Fiction
and Documentary in *Skins*

Most people think of Iktomi as coming in the form of a spider. He
could just as easily be a rock. And maybe he entered your brains when
your head hit that rock. . . . Remember, human beings don't control
anything. Spirits do. —*Skins*

Chris Eyre's film *Skins* is about the relationships between siblings, like *Naturally Native*. And like *Powwow Highway* and *Smoke Signals*, it tells the story
of the relationship between two very different men, in this case, the two Yellow Lodge brothers: the hardworking tribal policeman Rudy (Eric Schweig)
and the older Mogie (Graham Greene), an unemployed Vietnam veteran and
chronic drunk. The plot of *Skins*, like the plots of the other films, moves
toward and revolves to a large extent around a specific death. Mogie dies
of alcohol-related liver failure only near the end of the film, but the viewer
gets an indication of the likelihood of such a fate as early as the opening sequence. The film's use of a documentary-style overview of the quality of
life on the Pine Ridge Reservation in South Dakota in a sense foreshadows
Mogie's death.

    Skins is a narrative film based on a novel by the same title (1995) by Paiute
writer Adrian Louis, but it opens with an evocation of a different genre altogether. As if it were an actual documentary, the film's opening sequence offers
an overview of its geographical and cultural setting, Pine Ridge Reservation
in South Dakota. The film immediately establishes the context for Mogie's
death as it acknowledges and calls attention to a world that exists outside the
film itself. At the same time it serves to educate the viewer by offering what
is ostensibly reliable information that a non-Indian or nonreservation viewer
might otherwise not have. In this context the viewer is cued to assume that
the information so delivered is both accurate and important to the narrative
events to follow.

    Those narrative events, in brief, are as follows: tribal policeman Rudy Yel-
low Lodge is called to a crime scene and gives chase to two men who have just
murdered a young man named Corky. Rudy does not catch them because he

falls and hits his head on a rock, but he does recognize one killer's brightly colored shoelaces, which allows him later to identify one of the perpetrators as a suspect. A few days after this initial event, Rudy overhears the two murderers incriminate themselves, whereupon he disguises himself and attacks the two killers, bashing their knees with a baseball bat. He thinks that Iktomi the Trickster is messing with him, controlling him, and actually turning him into a vigilante. Rudy later undertakes another vigilante act. He sets fire to a liquor store, unaware that at that very moment his own brother Mogie, the drunk, is on top of the store, trying to get through the skylight to steal liquor. Mogie is severely burned, but survives only to die shortly afterward from cirrhosis of the liver, a result of his heavy drinking. Rudy's final vigilante act is to carry out a version of one of Mogie's last wishes, to deface Mount Rushmore. In these ways the film artfully blends several themes relevant to this study: even though an important character dies, much of film's focus is on his life, and despite the death of a main character, much of the film's emphasis remains on those who survive the person who dies. In this case the survivors whom the viewer has come to know are Rudy and Mogie's son Herbie (Noah Watts). *Skins* also offers a balance between the very real world of reservation life in general and another very real but very different world, the one controlled by Iktomi, the shape-shifting trickster.

From the start, the film provides the viewer with a very realistic account of life on the reservation. The opening shot is a brief aerial, a flyover of the Badlands, cutting to interspersed credit titles and shots of the reservation town of Pine Ridge. An audio clip of the voice of President Clinton reading from the text he delivered on his visit to Pine Ridge in July 1999 accompanies these opening shots: "We're not coming from Washington to tell you exactly what to do and how to do it; we're coming from Washington to ask you what you want to do and tell you we will give you the tools and the support to get done what you want to do for your children and their future." An aerial shot of the Mount Rushmore national memorial site immediately follows Clinton's voiceover, and, in a shot that foreshadows the film's final sequence, the viewer sees the carved-stone heads of four previous U.S. presidents gouged out of the mountain. A male voiceover explaining the setting accompanies this visual: "In the shadow of one of America's most popular tourist attractions, South Dakota's Mount Rushmore, some sixty miles southeast, lies the poorest of all counties in the U.S., the Pine Ridge Indian Reservation." With a cut to the cemetery at Wounded Knee, the voiceover continues: "Wounded Knee: located in the middle of Pine Ridge, the place where hundreds of men, women, and children were killed by the U.S. Army in 1890. Today it's known as the Massacre at Wounded Knee." Extreme long shots of the Pine Ridge community follow. These shots are again interspersed with credit titles and are followed by a female voiceover explaining that 40 percent of Pine Ridge residents live in substandard housing, that there is 75 percent unemployment on the reservation, that the rate of deaths from alcoholism is nine times the national average, and that life expectancy is fifteen years shorter for people on Pine Ridge than across the nation at large. The film cuts to a close-up of a man being interviewed, evidently a Pine Ridge resident. He has this to say: "I believe that America is big enough; it's powerful enough; it's rich enough, you know, to really deal with the American Indian in the way it should be done" (*Skins*). Regardless of what could be done or should be done, as the viewer is about to witness, the character Mogie lives in substandard housing, he is unemployed, and he dies of cirrhosis of the liver, directly related to his alcoholism.

Brief shots of President Clinton working the crowd follow the interview clip, presumably during that 1999 visit. In a brief critique of the film, Houston Wood comments that the "mockery of such oft-repeated official promises then plays across the screen throughout *Skins*" (31). The film makes no further overt mention of Indian Nation versus U.S. politics, however, despite the promise of overt political engagement the opening suggests, and it essentially drops reference to any theme of broken promises once it enters Pine Ridge. Similarly, other than one brief dinner-table discussion about American Horse and his testimony at the trial in Washington, D.C., concerning the Wounded Knee Massacre, the film lets the history of Wounded Knee, mentioned in the opening sequence, stand as mere backdrop or implied background, not explicitly or directly touching the daily lives of the characters represented.

This documentary-style opening sequence is worth pausing over in some detail, regardless of how the film may or may not follow through with the suggested political engagement, however, because the opening shots do establish a specific context for the rest of the film. The visual and aural effects of the establishing sequence give the film its undeniable feel of a documentary, initially at least, and these effects insist, as documentaries do, on the existence of a real world, one that exists outside the film. We can take a statement Bill Nichols makes in a different context and understand it as equally germane with regard to *Skins*: "Filmed fictions take advantage of the same indexical bond as do documentaries. (The establishing shots of Mount Rushmore in *North by Northwest* are every bit as indexically bound to their referent as are similar shots in any travelogue)" (150). Similarly the establishing shots in Eyre's film reach across genres as they insist on an indexical relationship between image and referent.

The voiceovers too are presented as if they are coming from newscasters, and the inclusion of the audio clip from Clinton's speech further augments the sense of the film's actually being a documentary. The documentary-style opening is echoed later, when a newscaster (Jenny Cheng), as a character within the fiction of the film, actually does describe the liquor industry just two miles south of Pine Ridge, across the state line in the tiny town of

Whiteclay, Nebraska, as a part of the main action of the film. According to the newscaster's report, many Pine Ridge residents visit this town to buy liquor. The viewer sees the newscaster as she is being filmed and hears her report on the liquor business in this tiny border town:

> Tonight's subject: the multi-million dollar liquor business generated in this small town of Whiteclay, Nebraska, population of only twenty people. Some accuse these white liquor store owners of being bloodsuckers who make a living off Indian misery. . . . Indians drinking beer and cheap wine, this sad cliché is brought to stark reality every Friday night, payday for the Indians on the Pine Ridge Reservation, who then flood the border towns like this one to buy alcohol which is outlawed on their reservation. (*Skins*)

This newscast, thirty-three minutes into the film, coupled with the documentary-style opening sequence lends an unmistakable air of authenticity and realism to a film that is very realistic anyway. According to director Chris Eyre, *Skins* "is the most realistic Indian movie ever made" (Chaw).

In the face of an insistence on such realism, however, the filmmaker contrasts this documentary-style insistence on a particular worldview with an altogether different conception of reality, one that makes manifest the power of Iktomi, a Lakota trickster spirit. Eyre renders the contrast explicit at one moment, for example, when Rudy sees the newscast on his television while he is constructing tobacco ties as a part of his own healing ritual. As Rudy knots the ties, the viewer hears nondiegetic music associated with healing, Robbie Robertson's "Peyote Healing," the same music, incidentally, that accompanies a healing moment in a film coproduced by Chris Eyre, *The Doe Boy*, the subject of the next chapter. The filmmaker thus melds the manifestations of two different worldviews into one scene.

The first narrative scene in *Skins* is actually a flashforward that introduces the viewer to Iktomi. The scene depicts tribal policeman Rudy Yellow Lodge as he drives his squad car up to his house and goes straight into the bathroom to wash what seems to be camouflage off his face. Because the scene is a flashforward, the viewer cannot yet know the actual context, but what the viewer does know is that, as Rudy washes his face, he sees a spider on the lavabo. That spider crawls across the back of the sink, and the shot is accompanied by another voiceover (this time Rudy's own voice), explaining what is going on: "Iktomi, the trickster spider, a Lakota spirit, had reappeared in my life." This flashforward cuts immediately to a flashback: a black widow spider bites the ten-year-old Rudy (Dillon Nelson). When he curses "that damn bug," his older brother Mogie (Canku One Star) explains to him, and hence to the viewer as well, the seriousness of the incident: "That was no bug, Rudy. Iktomi got you. The trickster. He likes to sneak out and mess with people's lives" (*Skins*). These two early sequential scenes, the adult protagonist's

seeing a spider and the child's being bitten by a spider, immediately introduce the viewer to Iktomi. Later in the film, Ed Little Bald Eagle (Myrton
Running Wolf) explains further to Rudy some of the complexities of Iktomi:

> ED: Skins have forgotten the forces that live around them.
> RUDY: I think Iktomi's playing with me.
> ED: Most people think of Iktomi as coming in the form of a spider. He could just
> as easily be a rock. And maybe he entered your brains when your head hit that
> rock. . . . Remember, human beings don't control anything. Spirits do. (*Skins*)

The juxtaposition of early scenes, a flashforward and a flashback, have the
effect of contrasting the ultrarealistic documentary-style opening sequence
with the mystical but equally realistic scenes that introduce Iktomi, the
trickster, the spirit that likes to mess with people's lives. The viewer is given
enough information in both cases to feel included. The film introduces economic and social conditions on the reservation and subsequently Iktomi. Specifically, Iktomi seems to have turned Rudy, the conscientious and hardworking tribal policeman, into a lawbreaking but equally hardworking vigilante.
Indeed, Rudy's antics as a vigilante drive the plot of the film.

Spirit power seems to be in control of Rudy's actions when he destroys
the knees of two young Indian men as punishment for their having murdered
(and according to the novel but not mentioned in the film, sodomized) a fellow member of the tribe (see Louis 61–62). It is also a spirit power that directs Rudy to set fire to a liquor store, and thereby cause him to accidentally
burn his brother Mogie, almost to death. After Mogie dies of liver failure,
not as a result of the burning, Rudy carries out yet another trickster act, a
watered-down version of his brother's last wish, to deface the Rushmore National Monument. Rudy's culminating act as Iktomi-inspired vigilante is to
pour oil-based red paint on Washington's nose. Although the viewer might
be tempted to read Rudy's final act of defacing the monument as triumphant,
the film ends almost as darkly as it opens. It does not seem to resolve the
problems it introduces in the opening sequence, problems such as poverty,
unemployment, and alcoholism. Those problems remain, but the film does
suggest hope in that Rudy is ultimately seemingly able to incorporate Iktomi
into his life in ways he is initially unable to do.

One of the effects of fusing fiction film with a documentary-style opening
and embedding the newscast within the fiction of the film is in large measure a means both to educate and to include the non-Indian viewer, to partly
explain a world that might otherwise remain too foreign for that viewer to
appreciate. Additionally, in a sense, the documentary-style opening serves to
authenticate the narrative to follow. This is real, the film insists; it exists in the
world outside the film itself. As Bill Nichols describes the effect in *Representing Reality: Issues and Concepts in Documentary*, expository documentary

offers "realistic representation of the historical world": "The expository mode emphasizes the impression of objectivity and of well-substantiated judgment. This mode supports the impulse toward generalization handsomely since the voice-over commentary can readily extrapolate from the particular instances offered on the image track. . . . Knowledge in expository documentary is often epistemic knowledge . . . in compliance with the categories and concepts accepted as given or true in a specific time and place" (33, 35). The film thus insists that alcoholism on Pine Ridge in general and a specific man like Mogie with a drinking problem are real. By extension, given such a documentary-style mode insisting on the real world outside the fiction of the film, Iktomi the trickster, whether spider or rock, is real as well, and the viewer needs to be made aware that such is the case. Nichols argues that what "each text contributes to this stockpile of knowledge is new content, a new field of attention to which familiar concepts and categories can be applied. This is the great value of the expository mode since a topical issue can be addressed within a frame of reference that need not be questioned or established but simply taken for granted" (35). The information presented as fact in the documentary-style opening sequence can be said to affect the viewer's perception and understanding of the narrative fiction that follows, and a documentary-style opening in itself situates the viewer in a special relation to the narrative about the power of Iktomi in the life of a tribal policeman.

The dialogue between two genres, between the fiction film and the documentary, demonstrates an insistence on the vividly real everyday life on the reservation as well as the very real power of Iktomi. With its blending of documentary and narrative film forms, *Skins* suggests that one must come to terms with the traditional Iktomi as well as Lakota history in order for the culture and the people to make sense of their present world and to survive in it. The film suggests that if one lacks the ability to incorporate and control the traditional in the contemporary world of border-town liquor stores, into the day-to-day on the reservation, the result is lawless vigilantism, hopeless alcoholism, alienation, or death.

One of the ways the film emphasizes the importance of a fully informed existence is by introducing and explicating Rudy's turning to his friend Ed Little Bald Eagle for help. Eyre is careful both to include the viewer and at the same time respect the privacy and honor the sacredness of the sweat ceremony itself in this sequence. After setting the liquor store on fire and thereby accidentally burning Mogie, Rudy visits his friend Ed, hoping for a cure. During the scene of several men preparing for the sweat, the viewer hears about the procedure by means of a voiceover: "Rudy, I'm glad you've come here today. We all know why you are here. So all of us in here, we're going to gather our minds, and we're going to make our minds, and our hearts, and our prayers one. We are all going to pray for this young man. We're going to help him to see and to hear the things that he needs to hear and needs to see. So at this time we're going to pray" (*Skins*). This voiceover in Ed's voice is followed immediately by a visual blackout. During the long take blackout (about twenty seconds of film time), the viewer hears a Lakota-language voiceover but sees only a black screen. Eyre manages to share with the viewer the importance of the sweat without exposing any of the sacred or ritual aspects of what is passing inside the lodge. He is able simultaneously to not completely exclude and not fully include the viewer. Played in this way, the scene suggests a significant difference from earlier Indian and non-Indian films. Other films—such as *A Man Called Horse* with its sweat lodge scene, *Thunderheart* with its problematically explicit Ghost Dance scenes, for example, or even *House Made of Dawn* with its elaborate Peyote ceremony scene—exploit sacred ritual for dramatic effect. *Skins*, in contrast, sensitively acknowledges the importance of the ritual without exploitation and without exposing the sacred.

In addition to addressing seriously and realistically the role of Iktomi in Rudy's life, the film also acknowledges the importance of confronting the painfully real and significant issue of alcohol abuse on Pine Ridge. The fiction film does not shy away from a somewhat brutal but honest depiction of how heavy and habitual drinking might manifest itself on the reservation. By means of the opening documentary sequence, the film instructs the viewer immediately concerning the role that alcohol plays. There are several shots of men drinking or lying on the ground drunk in that sequence, and through the voiceover the viewer knows that on Pine Ridge "death from alcoholism is nine times the national average" (*Skins*). The viewer knows full well that the film takes the issue seriously, as is evident from the scenes involving Mogie's drinking, from the scene incorporating a newscast about Indian drinking, and from the initial voiceover about the border-town liquor industry. Indeed, in this sense, the film reflects the spirit of the novel that provides the source material. Adrian Louis writes forcefully:

> Earlier that week [Rudy] had read the yearly federal crime statistics for the reservation. Their fifty-by-hundred-mile cut of land on the high plains of South Dakota was roiling in anarchy. Each of the eighteen thousand residents was touched by some form of pain, some degree of rez madness or sadness.
> In the past year there had been nine thousand, two hundred and five drug- and alcohol-related arrests. (Louis 93)

Given the novel's emphasis on drinking, the film can certainly be said to offer a fair adaptation of its source material. André Bazin writes that "all it takes is for the filmmakers to have enough visual imagination to create the cinematic equivalent of the style of the original, and for the critic to have the eyes to see it. . . . [W]hat matters is equivalence in meaning of the forms" ("Adapation"

20). Adrian Louis's novel includes no documentary-style segments as such, with the exception perhaps of Rudy's reading a newspaper, a literary equivalent. Louis does write, however, that

> in America, all the towns bordering Indian reservations made money off Indians in one way or another and then they treated the Indians like animals when their money was gone. All these towns profited from Indian misery, and maybe they always would. But Indians could bitch and moan all they wanted to. The border towns were not their worst enemies. They, themselves, were. . . . [T]he white man had oppressed them for centuries, but from his oppression, Indians had learned to oppress themselves.
>
> Rudy's job as a cop was to save Indians from themselves. (57)

The film raises important issues through its documentary style and through its depictions of life on the reservation that parallel the issues of the novel. These issues beg to be resolved or at least addressed once they are raised, and if they are not resolved, the viewer is left discouraged. If Rudy is consoled or the viewer finds his act of vandalism at Mount Rushmore a form of triumph, they have merely managed to overlook the circumstances that motivated the act in the first place. In this context, one question the film's finale raises is whether or not the actions of an Iktomi-inspired vigilante tribal policeman have done anything to save Indians from themselves.

Like Sherman Alexie, who has been accused of reinscribing the stereotype of American Indians as overwhelmed by alcohol addiction in his depiction of Mouse's death in *The Business of Fancydancing*, Eyre runs the risk of falling victim to and perpetuating the same unfortunate stereotype. It can be argued, however, that these directors circumvent such stereotypical, reductive presentations by refusing to reinforce any simple-minded understanding resulting from stereotypes in general. Eyre presents other Indian characters instead, specifically and especially Rudy in this case, who manage their drinking. They are not teetotalers; rather they are perfectly able to drink alcohol in moderation. Similarly, in *The Business of Fancydancing* Alexie depicts only the character Mouse as one who suffers from drug abuse and addiction. The film does not present any of the other characters as unable to manage their use of alcohol and other drugs. Such balance in these films defies the stereotype at the same time it allows the film to make an honest presentation. *Skins* and *The Business of Fancydancing* thus stand in contrast to films such as *Smoke Signals* and *Naturally Native*, for instance, which offer little in the way of a middle ground. As presented in the latter two, a character either follows a regimen of strict abstinence or drinks to drunkenness: Victor has never had a drop of alcohol in his life, and Steve in *Naturally Native* is equally abstemious. Their counterparts run the risk of becoming alcoholics: both Arnold and Vickie, for example, are tormented by the urge to drink; for both it seems to be either all or nothing. Granted, Tanya in *Naturally Native* manages a drink or two on her dinner date, and although that indulgence itself is not the cause, she does end up in the hospital that same evening. Such a filmic connection between drinking and violence or drinking and inevitable alcoholism certainly implies that any alcoholic consumption for American Indians must indeed be very dangerous. In this sense, both *The Business of Fancydancing* and *Skins* offer fuller, more nuanced and more realistic depictions of alcohol consumption and illicit drug use.

Another stereotype that contemporary American Indian filmmakers must confront in addition to depictions of drunkenness, of course, is the common depiction of the historical Indian as presented in Hollywood Westerns. In *Skins* Eyre alludes to these historical depictions in at least two different ways. First, as noted above, the documentary opening makes mention of the 1890 Wounded Knee massacre, and later in the film the characters watch a Western on the television, the watching of which inspires a conversation about the historical Red Cloud in the context of the 1890 massacre. A second method Eyre employs as a means to include an historical perspective is to juxtapose shots of historical photographs with those from within his film itself. To include these photographs, Eyre makes visible for the viewer the details of what Rudy envisions when he lies unconscious on the ground after falling and hitting his head on a rock. The man's vision, as it were, comes to him in the form of images superimposed on the night sky, a series of shots comprised of historical stills and clips from the film itself. Like several other American Indian films, *Skins* thus also weaves still photographs into its fabric. In this particular scene, the film intersperses shots of "historical" photographs with shots, almost as stills, from the film itself. When Rudy hits his head on that rock, he flashes to photographs; or perhaps one could say, Eyre uses shots of photographs to suggest what visions or hallucinations come to Rudy out of the starlit night sky as he lies on the ground virtually unconscious.

The sequence consists of a series of seven shots: historical stills interspersed with clips from the film itself, but the film clips have in common with the other stills that they are also black and white. Rudy first sees a photograph of four Sioux men seated in front of an interpreter. Though the viewer has no way of knowing this from within the film, the shot is of the Red Cloud delegation, including Little Wound, Red Cloud, American Horse, and Red Shirt. This shot will be echoed later in the film with a T-shirt that Rudy buys shortly before Mogie's death. The print on the shirt pictures the same four men, but on the T-shirt these four replace the heads of the four U.S. presidents of the Mount Rushmore memorial. In the brief glance the viewer gets of the shirt, these four seem very similar to the four from the photograph of Rudy's Red Cloud Delegation vision. As if to emphasize the connection between the photograph, the T-shirt, and Mount Rushmore, the filmmaker

Re-envisioning Rushmore. *Skins*. Screen Capture. First Look Media.

actually leaves out Red Dog, one of the five Indian men in the original photograph. Rudy next envisions an abused woman holding a child. The viewer cannot yet know who this woman is, but she does appear in the film: Rudy will respond to her emergency call for help later in the narrative. She has been beaten by her husband, the father of her child. This shot is followed immediately by a second historical shot, this one of a well-known photograph of the 1973 occupation of Wounded Knee: two men stand guard with rifles in hand. The 1973 Wounded Knee shot cuts back to the film with a shot of Corky Red Tail (Yellow Pony Pettibone), the young man who has just been murdered. This shot cuts to a shot of the shoe and shoelaces of one of his assailants. The next shot, the third in the series of Pine Ridge history, is of a photograph of the 1976 extradition arrest of Leonard Peltier, again with no identification of the man or the reference within the film itself. Peltier was accused of shooting two FBI agents at Oglala and was extradited from Canada in order to stand trial. The circumstances of his extradition, arrest, and trial remain controversial, and the photograph thus fits thematically with the others. The photograph implies that mainstream America's biased treatment of Indigenous people is legal and political as well as social. Red Cloud's delegation testified before Congress concerning the 1890 massacre at Wounded Knee, and Peltier took the fall for the shooting deaths of the FBI agents in 1973. The final visual of Rudy's hallucination is of the spider crawling along the back of the bathroom sink. This is an image that the viewer can and does recognize by this point in the film. Its placement at the end of the sequence suggests that Iktomi is indeed linked to if not responsible for the events depicted as flashing through Rudy's unconscious.

In sum, there are two flashbacks to the murder Rudy has just witnessed and two flashforwards, the first of the abused woman whom the viewer has not yet seen and the second of Iktomi crawling quickly across the bathroom sink. These two shots are interspersed with the visions of the photographs of nineteenth- and twentieth-century Sioux history. At this moment in the film, the viewer has already seen this spider in a flashforward, but ironically Rudy has not yet seen it, so in this sense the viewer has a specific knowledge of the future that even Rudy himself lacks. He will see the spider only after he attacks and beats the two young men for the murder of Corky later in the film. Despite the film's nod to documentary and its realism, the use of these photographs further enhances or extends its otherworldly feel, mixing as it does the realism of historical photographs with the visionary power evidently emanating from Iktomi. Shots that turn out to be of contemporary incidents on Pine Ridge combine with the historical photographs to suggest the importance of that history to the present at the same time they insist on a refusal to succumb to it. That is, these photographs acknowledge that the future grows out of the past yet is not completely circumscribed by it. In that they include flashforwards, the images insist that there is a future, however difficult and complicated the present is and however difficult and complicated the past might have been.

The juxtaposition of photographs in Rudy's hallucination works in ways very similar to how Mackenzie's juxtaposition of photographs works in *The Exiles*. Mackenzie, we remember, juxtaposes shots of photographs by Edward Curtis with photographs of the actual actors in his own film, imbuing significance to his actors as subjects of such photographs. *Skins* insists on the significance of those photographed, whether recognizable historical figures such as American Horse and Leonard Peltier or contemporary individuals living on the Pine Ridge Reservation. As mentioned above, "to photograph is to confer importance. . . . [T]here is no way to suppress the tendency inherent in all photographs to accord value to their subjects" (Sontag 28). As do the stills in *The Exiles*, the stills pictured in Rudy's vision in *Skins* recognize and honor as well as acknowledge a debt to and connection with the past. At the same time, they incorporate the present and look to the future.

Skins does not identify the historical photographs, and in this sense, Eyre asks a lot of the viewer as he privileges audience members who would recognize such shots. The film may be framed by views of the monuments at Mount Rushmore, but between the images of the frame are images of American Indian heroes who are still important to the film's present: Red Cloud, those who occupied Wounded Knee in 1973, and Leonard Peltier, for example. Although the references might appear obscure to some viewers, that obscurity is part of the point; they should not be! Eyre's film embodies a form of visual sovereignty in that it refocuses the dominant gaze. From outside the "national orthodoxy" and outside the "national outlook," to use Barry Barclay's phrases, it asks its viewers to see actual American heroes on the ground rather than the iconic images of dead presidents on the mountaintop (Barclay 9). Especially noteworthy, of course is that those actual worthies in the photographs are American Indians.

The use of this series of images serves to realign what actions and which people might be thought of as heroic as it also serves to link past and present and to look to the future. The series of images does not invite the viewer into an inner circle in that there is no filmic explanation for any of the three photographs. In terms of including and educating the viewer, Eyre is more considerate of the uninitiated viewer in the context of the massacre at Wounded Knee than he is with Rudy's vision. Here the film is careful to inform, educate, and include the viewer, beginning with the opening documentary-style reference to the massacre and then with Rudy and Mogie combining to explain its significance to Mogie's son Herbie late in the film. With this explanation, *Skins* reflects the source material, in that in the novel too the connection between the historical Wounded Knee and present-day Pine Ridge is important. Adrian Louis writes that "throughout [Rudy's] whole life, what happened at Wounded Knee in 1890 had been a recurring nightmare" (36). The film reflects the frequent references to and verbal pictures of Wounded Knee evident in Louis's novel. At one point the author quotes from American Horse's comments before the Commissioner of Indian Affairs in 1891. After the soldiers shot and killed most of the people, mostly women and children, he writes, *"All the Indians fled in three directions, and after most of them had been killed, a cry was made that all those who were not killed or wounded should come forth and they would be safe. Little boys who were not wounded came out of their places of refuge and as soon as they came in sight, a number of soldiers surrounded them and butchered them right there"* (36, original emphasis). In the film, complementing the much earlier shot of the photograph of American Horse and the reference to the massacre in the documentary-like opening sequence, Eyre provides a narrative account as part of the plot of his film. Rudy begins the explanation, and Mogie takes over, explaining to his son Herbie, and thus to the viewer, about American Horse's trip to Washington, D.C., to testify at the trial concerning the soldiers responsible for the Wounded Knee massacre:

HERBIE: Who was American Horse? . . .
RUDY: He testified at the trial of the Wounded Knee Massacre. At that time all Indian religious ceremonies were banned by white men because they were afraid of them. Now, up on the Cheyenne River Sitting Bull resisted, so they shot him. And Big Foot knew that he and his people had to flee the area immediately. So they came to Pine Ridge, and when they camped out, the Wounded Knee troopers of the 7th cavalry . . .

MOGIE: The 7th Calvary was called in to escort them to the reservation. And the soldiers disarmed them. Wounded Knee was nothing but a damn massacre of women and children. American Horse testified before Congress.

HERBIE: What happened after American Horse testified?

MOGIE: They were all given the Congressional Medal of Honor. (*Skins*)

As Mogie speaks his lines, he is on the verge of tears. This man, who immediately after being nearly burned to death can make jokes with his brother, nearly cries at the thought of what happened at Wounded Knee in 1890, over a hundred years earlier. Eyre thus stresses the continued importance of that historical moment, insisting that the aftershocks of that massacre are still being felt on Pine Ridge.

Roger Ebert, writing for the *Chicago Sun-Times*, claims that *Skins* is "just as humorous and more engaging than *Smoke Signals*" (Ebert). Despite this assertion, the film actually seems to lack almost any humor at all and seems to have a much grimmer outlook than Eyre's earlier film. There are exceptions, of course, as in the humorous scene in which Mogie surprises Rudy by tackling him during a football game at a tribal policemen's picnic. The picnic scene is thematically related in that it recalls an incident from Mogie and Rudy's high school football days, but the flashback depiction of those days is anything but humorous. In the flashback to a game day, the viewer sees the brothers' parents in the stands as they begin to quarrel. Their father Sonny (Gil Birmingham) pushes their mother Evangeline (Renae Morriseau), and she falls in the bleachers so that her skirt is hiked up. In the film the boys run from the playing field into the stands to help her, and both the film and the novel make explicit how such a public display between family members is an embarrassment for the two young boys: "Between themselves, Rudy and Mogie never had any shame about being so *onsika*, so destitute and out of step with white America. Like most Indians, they got their shame from how the white people looked at them. Now the *wasicus* had been given a view of how these Indians *really* were. . . . Red panties! His mom's panties!" (Louis 139, original emphasis). In the film, the flashback to this event focuses on the boys' efforts to protect their mother from their abusive, drunken father, and the film radically lightens and softens what in the novel, in contrast, is a somewhat darker experience. As in the film, Rudy of the novel, still dressed in his football uniform, drives his unconscious father to the police station, but when he gets back to the house, according to the novel, he witnesses through the living room window his brother Mogie masturbate on top of his mother, who has passed out on the couch. Clearly, screenplay author Jennifer D. Lyne and director Eyre choose to protect the viewer from this complication in Mogie's character and to take some of the edge off the severity of Louis's depiction of the boys' adolescence. But even without the complication of Mogie's Oedipal actions, the scene suggests the grimness of the boys' lives.

The very tenuous or fragile family connection as represented in the film reflects the source novel's concern with the importance of family and tribal ties. According to Louis, "In the old days, it was the family, the band, the tribe that came first. The individual and his acts were only good if they did good for the people. Rudy knew that had changed for the most part. The family unit was mostly broken now and he figured that was what all the white Indian experts meant when they quoted Black Elk's statement 'the sacred hoop is broken'" (21). If Mogie's tackling the show-off Rudy at the picnic seems humorous, it also reinforces the very serious notion that the individual and his acts are important only in relation to the people as a whole. Mogie's surprise tackle and the subsequent fight between the brothers brings this home implicitly as it explicitly demonstrates that the family unit is still somewhat ruptured, if not broken. Ironically, as a result of Mogie's death, family ties may well be more tightly established. Mogie's dying wish in a letter to Rudy, which the viewer hears as a voiceover, is that the younger brother look after the nephew: "You must do one thing for me. You must take care of Herbie. You made a life for yourself, and you are someone he can look up to" (*Skins*). The viewer has already seen Rudy taking care of Herbie to some extent, and the film gives the viewer no reason to think that he would not continue to do so.

In its relatively somber depictions of reservation life, *Skins* contrasts rather starkly with the relatively happy and humorous film *Smoke Signals*, in which Victor seeks and achieves a sort of reconciliation with his deceased father, and with the happier still *Naturally Native*, in which the sisters seek and find their tribal roots and extended family at the same time they make commitments to their relationships with their men and also secure funding for and begin their promising business venture as they are welcomed back into the thriving community of their heritage. On first viewing, *Skins* seems to offer very little promise of a bright future, or if it does, that promise is carefully embedded in what at first is a depiction of a much starker and more hopeless world. The dramatic tension in *Skins* is split between Rudy's reckoning with Iktomi and Mogie's drinking and death, and the resolution of this tension seems at first to offer Rudy only a pyrrhic victory, if any victory at all. The final subversive act of defacing Mount Rushmore does not appear to be particularly satisfying or helpful in the face of the problems and issues the film raises: excessive drinking, domestic violence, random murder. In this sense, *Skins* echoes *Powwow Highway*, which, according to some scholars, also raises several serious issues but finally leaves them essentially unresolved (see Arnold 355). But the final scene in *Skins* deserves contextualizing and parsing.

Mogie suggests shortly before his death that he and Rudy blow Washington's nose off the face of Mount Rushmore, but Rudy balks. After Mogie's death, however, Rudy climbs to the top of the mountain, and with the help of Iktomi pictured as a spider crawling along the top of the paint can, he does splash the monument with red paint. Not the act itself so much as its immediate aftermath suggests that *Skins* can indeed be said to offer solutions to pressing problems. After Rudy has defaced the monument by throwing the five-gallon bucket of red paint over Washington's forehead and climbed back down the mountain, he stops his vehicle to look back at the effect of his action. Rudy and the viewer see the red teardrop as if it is running down the side of Washington's nose. Rudy smiles. It is at the moment of this smile that Rudy is especially interesting. For in this instance, at least, he is superior to his destiny. He is able to bring Washington to cry a bloody tear with this act of vandalism, and the act thus has symbolic importance in a way that echoes the symbolic importance of the promises President Clinton makes in the film's opening sequence: "we will give you the tools and the support to get done what you want to do for your children and their future" (*Skins*). But the act occasions yet another important result: it brings Mogie back, not exactly literally, of course, but certainly figuratively. After Rudy begins to drive away, he sees a young man, headed in the opposite direction, hitchhiking. Rudy recognizes him, and the viewer recognizes him, as the teenage Mogie (Nathaniel Arcand). At the moment Rudy sees and recognizes him, he speaks aloud his name. Here the film ends, but in this sense, Mogie survives that ending.

As suggested by the complexities of the plot and the juxtaposition or fusion of two genres, documentary and narrative fiction, *Skins* is much richer than an analysis merely of the death of Mogie would suggest. That is, the film fits the paradigm I am suggesting of so many American Indian films. It includes a focus on the death of an Indian person as a major plot element, yet it insists on the importance of that person beyond death. *Skins*, in this instance, moves beyond that paradigm to explore Iktomi's role in contemporary reservation life. In the film's last moments the viewer sees Mogie as a teenager—young, alive, and on the go—followed by a cut to Mogie as a child carrying Rudy on his back, as seen in the beginning of the film. Where there is such hope and vision, there is life beyond the literal death. Like several other films, *Skins* depicts the death of a main character, sets a context for that death, and then moves beyond any dying-Indian stereotypes by setting a context for that life, refusing in a sense to let the character die, and insisting on their presence and promising the continuance of those characters who do literally survive the end of the film.

ELEVEN

The Stories Pour Out

Taking Control in *The Doe Boy*

Nobody cares how much blood runs through a deer. But everyone
wants to know how much blood runs through an Indian. It's kind of
hard to tell, unless you cut one of us open and watch all the stories
pour out. —*The Doe Boy*

The opening sequence of Randy Redroad's film *The Doe Boy* depicts three
young boys as they race one another through the woods. A series of alternat-
ing shots make up the scene: a handheld camera lets the viewer see what the
running boys see; medium close-ups of their running show them exerting
themselves, and long shots provide the viewer a sense of perspective. A crane
shot zooms to an asthmatic runner as he pauses to use his inhaler. Preceding
these opening shots of the boys is a very brief shot of a deer, and a medium
close-up shows the buck to have a string of red and black beads around his
neck. If not a flashforward itself, the shot of the deer at least foreshadows the
hunt and chase that will take place at the film's climax. The shot of the deer
notwithstanding, though, the emphasis of the opening is clearly on the boys
and their running.

   This establishing sequence recalls a non-Indian "Indian" film that also begins with shots of three people sprinting through a forest: Michael Mann's
The Last of the Mohicans. Hawkeye (James Fenimore Cooper's Natty
Bumppo is Nathaniel Poe in the film and is played by Daniel Day-Lewis),
Chingachgook (Russell Means), and Uncas (Eric Schweig) lope through the
woods at the opening of this remake of a 1936 adaptation of Cooper's 1826
novel. In Mann's film, the three men run through the woods in pursuit of a
deer, as the viewer finds out soon enough. Although the similarities in the
openings of the two scenes definitely suggest a conscious intertextual reference, there are several differences that hint at the ironies implicit in *The Doe
Boy*'s allusion to *The Last of the Mohicans.* Perhaps the most obvious differences are that the runners are boys, not men, and that they are racing one
another rather than chasing the deer. In contrast to the hunting scene opening *The Last of the Mohicans*, as well as to the gruesome depictions of war
and death throughout Mann's remake, the opening moments of *The Doe Boy*

are innocent and jovial. The runners are just kids racing for fun, and the unharmed deer wears a colorful necklace. For the boys, the reward for winning the footrace is to be a soft drink. This difference becomes especially significant when the character Hunter, Doe Boy, later in the film confronts a deer, hesitates, and opts not to shoot the same deer that the viewer sees at the very beginning of the film. Hawkeye in *The Last of the Mohicans* has no such hesitation: after bounding through the lush woods ahead of his two fellow hunters, two Indian men, he stops dramatically, shoots, and kills the running deer quickly and efficiently. It is not clear what purpose the opening scene plays in the overall film, except perhaps to demonstrate the excellent physical qualities of the three men and show what great outdoorsmen and hunters they are, and emphasize that the non-Indian is the fastest and evidently the best shot with a rifle. In *The Doe Boy*, the opening race is much more thematically linked to the rest of the film. It establishes the relationships between the boys, foreshadows the ultimate, climactic deer hunt, and introduces the viewer to the fact of Doe Boy's hemophilia.

It is important to linger on a comparison between the two films not least because beyond the particular, a comparison makes evident some of the many ways Indigenous film can talk back in general to mainstream cinema. That is, the specific points of comparison make evident some of the subtleties and intricacies of reversing Hollywood's hold on the popular imagination. The instance of Mann's film is especially pertinent as an example because of the overwhelming differences in budget and distribution between *The Last of the Mohicans* and *The Doe Boy*. The former, distributed by 20th Century Fox, had a very wide release, opening in September 1992 on 1,856 screens. The film grossed almost 11 million dollars its first weekend. The total gross was approximately 75 million, easily justifying its estimated 40-million-dollar filming budget and its perhaps as much as 15-million-dollar advertising budget (see Fox). In November it opened in Great Britain, and its British run grossed over 5 million pounds. By the end of the year, the film had opened in ten different countries. *The Doe Boy*, in stark contrast, had an estimated budget of 1.6 million, was distributed by Wellspring, and opened at the Sundance Film Festival. It won several awards during the year at various other festivals, including the American Indian Film Festival in San Francisco, but it was not earning money nor was it being distributed to any fanfare. As these numbers make clear, the Hollywood film enjoyed a massive audience, and those viewers inevitably came away with its images in their heads.

The immense imbalance between the respective films' power to influence viewers suggests the importance of one's appreciating *The Doe Boy* as a necessary corrective to Hollywood's (mis)representations. Several points of comparison between the two films serve to demonstrate the ways in which *The Doe Boy* does indeed talk back to Hollywood, both specifically and generally.

The device of calling attention to such mainstream cinema and then moving beyond the limitations of merely talking back offers Redroad the opportunity to establish ways in which his film gives American Indians their own voice as it allows them to tell their own stories.

In the opening moments, *The Doe Boy* offers an intertitle: "Tahlequah, Oklahoma, 1977"; this stock device for providing the date and place of the film's action also echoes an initial intertitle in Mann's film. The viewer can thus deduce that Doe Boy and his friends run through the woods 220 years after the action of *The Last of the Mohicans*, which is set, as a series of intertitles denote, in "1757," and in "The American Colonies" during "the 3rd year of the war between England and France for the possession of the continent." The intertitles alone suggest the grandiose and epic nature of one film and the local focus of the other. In addition to the similarities and to any obvious and immediate differences between the two opening sequences, there is also thus a difference in the films' fundamental conceptions. *The Doe Boy* repudiates the fundamental lie underpinning the earlier film. The lie at the heart of *The Last of the Mohicans*, both novel and film, is that Uncas's death at the end of that film and at the end of Cooper's novel signifies the end of Native Americans as a whole and essentially the end of Native America. Another intertitle in Mann's film informs the viewer of this possibility: "Three men, the last of a vanishing people, are on the frontier west of the Hudson River." That title overlooks the fact that Nathaniel Poe is not Mohican, and not an American Indian at all. In one of the few instances in which Mann's film adheres to the plot and sensibilities of its source novel, the ending is of the death of Uncas. With a stunning backdrop of the Appalachians (the movie was filmed in North Carolina), his father, Chingachgook, offers a prayer to the Great Spirit: "Welcome him and let him take his place at the council fire." The grieving father then adds that "they are all there but one, I, Chingachgook, the last of the Mohicans." A few moments later, he says to Nathaniel, "The frontier pushes the red-man of these wilderness forests in front of it, until one day there will be nowhere left. Then our race will be no more" (*Last Mohicans*). Cooper's novel ends on the same note: "The pale-faces are masters of the earth, and the time of the red-men has not yet come again. My day has been too long. In the morning I saw the sons of Unamis happy and strong; and yet, before the night has come, have I lived to see the last warrior of the wise race of the Mohicans" (350). *The Doe Boy* makes manifest the lie at the heart of *The Last of the Mohicans*: contrary to the trope of the vanishing Indian, Redroad's film insists that American Indians survive the eighteenth, nineteenth, and twentieth centuries. Granted, Doe Boy, his friends, his mother, and grandfather are Cherokee rather than Mohican or Huron, but they are most certainly survivors. *The Doe Boy* thus exposes the lie embedded in the Hollywood mentality that keeps reiterating and recycling the same stereotypical "last-of" story in film after film after film. To echo a moment in *Smoke Signals*, one can list some such films: in addition to the numerous film and television versions of *The Last of the Mohicans*, there are *The Last of the Redmen* (1947), *Last of the Comanches* (1953), *The Last of His Tribe* (1992), and *The Last of the Dogmen* (1995), to name a few.

Another difference that the intertextual reference makes starkly evident is that in contrast to the physical perfection of the adult men in Mann's film, the runners in *The Doe Boy* are misfits. *The Doe Boy* challenges the stereotype and the abiding notion of the Indian as noble savage, fleet of foot, strong, and at ease and at home in nature, fierce and wild savages, relentless warriors. Redroad's boys are quite human. One of them is asthmatic, and another, Hunter, who only later earns the name Doe Boy, is the fastest and is a hemophiliac, "Band-Aid Boy," as the others call him. Hunter's physical condition affords Redroad the opportunity to emphasize the centrality of issues of blood and of identity based on blood quantum. Such considerations are important to Redroad's film as a whole in ways that are completely absent from Mann's film. At one point later in *The Doe Boy*, for example, Hunter accuses his white father of being the one responsible for his condition: "It's probably your blood that ruined me. It's a goddamned white disease" (*Doe*). Actually, of course, whether or not it is a "white-man's disease," a son cannot inherit hemophilia from his father, only from his mother. Regardless of the accuracy (or in this case, inaccuracy) of Hunter's accusation, however, the statement does emphasize the issues of blood, identity, and race relations that underlie the film.

As the boys stand panting after their cross-country footrace, the viewer hears an old man's voice. This initial voice-over makes explicit one of the connections between the deer the viewer has glimpsed and the boys. Marvin speaks the lines, quoted above, about how much blood runs through an Indian. The voice is that of Marvin Fishinghawk (Gordon Tootoosis), who, the viewer discovers, will be both a character and the narrator throughout the film. He is Hunter's maternal grandfather, and his initial comment about blood completely undermines the notion of using blood quantum as a means of determining American Indian identity. In this same passage, the speaker's use of the first-person pronoun *us* enables the narrator to self-identify as an American Indian man himself, and thus as one who speaks, one who tells his story, which is also Hunter's story, from an insider's point of view. In this way, the film establishes filmically the notion of self-determination and ultimately of visual sovereignty. An Indigenous man is in control of the story and of the history that story asserts. At the same time that Marvin undercuts the notion of blood quantum as a means to determine whether or not one is Indian, or what one's degree of Indianness is, he does nevertheless take a step toward identifying what it might mean, from his point of view at any rate, to be Indigenous. Indigeneity, he suggests, is determined not by how much "Indian" blood runs through a person's veins, but by the stories in that person. And thus, in a sense, Marvin Fishinghawk begins the *story* of the Doe Boy, the story of a boy who gets his name when he kills a doe by mistake. As the grandfather recounts the hunt and informs the viewer with a later voice-over, "There was a boy who shot a woman while his father slept, a boy with bullets in his eyes and arrows in his chest" (*Doe*).

In addition to defining the parameters of the film's themes concerning blood and identity, the opening intertextual reference also implies a comparison between the overtly military heroics that make up Mann's film and the place the military holds in Redroad's film. A major component of *The Last of the Mohicans* is the role the characters play in the battles between the French and the English. The Indians, of course, take sides in the war between these European powers. Mann's film glamorizes and valorizes military prowess and successful attacks and counterattacks, and the characters are heroic in relation to their military prowess. *The Doe Boy*, in stark contrast, questions that mainstream conception of a military man as heroic in several ways, most notably through depictions of Hunter's non-Native father, a failed fighter pilot, as a sometimes drunk who misremembers his own military past as being much more glamorous or heroic than it was.

In the same conversation in which Hunter erroneously accuses his father of contributing the white blood that made him a hemophiliac, the eighteen-year-old reminds him that he was never in the war in Vietnam. On some level, however, Hunter's father, Hank (Kevin Anderson), continues to think, or at least assert, that he was nevertheless a warrior, and he idolizes and glorifies fighter pilots especially. The film depicts the idolizer as a drunk wannabe soldier who laments, but at the same time denies, that he never saw action, and it pointedly undercuts the father's glorification of the military. At one point Hank says to himself as he watches the television, "They weakened their defense the day they lost me" (*Doe*). The viewer is cued to see his statement and the man at this point as pathetic if not outright laughable. He makes this somewhat hyperbolic pronouncement through blurry eyes as he drinks beer and watches a black-and-white war film. When Hank lists to Hunter's mother, Maggie (Jeri Arredondo), who works as a nurse, what he sees as disadvantages of his son's having a blood disease, he includes the obvious consideration that his son will never become a soldier:

HANK: He can't play sports, can't work with tools. They'll damn sure never take him in the military.
MAGGIE: Good.
HANK: It ain't good. Afraid he's gonna end up a nurse too. . . . His mother outlawed just about everything a regular kid does at his age. (*Doe*)

Hunter himself questions the prestige and glory of serving in the military when he insists that his father is one of the lucky ones because he did not have to serve in the military during the war in Vietnam. After Hunter tells his father that there is a difference between deer hunting and killing, his father responds:

HANK: Don't lecture me about killing, 'cause I been there and you ain't.
HUNTER: No you haven't. You missed the war, remember? You're one of the lucky ones who didn't have to go.
HANK: I didn't miss nothing. I did my time.
HUNTER: You didn't do anything. You think you were there, but it's all in your head. (*Doe*)

After this argument and his dad's hitting him, causing him to bleed, Hunter takes his father's gun, the gun the father has been so meticulously cleaning, and drives to the woods, evidently wanting to kill a deer and thus prove himself. According to Houston Wood, the film "puts special attention on an uneasy father-son relationship within a hunting culture where killing game is equated with maturity" (124). Hunter sits on the tailgate of his Malibu and shines a flashlight, the very hunting method practiced by his father and others, a method Doe Boy himself has just condemned. Before he sees any deer, however, he falls asleep. When he wakes in the morning light, he is so angry with himself for having slept the night through that he swings the rifle against a tree, breaking the stock right at the bolt. When he shows his father what has happened, the viewer sees the broken gun lying on the bed of the truck on a red-and-white-striped towel or blanket, something that looks very much like an American flag. The camera lingers a moment on the broken rifle on flag stripes. This shot cuts to the tattoo parlor where Hunter's childhood friends Cheekie (Robert A. Guthrie) and Junior (Nathaniel Arcand) are getting "U.S. Marines" tattooed onto their arms. The scene of Cheekie wincing in pain as he sits in a tattoo parlor signifies that he has enlisted, and the film thereby again seems to suggest that such endeavors are somehow less than heroic. The scene begins with an extreme close-up tracing the tattoo artist's own arm, completely covered, beginning with a figure holding a raised scythe, resembling conventional depictions of Death and tracing down to skulls beneath the Death figure. The camera catches the artist as he puts ink into the blood on Cheekie's arm, and in this way, both the filmic aspect and the narrative itself tend to emphasize the death and destruction rather than the glory and heroism associated with the military.

With the cut to the tattooing come lyrics to the song "Positively Lost Me": "You lost a lot when you lost me." Initially as if diegetic, as if the music is being played in the tattoo parlor, the sound becomes nondiegetic as it provides a sound bridge between the tattoo parlor scene and the scene of Hunter loading his car to move out of his parents house, just after his eighteenth birthday. The song lyrics can thus immediately be thought to refer both to the idea of a boy's going off to war and leaving behind the "best girl in the world," as Hunter says of his friend's girlfriend and to another boy's moving out of his parents' house as Hunter is doing. These particular lyrics can also be said to echo Hank's comment that he would rather work on the jets "than fly for those bastards," implying that they lost a lot when they didn't assign him to combat duty in the military. The song lyrics themselves are a bit ironic in that following the repeated line, "You lost a lot when you lost me," is the apparent lack of value of all but one of the objects that were actually lost: "six paperback books, and a dying tree, a looking glass, and a diamond ring" (Doe).

The Doe Boy is not primarily about war or the military, however. It is rather to some degree a film about hunting, yet through its references to hunters as former soldiers, especially Vietnam veterans, it insists on an analogy between war and hunting. Paralleling the motif of the military in the film, in other words, is the idea of sport hunting. Junior makes explicit for the viewer the connection between the two: "My dad will shoot anything that moves. Except he never hits nothing. He said when he was in 'Nam and they'd get attacked, he'd just shoot in the direction the bullets were coming from. Kind of hunts the same way too. Empties his chamber and hopes he hits something" (Doe). The humor inherent in Junior's statement is very dark. His reference to the two Vietnam veteran Indian hunters who can never actually kill a deer, who can't hit anything, foreshadows their eventually accidentally hitting Doe Boy's father, Hank. The humor at the same time undercuts or challenges the cliché of Indians as great hunters. In an early, lighter humorous exchange, Manny's son makes a similar point about his father's poor deer hunting skills:

MANNY: You know I ain't got one in three years.
CHEEKIE: Mom says you're cursed.
MANNY: Yeah, she does say that, don't she? This lucky little shit got a four-pointer last year. On a dead run.
CHEEKIE: Mom says the deer are holding a grudge against you 'cause you hit too many with your truck.
MANNY: Your mom says a lot of things don't she? (Doe)

Much darker is the humor surrounding the accidental shooting and death of Hank, but the viewer has been prepared for his death. When Hunter hunts as a boy, someone shoots and chips the bark off the tree above where he is sitting, where his father told him to wait. It is later in the film that Cheekie acknowledges to Hunter that his father can't hit anything, and when the viewer finally sees Bear (Norman Brown) and Manny (Gil Birmingham) actually hunting, it is clear that they do indeed simply shoot blindly into the vastness of the woods. They unwittingly shoot and kill Hunter's father, but they do not know it at first. Between shooting and discovering Hank's body, Bear makes a series of jokes, saying to Manny, "You couldn't hit your pocket with a goddamned quarter. . . . You couldn't hit the bottom of a toilet with a turd. . . . You couldn't hit water if you fell out of a damn canoe" (*Doe*). Meanwhile, Hunter's father has been shot and lies dead where he had been sitting in camouflage, waiting for a deer.

The depiction of Vietnam veterans as hunters offers one parallel between hunting and war, and Hank makes another overt connection when he also juxtaposes hunters and hunting with soldiers and fighting. In a conversation with Maggie he suggests that the young Hunter should be allowed to hunt, especially because as a kid Hank himself went hunting with his father, and he links the only two moments in his life when he seemed have the respect or admiration of his father:

> HANK: There's nothing like killing your first buck, man. I'll never forget the look on my dad's face when I killed mine. The only other time I saw that look was when I got into flight school. He was dead before I ever made him proud again. (*Doe*)

As Marvin explains to his grandson Hunter, and hence to the viewer, Hank's way of hunting is to wear camouflage and wait for a deer to come by. In defense of his method, Hank says, "I hunt like every other man in the goddamned state hunts." Worse still, the film suggests in this context, is that he has evidently hunted at night by using lights to blind and freeze the deer. Hank's way is repeatedly contrasted throughout the film with the way a "real hunter" hunts. Marvin defines for his grandson what that real hunter is: "That's Tommy Deer in the Water. Now there's a real hunter. He ain't no weekend warrior like your daddy. Always hunts alone. Only takes one arrow. . . . That's all a real hunter needs. Heard he got so close to one once, he hung some beads around its neck. . . . Remember, a good hunter always gives the deer a chance. You don't have to dress up like no tree and then sit around and wait for one to walk by" (*Doe*). Shortly after this conversation with his grandfather, Hunter does accompany his father on a hunting trip, and that is when he mistakenly kills a doe. But he does not provide an overt link between hunting and war. He does not become a hunter until the film's climactic scene, and of course he does not join the military.

The film seems to privilege hunting as a man's endeavor and a signifier of maturity, but at the same time it undercuts this apparent signification by ultimately suggesting that the real hunter does not actually kill the deer. Rather, in a sense, he counts coup by hanging a string of beads around the deer's neck. Indeed, the macho trappings of both hunting and soldiering, the hallmarks of the warrior cliché, are all overturned in the film's climactic scene. Building up to this requisite finale, Hunter makes all the necessary preparations, and in a sense the film heads toward this hunting sequence from its very beginning. Hunter as a young adult carries within himself the need to make up for his childhood mistake of shooting a doe. Since childhood, that is, he has heard his grandfather talk about Tommy Deer in the Water (James Smith Jr.), the real hunter. Hunter also has the failed attempt to hunt by nightlight and the breaking of his father's hunting rifle to make up for. All these plot elements point toward the film's need to culminate in a successful hunt.

Immediately preceding the actual hunt, Hunter prepares himself with his grandfather's help. Marvin constructs a bow, and Hunter an arrow, the one arrow a real hunter will need. "It feels good to make something," he tells his grandfather. For the actual hunt he paints his face and performs a smudging ceremony with his mother. As he makes ready for the hunt, the film offers nondiegetic music, Robbie Robertson's "Peyote Healing," the same version of the song director Chris Eyre uses to accompany Rudy (Eric Schweig) as he performs his own ritual healing ceremony with tobacco ties in *Skins* (2002). In addition to these ceremonial preparations, Hunter leaves his girlfriend Geri (Judy Herrera) a note and his identification bracelet. She reads the note while he is on his way to the hunt: "Geri, I used to wear this in case of emergencies. I think I've outgrown it" (*Doe*). These ritual preparations combined with the note and the beaded bracelet he leaves for Geri suggest that he has successfully straddled two worlds, and the note itself suggests that he has outgrown the need for this bracelet. The idea of his being mature or ready or grown up is made even more evident in a brief exchange with his grandfather just after he has finished making his arrow:

HUNTER: I guess now I just have to practice.
MARVIN: You don't need practice for what you're looking for Hunter. Just courage. And you're full of that. (*Doe*)

What the viewer discovers, however, is that rather than kill, Hunter needs all that courage in order *not* to shoot the deer. The grandfather's words suggest that the old man already knew as much.

The hunt begins with a chase scene in which both Hunter and the deer lope through the woods. The scene recalls the film's opening sequence and echoes again *The Last of the Mohicans*: a man runs through a forest in pursuit of a deer, and the shots cut between the hunter and the hunted. Once Hunter comes face to face with his prey, the viewer sees the beads around the deer's neck, sees the deer's eyes, and sees Hunter poised and ready, with bow drawn, just a few yards away from the stationary deer. In a series of about twenty extreme close-ups interspersed with medium close-ups, Hunter

Facing off. *The Doe Boy*. Screen Capture. Wellspring.

has his showdown with this animal. The shot editing here certainly gives the viewer the impression that hunted and hunter are staring at each other, almost intimately, and the filmic convention of shot/reverse-shot editing in this scene also suggests that Hunter and the deer are in some sort of conversation. They seem to come to an agreement through intense eye contact. An extreme close-up of the deer's eye, that is, is followed by an extreme close-up of Hunter's eye. A reestablishing shot shows the deer's proximity to Hunter as the young man stands with drawn bow. Finally, the deer lowers his head, an act that prompts Hunter to lower his drawn bow. The encounter has ended peacefully.

The deer evidently acknowledges the apparent mutual respect and trust or brotherhood between himself and his would-be killer by making a gift to him of the same string of beads that the viewer first sees around the deer's neck in the film's opening moments, as well as several times throughout the film. After the deer has vanished, Hunter finds the beads on the ground in front of him just after he has washed his bleeding hand in the river. A close-up of this necklace indicates that the clasp has not been opened, nor has the string been broken. The viewer thus knows that the string of beads could not have come off the deer's neck accidentally. The beads are a gift, pure and simple. Just before Hunter picks up the beads, Marvin in a voice-over sums up what has just happened: "There was a boy who dreamed of becoming a good story and made it happen" (*Doe*).

One promise the good story *The Doe Boy* makes but does not seem immediately to keep concerns the question Marvin raises, figuratively of course, at the very beginning of the film: "How much blood runs through an Indian?" Issues of blood, both literally and figuratively, are undeniably central to the film. When Hunter asks his new friend Geri what tribe she is, she tells him that she is a "little bit of everything pretty much: Pueblo, Navajo, Mexican, Spanish." He replies, "Damn, you're like an Indian gulash" (*Doe*). She does not, in her turn, ask him about his tribal identity, but the viewer knows that he has a white father and a Cherokee mother, and Cherokee maternal grandfather. Most immediately, the significance of Hunter's blood is that he has hemophilia. One early reviewer notes that Hunter's hemophilia "serves as both a metaphor for mixed-blood . . . and a constant reminder that he is as fragile as the doe he killed" (Bastian). Also important is that Hunter's condition serves to remind the viewer of the importance and complexity of questions of blood in a culture that determines status and identity by blood quantum. Although in a moment of anger Hunter wants to blame his father for his blood condition, his father cannot actually be the source of his hemophilia. This blood disorder is carried through the X chromosome, and males get their one X chromosome from their mothers. In the strictly biological sense, then, Hunter's mother Maggie must be an asymptomatic carrier and the one responsible for Hunter's hemophilia. This biological fact parallels another biological fact: Hunter's Cherokee heritage also comes from his mother's side. Whether or not either Hunter the character or Redroad the director is aware of the biology involved, the coincidence of the parallel of these blood characteristics carries weight in a film reflecting a society in which blood quantum or literal ancestry plays a role in one's political as well as one's cultural identity. Filmically, the thematic connection between blood and identity is made in the scene in which Hunter becomes a man, in a sense, in a single cut: as the young Hunter (Andrew J. Ferchland) needs medicine to help coagulate his blood after his hunting trip with his father, the needle goes into the arm of the young Hunter, but as it comes out, there is a cut to a close-up of the soon-to-be eighteen-year-old Hunter (James Duval), still needing the shot, but giving it to himself.

As Hunter moves toward maturity—in this film that in some ways tells a coming-of-age story—he turns almost exclusively toward his mother's and grandfather's Cherokee heritage, rather than toward his father's side of the family. For his eighteenth birthday, for example—that all-important birthday in terms of becoming an adult—his grandfather gives him a handmade flute. Marvin looks to Hunter to be the one to carry on the tradition passed to him from his father. Hunter takes on the responsibility and does indeed learn to play the flute. Another important rite of passage for the young man involves his father's passion, hunting. But even in this regard Hunter ultimately chooses his Cherokee grandfather's preferred approach over his father's. Hunter chooses to hunt with a bow and one arrow, and ultimately decides not to kill at all. In these ways, then, Hunter chooses one cultural bloodline over another. His choice and the upshot of his pursuit of the deer suggest that he has turned to his Cherokee heritage in another way as well. An apparent nod to magic counters his father's statement early in the film that there is no magic. The lines between the two worldviews are drawn clearly in an exchange that takes place just after Hunter has shot the doe, imagining at first that the deer had been a buck with antlers:

> MARVIN: He wanted a story to tell for the rest of his life. You napping while he shoots a woman probably don't cut the mustard.
> HANK: You ain't helping him any, filling his head with stories of magic beads and magic hunters. There ain't no magic around here Marvin. It's just real life. (*Doe*)

Yet the film insists that there is magic. Despite Hank's assertion, that is, there certainly seems to be magic when Hunter finds the necklace, as noted above. In the same scene he washes his hand in the river, and the viewer sees by means of an underwater close-up that the blood seems to clot on its own. Hunter then wraps the newfound bead necklace, the deer's necklace, around his own injured knuckles. The act implies that the beads have worked some sort of cure, even if only temporarily helping the blood to coagulate.

In conjunction with Hunter's hemophilia, the film raises the subject of HIV. Within the fiction of the film another Indian hemophiliac has recently died of AIDS, which he contracted from a blood transfusion. Hunter's doctor encourages him to be tested, and Hunter agrees to allow the tests to be run. The film leaves the result of the test unknown, and the lack of closure in this regard offers the filmmaker, symbolically at any rate, the opportunity to leave issues of blood ambiguous, unresolved. In this sense, the viewer does not get to know how much blood or what type of blood runs through an Indian. Ultimately, the film argues figuratively or ideally, it is immaterial. What matters is not the blood quantity, but the stories, as Marvin tells the viewer in the opening sequence.

The plot reinforces the definitiveness of Hunter's choice to imbibe the culture of his maternal grandfather and his mother rather than of his non-Indian father in that the film literally kills off the father before Hunter actually begins his deer hunt in the climactic sequence. With the father's death and the final hunting scene, *The Doe Boy* echoes and at the same time reverses a major plot element of *The Last of the Mohicans* and any number of other Hollywood (mis)representations. *The Doe Boy* does not depict a heroic white man who enters the lives of a group of Indigenous people and is quickly able to outhunt, outshoot, and outfight the people from whom he learns how to hunt and fight in the first place. Such is the case in such Hollywood blockbusters as *Last of the Mohicans* and *Dances with Wolves*. In Mann's 1992 film, we remember, the non-Indian man Hawkeye is the successful hunter and expert military man. In *Dances with Wolves* it is the non-Indian soldier Lieutenant Dunbar (Kevin Costner) who is depicted as having the best hunting abilities and as the one who can actually teach his Sioux friends how best to kill buffalo. Both of these films echo the earlier film *A Man Called Horse*, in which the non-Native man Horse (Richard Harris) teaches his captors how best to do battle with their enemies. As Eric Anderson writes of such Hollywood productions, "rather than trouble to celebrate the multicultural nature of American society . . . these filmmakers cater exclusively to white moviegoers, reassuring them that Richard Harris's Medicine Pole vow is somehow more screenworthy than any Native's ceremonial experience" (142). These mainstream films preempt any possibility of Native American centeredness when their non-Native protagonists "go Indian" and become inevitably better at being "Indian" than their Native American mentors.

In Redroad's film, in contrast, it is the American Indian children who are the successful hunters. Just as they are the ones running through the woods in the film's opening moments, they are the only ones in the film who actually kill or even have the opportunity to kill any deer. The notion that they are the successful hunters is ironic, however, in that, in the case of the character Hunter at any rate, the boy kills the wrong deer: he kills a doe. Redroad's reversal is further augmented in that his film repeatedly cues the viewer to ridicule the white man's hunting methods by repeating the grandfather's scornful assessment of how Hank hunts. It is, after all, while Hank sleeps under his tree that the young Hunter shoots the wrong deer. Ultimately, Hank's hunting method—sitting, waiting, and even sleeping under a tree until the other hunters chase the deer to him—costs him his life. At the same time the film kills off Hunter's father, however, it refuses to place the adult Indian hunters on any pedestal. No special hunting skills are attributed to American Indians. Hunter kills the wrong deer, and it is the inept and careless Indian hunter Manny who accidentally shoots and kills Hank. In this way Redroad can be seen to be spoofing both Hollywood's ongoing contention that white men make better hunters and the concurrent and contradictory stereotype that American Indians are naturally good hunters and live in graceful harmony with nature. The exception, one could, argue would be Tommy Deer in Water, but whatever his reputation as a great hunter, the viewer never sees him actually shoot a deer. The old man Marvin, too, who talks as if he knows all there is to know about hunting skills, actually does not seem to hunt at all.

The character of Hank allows Redroad to reverse another Hollywood stereotype, that of the Indian as drunkard or alcoholic. In this sense *The Doe Boy* challenges not only Hollywood depictions but also even those in other recent American Indian films such as *Smoke Signals*, *Skins*, and *The Business of Fancydancing*, films in which Native American characters are shown to have serious, potentially fatal drinking problems; indeed, films in which alcoholism is presented as an exclusively Native American disease. In Redroad's film the chronic drunk is not an Indian at all but the non-Native man. The director depicts the Indian characters as drinking responsibly or not at all, whereas he depicts Hank as often drunk, and almost always with a can or a bottle of beer in his hand. When drinking, Hank babbles about the military prowess he never had, indulges in self-pity, and even at one point cuffs his hemophiliac son, causing him to bleed. This is not to say that Hank is not also a complex character; he is not merely a drunk. He has a touching scene when he dances gently with his wife and another when he visits and reconciles with his son.

Another significant reversal of Hollywood tradition in *The Doe Boy* is the wonderfully ironic depiction of a non-Indian man as the one who does not survive the end of the film. Just as the film reverses the opening scene of *The Last of the Mohicans*, a film that ends with the death of the Mohican character Uncas and leaves only the old man Chingachgook, *The Doe Boy* ends only after the death of its leading white character. That two Indian men are responsible for that man's death and that their shooting him is completely accidental adds another layer of irony to the reversal. The film simply does not allow room anywhere to establish a stereotype. Meanwhile, a triumphant, independent American Indian man survives the film's ending. Hunter, the Doe Boy, has made ritual preparations for the hunt, has made his own decision not to kill the deer, and has performed a form of ritual cleansing by washing his hand in the river and wrapping the deer's beads around it. After Hunter decides not to shoot the deer, he walks to the river to wash his hand and is accompanied by a voice-over by his grandfather Marvin: "There was a boy who was part deer and part bird, part science, and four-leaf clovers. There was a boy who dreamed of becoming a good story, and made it happen." This final voice-over echoes the initial comment, quoted as the epigraph to this chapter: "Nobody cares how much blood runs through a deer. But everyone wants to know how much blood runs through an Indian. It's kind of hard to tell, unless you cut one of us open and watch all the stories pour out" (*Doe*). The story that pours out of Hunter is his own.

Randy Redroad's clever and ironic reversal of the long-standing Hollywood trope of the dead Indian or the last of the Indians challenges and undercuts Hollywood's monopoly on representation. *The Doe Boy* can stand as a prime example of how an Indigenous filmmaker can both talk back to the traditions of first cinema and at the same time create a film on his own terms, a film that moves well beyond merely talking back. Hunter stands up from washing his hand and finds the string of beads, as if a gift from the deer. In the film's final scene, the film flashes back to the young Hunter in his shoulder pads and hunting gear. This version of the episode differs, however, from what the viewer saw earlier in the film. This time, in this version of the story, rather than one of his father's rifles, the boy carries a bow. As he faces the camera, he lifts that weapon, and his action is accompanied by what seems to be a celebratory shout. The shout seems to emanate from this boy, who is part bird anyway, and it sounds very much like a hawk's cry. This shout completes the reversal. Hunter takes complete control of his own story, even rewriting it. And Redroad suggests a cinema of sovereignty by creating a character who does so. The boy's first hunting trip is marked by struggle with his non-Indian father about how to dress, where and how to hunt, and finally whether to hunt a doe or a buck. In Hunter's brief revision of that history in the film's final shot, he demonstrates that although the past continues to influence the present, it is the Indigenous character who controls that present, who writes the past, and who looks toward a future.

TWELVE

Telling Our Own Stories

Seeking Identity in *Tkaronto*

The time for you people telling our stories is over. . . . I'm done
being asleep. —*Tkaronto*

Métis director Shane Belcourt's feature-length narrative film *Tkaronto* tells
the story of two young urban Indigenous Canadians who arrive in Toronto,
and because they stay at the same house, they meet, spend time together,
and share with each other their stories. Jolene (Melanie McLaren) has come
to the Canadian city from Los Angeles to interview Max (Loren Cardinal),
an Ojibwa elder, as a part of her project to interview, photograph, and paint
portraits of several such elders. The Métis man Ray (Duane Murray) has
come from Vancouver to market his idea for an Aboriginal television series.
The film's plot traces the growing connection between these two main characters as they do the work that has brought them to the city and as they simultaneously ponder the significance of their Aboriginal identities.

Tkaronto is not a film that features the death of an important character,
but it does include mention of the deaths of people significant to the characters, and Jolene's project implies a perceived need to capture and preserve stories and images of some of the tribal elders, a project similar to Will's photograph calendar in *Medicine River*. In addition to this implication and to the
brief references to deaths, the film has themes in common with several other
films under discussion in this study. It melds a documentary style into its fictional framework, as do *Skins* and *The Exiles*, for example, and like *Naturally
Native* it both features an Indigenous woman in a leading role and traces the
experiences of characters who seek a sense of Indigenous identity. As part of
its depiction of this identity search, *Tkaronto* also identifies the hold Hollywood (mis)representations can have over a Native person's sense of self.

In the opening scene of *Tkaronto* Jolene is in the midst of interviewing
Max about his Aboriginal identity. The scene is, or appears to be, straight
interview, and in these opening moments the viewer has no way of knowing otherwise. The film thus immediately and pointedly recalls or alludes to
the long-standing documentary mode of the interview. This form of interac-
tive documentary, according to Bill Nichols, "stresses images of testimony

or verbal exchange and images of demonstration" (44). The form has the capacity to readily demonstrate the validity of what the interviewee relates. In *Tkaronto* the effect is achieved with a series of shot/reverse-shot close-ups between interviewer and interviewee, the young Ojibwa woman Jolene as she interviews the Ojibwa elder Max. She records his responses to her questions, and after the interview proper, she takes a few photographs. Her project within the fiction of the film, the viewer finds out only later, is to interview and paint portraits of several elders. She apparently uses the taped interviews as inspiration as she draws from the photographs she takes at the end of the interviews. The effect that director Shane Belcourt achieves with this use of a documentary format is to suggest, as documentaries do, a real world outside the documentary itself. The film can be seen as authoritative and instructional in the same way one perceives documentary to be authoritative and instructional. Even though it is not actually a documentary, *Tkaronto* does seem to impart important real world information by borrowing the style and tropes of the genre. It relays information about some of the identity issues that are very real for the characters at the center of the film and, implicitly at least, for the viewers as well.

In addition to recalling the genre of the documentary, such an opening scene sets the stage for a major thematic component of the film. Both Jolene and Ray will turn to and rely on Max to help them understand who they are and what it means to be Canadian Aboriginal. The first scene surely indicates that *Tkaronto* is very much a film about identity, and Max's comments sound a thematic note that will resonate throughout the entire film. Belcourt's film thus takes on an issue that is important to Indigenous art forms in general and film in particular. In introducing her book, *Wiping the War Paint off the Lens: Native American Film and Video* (2001), for example, Beverly Singer maintains that "one of the most important issues facing American Indians concerns the question of identity. . . . What really matters to us is that we be able to tell our own stories in whatever form we choose" (1, 2). Belcourt himself acknowledges that in writing the script he was investigating his own questions: "Putting my heart on my sleeve and exploring my identity issues" (qtd. in Jason Anderson).

The interview and its topic offer first-time director Belcourt the immediate opportunity to confront stereotypes as they are related to identity. The film's very first words set the stage for this confrontation as Max asks specific rhetorical questions: "Who are you and I? Are we what people see? What do they see when they see us?" (*Tkaronto*). Max segues into talking about issues of identity, but with these initial questions he simultaneously asks the viewer to (re)consider what presumably non-Native people see when they see Aboriginal people. Max's questions suggest another: Do these people see the stereotypes they have absorbed from the media and elsewhere? Such a question and the hint of any mainstream tendency to stereotype Native peoples link thematically with the film's interest in issues of Aboriginal identity. Later in the film, for example, Ray explains his ambivalent feelings about his own Métis heritage, especially after having seen the film *Dances with Wolves* as a child. He tells Jolene that he remembers that the film confused him and that afterward he felt the need to learn what it meant to be Métis. He tells Jolene that he wanted his father to send him to a camp so he could actually learn how to be Aboriginal. *Tkaronto* calls forth such stereotypes as those presented in a mainstream Hollywood Western, and once it makes the viewer conscious of them, it questions them. Most immediately, the film challenges them by presenting complex contemporary Aboriginal characters as leads who most certainly do not fit the stereotypical mold. Crucially, these people are twenty-first-century urban professionals rather than nineteenth-century plains warriors. The film contextualizes their complicated lives, and they survive the film's ending.

The film addresses identity issues, in a sense, even before the opening interview scene in its very title. According to Belcourt, the word *Tkaronto*, pronounced something like /garondo/, is the Mohawk word that French explorers adapted in naming Toronto. It means "where there are trees standing in water," which is a reference to the fact that the settlement that became the city of Toronto was a place with a series of posts in the water to support a fence for corralling fish—they can swim into it, but they cannot get back out of it (see Jason Anderson). Like the fish in such a weir, one could argue, the two main characters feel consciously trapped and limited by their sense of alienation from their own indigeneity, Ojibwa or Métis in their respective cases. Jolene and Ray are both caught between the lives they *must* live in mainstream contemporary urban Canada (or Los Angeles in Jolene's case) on the one hand, and the sense that they *want* to be aware of and connected to their Aboriginal heritage on the other. As the two attempt to work through their respective identity issues, they discover each other, and they also discover that they are working through other, perhaps related, issues as well. Both of them have questions about their being married to non-Aboriginal people, and in this sense the film asks much the same question that Anishinaabe writer Gerald Vizenor asks: "Must we be severed from the dreams and tribal visions to survive in cities?" The film responds to the question in much the same way as Vizenor himself responds to that question: "The Métis, or mixedblood, earthdivers in these stories dive into unknown urban places now, into the racial darkness in the cities, to create a new consciousness of coexistence" (*Earthdivers*, quoted in Pulitano 146).

Jolene identifies herself as Ojibwa, and she is married to a non-Indian, would-be actor, whom the film's viewer never meets and who seems to have no interest whatsoever in Jolene's cultural heritage. Jolene senses that since their marriage she has changed but her husband has not. The viewer knows very little about this husband, only that he does not return her phone calls. She has a few brief exchanges with Ray about him, and in one of them she explains how she feels:

JOLENE: Tom and I, we have these powerful dreams about each other. Even before we got together we had these dreams where I'm a nurse in a bunker and he's a soldier fighting on the front lines, and the war separates us and we never do make it back to each other. So it's like in the past lifetime we both died and in this life we made it back to each other. So it just doesn't seem fair that it may not work out again, you know.

RAY: Yeah, but listen, if you guys have this mythological way of looking at relationships, I think that's pretty great and I think it gives it a better chance of working than most.

JOLENE: Or more pressure to hang on when you shouldn't. (*Tkaronto*)

Jolene and Ray turn to Max, the man interviewed in the opening sequence, with their questions about what it means to be an urban Aboriginal. Jolene's concern is most immediately about how a somewhat disconnected Ojibwa person such as herself can learn to pray. Ray is concerned with his Métis identity. He wonders how to contextualize his being married to a white woman and his becoming the father of her child. As Max educates the characters throughout the film, he also implicitly educates the viewer. The film's documentary-style opening and its educational interludes hint that in order for the viewer to appreciate the characters' search for identity an understanding of the culture and context to which the characters belong is necessary. The documentary elements Belcourt incorporates into his film facilitate this understanding, and hence the film's overarching theme of finding or coming to terms with one's identity, or with discovering what it means to be an urban Indigenous person in the twenty-first century, can find expression.

After the opening interview, Max presents Jolene with an eagle feather as a way to thank her and honor her for the work she is doing, the work that is, as he says, helping to heal "all our people" (*Tkaronto*). Jolene's project, the viewer soon learns, as mentioned above, is to interview and then paint portraits of several elders. With the presentation of the feather comes a lesson from Max detailing its significance. Belcourt uses this moment to inform the viewer of the significance of the feather from Max's perspective:

The eagle feather is the highest honor we have within our culture. He is admired by our people because he flies higher than all the other birds. He's considered to be a messenger for us; he takes our prayers to the Creator. The eagle has great strength and represents honesty, and when you hold an eagle feather, you are compelled to speak our truth. The wings of the eagle feather represent balance, and the quill at the center represents the path you are on in this life from birth

Urban Aborignals. *Tkaronto*. Courtesy of Shane Belcourt.

to death. And no matter how far you stray in one direction or the other, you'll always return to the center, the path you were meant to walk on. (*Tkaronto*)

This lesson is perhaps more germane to the actual plot than a similar lesson in *Naturally Native* about the dream catcher or the inappropriateness of certain sports mascots, but it is nonetheless similarly a moment during which the film pauses and instructs the viewer as well as a character in what can be seen as a proper way to understand and appreciate the meaning of a specific element of the culture. Given the necessity for the explanation in the first place, it is evidently addressed to an outsider. Although Jolene, like Max, is Anishinaabe or Ojibwa, she is outsider enough to need an explanation of the place of the eagle feather. Without the background to understand this significance, neither Jolene nor the viewer would be able to appreciate Jolene's subsequent desire to learn how to use that feather in prayer. Belcourt is candid about the origins of the idea for Jolene's search. He recalls that her "entire spiritual journey was motivated by a conversation [he had with his] sister, acclaimed Métis artist Christi Belcourt": "We just put our cards on the table and said to each other, 'You know, I don't know how to pray, I don't know how to speak our language, I have to do something about this. Otherwise, who am I?' . . . So, I knew that Aboriginal identity would be the central theme of *Tkaronto*. I also knew that it had to be set in the urban environment" (Belcourt).

Tkaronto includes several educational moments similar to Max's explanation of the feather. With these moments the film takes the care and the actual film time to provide the viewer with detailed cultural information. One reviewer finds fault with this aspect of the film: "There are far too many scenes explaining the significance of symbols, traditions and historical information" (Sasano). As this reviewer implies, perhaps inadvertently, it is important to notice such scenes, but the argument that there are too many of them ignores a point crucial to the film: without a grounding in some of the cultural aspects that Belcourt presents, much of the import of the film would be lost on the uninitiated viewer, whether Native or non-Native. And without precisely the sorts of explanations Max shares with Jolene and Ray, the unschooled viewer would be unable to appreciate the cultural significances of eagle feathers or what it means to pray in the way Jolene wants to learn. Thus much of the argument of the film would be lost.

It is instructive to take the example of literary studies in this context. Scholars of Native American literature often concern themselves with arguments about the importance of knowing something of the culture depicted in literature they study. As Louis Owens points out in *Other Destinies*, for example, the audience for Native texts "will likely consist of a heteroglot gathering, including tribal relations[;] . . . Indian readers from the same or other tribal cultures who may not be familiar with the traditional elements essential to the work but who may recognize the coercive power of language to 'bring into being'; and non-Indian readers who approach the novel with a completely alien set of assumptions and values" (14). In his book *Red on Red* Craig Womack argues that "Native literature, and the criticism that surrounds it, needs to see more attention devoted to tribally specific concerns" (1).

One can make the corollary argument in the context of film: to appreciate Indigenous North American film more fully, one must make the effort to understand some of the Native context from which the film derives or to which the film alludes. As Stuart Murray writes in the context of Fourth Cinema, the viewer needs "to understand the cultures from which [the film] comes, and that it is aimed at these cultures first and foremost in terms of its audience. It is impossible to engage with the films only at the level of the image, or through critical readings that seek to approximate the filmic content by way of analogy to non-Indigenous narratives" (18). Because of the very real, even palpable, difference between the two media, written text and film text, such cultural information must be delivered differently. In the midst of watching a film one can hardly pull down a book or search the Internet concerning the significance of eagle feathers in Anishinaabe forms of prayer. Therefore, the filmmaker must actually present some of this information for the viewer. In *Mediation in Contemporary Native American Fiction* James Ruppert argues that Native American artists use "the epistemological frameworks of Native American and Western cultural traditions to illuminate and enrich each other" (3). Mediation can be said to take the form of such embedded filmic moments for Belcourt in directing *Tkaronto*, as when Max offers

Jolene a lesson on what the eagle feather means. Such moments are critical to the viewer's understanding and appreciation of both the plot and the thematic elements of the film, and they ask that the viewer practice patience and perhaps engage somewhat differently from the way a viewer watches a mainstream Hollywood production.

Another instance of such an instructional moment and the need for it within the fiction of *Tkaronto* comes after a conversation Ray has with the television-show producers. Kevin and John ask Ray questions about his Aboriginal heritage in this scene, and the Métis man offers them a précis, a concise overview of what it means officially to be a Canadian Aboriginal. He provides information that they clearly need and that any unschooled viewer may also need:

> KEVIN (to John who has just entered the room): Ray's half Métis [pronouncing the s: /mɛtis/].
> JOHN: Good, that qualifies.
> KEVIN: It just says "Canadian Aboriginal." So . . . ?
> JOHN: Is that going to be a little bit of a problem?
> RAY: No, no. You see, there are three aboriginal groups in Canada: there's the First Nations, the, ah, "Indians"; then there's the Riel People, the Métis; and then the Inuit are the people up in the Arctic Circle. . . .
> KEVIN: . . . So, if you're only half Métis [this time he pronounces the word more like "meaty": /miti/], that means you're twenty-five percent Indian, right?
> RAY: I don't think it works like that. (*Tkaronto*)

After completely missing the point that Ray makes about the Aboriginal groups, John and Kevin are content only after Ray shows them his Métis Nation card. The embedded explanation of Canada's Aboriginal groups is brief but necessary to the film in that it highlights the importance of identity in a very literal and "official" sense. The explanation is explicitly necessary for the characters Kevin and John, and it is implicitly necessary as a means to educate the viewer. The exchange also exposes the problematics of anyone's needing such an identity card in the first place. The exchange allows the film to call into question such notions or understandings of tribal affiliation and identity, especially when it comes to blood quantum. Louis Riel, as quoted in Joseph Kinsey Howard's *The Strange Empire of Louis Riel*, had this to say: "Why should we concern ourselves about what degree of mixture we possess of European or Indian blood? If we have ever so little of either gratitude or filial love, should we not be proud to say, *We are Métis*" (qtd. in Vizenor, *Earthdivers* x, emphasis in original).

Belcourt juxtaposes this scene—which is comic despite, or because of, the buffoon-like qualities of the two television men—with a scene in which Jolene listens to part of the tape of her interview with Max. The film cuts from the scene of Ray at the television station offices to Jolene listening to Max and then back to Ray. This crosscutting suggests not only that the two moments are apparently happening at the same time but also that they are thematically congruent. As she listens to her tape, Jolene and the viewer hear Max speak further about identity, and his words offer a welcome and sober antidote to the absurdity of the cultural misunderstandings exhibited by John and Kevin. The film's return to the taped interview recalls the genre of the documentary and with it an indication of the real-world importance of identity issues that Aboriginal people face daily, as exemplified by Ray's encounter with the two television executives. Jolene sketches Max as she listens to the tape, and meanwhile the viewer listens along. Max's voice is on tape, and his reference to "studies and other reports" actually lend credibility and authority to what he has to say. The viewer is cued as one is when viewing a documentary to assume that as the interviewee Max offers trustworthy information applicable in the world outside the film. According to Bill Nichols, "We expect to apply a distinct form of literalism (or realism) to documentary. . . . We prepare ourselves not to comprehend a story but to grasp an argument? We do so in relation to sounds and images that retain a distinct bond to the world we all share" (5). The film is thus able to reach outside its own specific fiction, as it were, to insist on the importance of identity issues in general:

> MAX [on tape]: Getting to the core of who you are and identifying yourself with your people is the foundation of any identity formation. And we know through studies and other reports and things that when aboriginal people find their way back to the culture and identify with it and practice it, it really gives them a strong sense of identity and who they are. They do better in everything. They can participate fully in this society. You know when we see the immigrant societies come into Canada, they come with their institutions in tact. They come with their identities formed, and solid. So they can participate and then they engage in the Canadian vision or milieu or whatever we want to call it; and they're successful. But when you look back at the history of Aboriginal people, their institutions and their ways of doing things were attacked, severed, and destroyed. So we're now in a position where we have to rebuild those institutions and rebuild those frameworks, in order to build stronger individuals so we can participate within the Canadian society. (*Tkaronto*)

Ironically, it is Ray who at this moment in the film is most actively trying to participate in the wider more general urban society, and in doing so he confronts mainstream ignorance and institutional racism evident in the television company's interest in quotas and questions of blood quantum.

Shortly after Max gives Jolene the eagle feather, there comes another sequence in which Belcourt again provides Max the opportunity to offer her, and hence the viewer, instruction. He instructs her on how to pray with that eagle feather. The sequence is important enough that it essentially stops the action of the film, and focuses on the documentary trope of a person in a position of authority sharing factual knowledge. The evocation of the documentary suggests again that such information has relevance in the world that exists outside the film itself. Belcourt evokes the documentary genre at the same time he subverts it in this sequence. A series of crosscuts juxtapose Max's explanation with shots of Jolene in two different locations. In some shots she sits at a table in Max's home listening to him; in others she kneels alone in a grassy field, actually seeming to pray. As she sits across the table from Max, she confesses that she does not know how to pray: "I feel like I should know how to do this. You know, I'm Anishinaabe. My parents are First Nations. My ancestors were First Nations. Isn't this something that all aboriginal people should know how to do?" Jolene gives him a very detailed account of how she doesn't know what to do or how to do it. "I feel ashamed because I'm not sure if I'm smudging the right way, you know. I'm not sure if I'm holding the eagle feather the right way. I'm not sure if I'm praying the right way" (*Tkaronto*). Jolene's questions provide Max the opportunity to instruct both her and the viewer in what it means to pray. As the film makes this verbal gesture, the visual texture is extremely rich. The film cuts between close-ups of Jolene and Max as they talk, and Belcourt intersperses flashback or flashforward shots of Jolene somewhere outdoors, somewhere in nature, as it were, attempting to pray. During their lengthy conversation, which takes about nine minutes of film time, there are a total of ten cuts to Jolene in the meadow, each just a few seconds in duration. The first cut is to Jolene standing in a field of knee-high, golden grass, which is surrounded by trees. Other cuts show her sitting or kneeling in that field, lighting the sweet grass she has brought with her, wafting it toward herself, and unfolding the feather from its fabric sheath. The sequence also includes several close-ups of flowers and the grass in the field. Jordan O'Connor's slow, quiet, nondiegetic string quartet music plays softly throughout the entire sequence.

Max begins his lesson with a story, a parable, so to speak, and his response is worth quoting in full as a demonstration of how much the film centers on and pauses over this instructional moment.

> You know, when we first moved here, there was no tree out front; it was just lawn. And then one day I saw this seedling in the corner, and I decided, "I'm going to let that grow." And it's been many years, and over the years that tree has become my friend *and* my teacher. And there's still lots I'm learning from her. You see, our people, everything we learned, we learned from nature. Our songs. Our dances. Our ceremonies. Even our prayers. We observed the plants and how they grew. And the animals. What they did. What they ate. How they survived. So when we pray, we give thanks to Mother Earth for giving us life, and all life depends on her. And we give thanks to the plant life, to the trees, the medicines, everything that grows. Because all animal life depends on plants. And we give thanks to the

insects. The animals. The fishes. The birds. Because we need them to survive. You see, human beings are the weakest in creation because we depend on everything for our existence. When we pray, we give thanks to the Creator and all these things. We acknowledge their gifts. And the gratefulness that we feel because they give of themselves, so we can live. You see our people like to keep things very simple. Nothing was very complicated. So when we pray, it's just a matter of gratefulness. And everyone can do that. (*Tkaronto*)

The detail and length of Max's response to Jolene indicates its importance. In film time alone it holds a relatively significant place, and the import of what Max has to say is crucial to Jolene's understanding of what it means to pray. Max offers his tree parable and a nod to the significance and role of "Mother Nature" in his own life, and in the life of the Anishinaabe people generally, before finally coming back to Jolene's specific question about how to pray. The moment's importance is further emphasized in that the film returns to the meeting between Jolene and Max when later that evening Jolene reports to Ray more of what Max has said to her.

As Jolene takes lessons and gains an idea of what it means to pray, Ray has concerns about what it means to be Métis, especially since his white wife, who has remained in Vancouver, is expecting a child and has been sending Ray texts regarding her pregnancy. The father-to-be worries about fatherhood in general, and in particular he worries about how he will explain to this child (known to be a boy through a text from the mother) that even though he has a white mother and a white paternal grandmother, he is nevertheless Métis. Like Jolene, Ray turns to Max for advice. The film presents Max with yet another opportunity to offer a lesson concerning identity: "I tell you, it can be tough for people with mixed ancestry. But there is such a thing called 'blood memory.' The same blood that's in me, in this part of the world, it's also in you. And it will be in your son, or daughter, and that blood memory will know what to do. And it will feel the call to come and join the same circle that you and I sit at together. These blood relations can't be measured. But as long as you come to the circle, your kids will follow" (*Tkaronto*).

Ray is confused about facing fatherhood in general, but he is especially confused in the context of his being Métis. His confusion is worked out filmically in his imagination. That is, in at least three different scenes, the viewer has the privilege of seeing what is going on inside Ray's head rather than what is actually happening, as it were. Belcourt turns to the surreal to allow the viewer to visualize Ray's confusion. At one point, for example, he sees a man pushing a baby stroller, and this sight initiates Ray's first hallucination. The man turns to Ray, the expectant father, and makes the comment that this is not so bad, this fatherhood thing is not so bad, and he then pours gasoline over himself and lights a match. Before what is certain to be a rather gruesome explosion and burning, the film cuts to Ray as he wakes from his dreamlike trance. The sidewalk is empty. In another similar but less potentially gruesome scene, Ray is browsing through merchandise in a children's store, and in response to a sales clerk's approaching him, he seems again to hallucinate. After a short, realistic exchange with the clerk, Ray imagines her laughing at him in scorn, laughing wildly and loudly at how unprepared he is for fatherhood, and laughing at his confusion and about his ignorance concerning a baby's needs.

Ray's fear about fatherhood in the context of the baby that is on his way is a bit confusing filmically in that he at one point tells Jolene that he lives in Vancouver with his wife and three kids. Whether this is an editing oversight or a suggestion that here Ray is making a joke about bourgeois nuclear families is not clear, but his sincere concern about the new baby is clearly evident. Finally, at the film's end, he has a hallucination that is not related to fatherhood; it concerns the goings-on of the two television executives and their boss to whom he is trying to sell the idea for his show. About these quasi-surreal moments in the film, the actor Duane Murray (playing Ray) noted that such scenes were indeed meant as a filmic way to offer a visual marker for Ray's internal confusion (see Duane Murray). Belcourt uses the same filmic technique for all three scenes to link the confusion Ray feels about his immanent fatherhood with the misgivings and doubts he has about working with these television show producers.

Ray is in Toronto in the first place to sell his work for television, but he decides not to allow them to use his script after all. The scene preparing the viewer for his decision moves in and out of the surreal, again suggesting his confusion. Kevin and John present to Gail, their boss, the ideas they have for the television program based on what Ray has written, maintaining that the lead character in what is to become the series need not be played by an Aboriginal. Ray seems overwhelmed and disgusted by the conversation in which Gail and the others contribute this:

> GAIL: It would be really great to have some fun with Indians again. It's all gotten so serious. . . . The whole residential school situation, for example. . . . Or the various whales.
> KEVIN: Or the booze.
> JOHN: Or the being raped by the white man of history.
> KEVIN: Been there, done that. (*Tkaronto*)

The initial realism of the scene suddenly gives way to an exaggerated version of what these television people are saying, and this is the film's way of getting inside Ray's head. It is a method for visually depicting the confusion and indignation he feels. Ray is indeed displeased and disappointed, and once he comes to his senses again, he tells them he cannot do it. He confronts and challenges the others by getting angry: "You know who should play the aboriginal in an aboriginal story?" he asks: "How about a goddamned aboriginal? How does that float you, huh?" As he is leaving the room in disgust, he adds this:

> You say I'm twenty-five percent Indian. What the hell does that mean? Tell me, what does it mean? Point to it. Point to me the part that's twenty-five percent. Is it my foot? Is it my arm? Is it my face? You know what? You stole our bundles. We bided our time. You stole our land. We bided our time. Now you're trying to steal our stories? You know what, the time for you people telling our stories is over. We all said our nation would sleep for a hundred years. Guess what people? Time's up. I'm done being asleep. (*Tkaronto*)

A part of the richness of the film is that although it is on one level a story concerning Indigenous identity, it moves from this specific issue to a different level, to a much larger one, becoming a treatise on human identity in general. As Belcourt himself says, "This is what I find so ironic about life . . . that by going so personal, it becomes universal" (qtd. in Punter). The film itself seems to ask and prompts the viewer to ask, "Who are these people?" Not who are these Indians, not who are these Aboriginals, but who are these two young urban professionals, Ray and Jolene, who happen to be Indigenous.

At the same time as it generalizes from its specifics, however, the film definitely does not lose sight of the issues of Aboriginal identity. The issue remains central, for example, in that for political and ethical reasons Ray ends up turning down his chance to sell the idea. Once he realizes that the would-be producers would steal and then pervert his story, he tells them he cannot work with them. Reviewers of the film suggest that the episodes concerning the buyers of Ray's story are both simplistic and overwritten. One could argue that they are almost unbelievable in the way they present and embody ignorance and racism. According to a review in the *Ottawa Citizen*, for instance, "the media types come across as . . . cartoonishly bigoted" (Sasano). Another reviewer supports Belcourt's choice, however, writing that "men and women in the TV industry are more than happy to exploit his native status as well as his stories. Belcourt makes his point even if the tone of buffoonery in such scenes seems out of place with the wry humour that dominates elsewhere" (Al-Solaylee). It is, however, important for the film to establish explicitly Ray's reasons for turning down a contract with these particular people. As he tells his wife over the phone, they simply "are not a good fit" (*Tkaronto*). The film must demonstrate an explicit reason in order to illustrate that he leaves Toronto with his identity intact, even if he is leaving without a contract. The buffoons Kevin and John provide that explicit reason. His confronting these would-be producers is his defining moment as a professional, as an artist, and as a Métis man.

His defining moment as a husband and father-to-be comes in the scene of the previous evening in which he refuses to have sex with Jolene. The thematic element of Ray's working though his impending fatherhood parallels the scene in the producer's office when he hears over and over the words of the producers as they articulate their ideas of how to use his material. The filmic link serves to emphasize the thematic: Ray's confusion and insecurity over becoming a father is integrally tied up in his refusing to sell out his Indigeneity in order to sell his work. At one point he tells Max that one of the reasons he is afraid to become a father is that he fears that he won't know how to respond to his child's questions about identity, especially about Métis identity. Similarly, Ray refuses to sell his television series idea because to do so to this particular group would be to give away, or allow to be stolen, his stories. This he refuses to do.

The evening before this final encounter with the television people and his departure, he and Jolene dance for a while in the kitchen, and she says that she thinks they are doing more than dancing. At this point, for the first time in their relationship, she leans to kiss him. He turns away from her, saying he cannot. As the viewer knows, but not Jolene, he has just gotten a text message from his wife: "Ultrasound was good. It's a boy" (*Tkaronto*). After being turned down by Ray, Jolene goes to her room, cries, and takes off the bright red ceremonial dress—a gift from Max's wife, Linda (Cheri Maracle, Tyendinaga). In the meantime Ray, for whom this encounter has also been difficult, steps outside, looks again at the text message from his wife, and he too cries. Separately then, they cry together, and both are alone, but for different reasons.

With the news of the pregnancy, of course, the film looks forward, beyond its own ending. That same night, as the viewer discovers only the next morning, Jolene paints a portrait of herself, and this self-portrait also reaches beyond the end of the film. It signifies that the young woman has somehow come to terms with her identity, has found herself. That is, she typically does portraits of elders, "prominent aboriginal leaders" (*Tkaronto*), as she describes the people she interviews and paints. These individuals have presumably come to terms with themselves and their identity and are in a position to share some of their wisdom and insights with others, with younger tribal members like Jolene, for example. This is certainly the case with Max, the one elder the viewer actually meets. Thus, in that Jolene paints a self-portrait, the film implies that she herself has somehow matured, has somehow arrived and is therefore worthy of a portrait in ways similar to, or analogous to, the way any particular elder might be worthy of a portrait. This contention is borne out in that the film's final sequence includes shots of Jolene back in the grassy meadow praying. The sequence suggests that she has indeed learned from Max and that she is coming to terms with her Ojibwa identity. She is able to pray.

The portrait has significance beyond its serving as a manifestation of Jolene's maturity and her coming to terms with her identity. What is also noteworthy about this self-portrait as the final tableau in the film is the obvious fact that it is a self-portrait. With this portrait the film becomes self-reflexive: here is a Native woman representing a Native woman just as Métis director Shane Belcourt represents Aboriginal people in his film. The painting is the very literal means by which and through which Jolene is able to tell her own story, to represent herself. Within the text of the film her doing so parallels Ray's insistence that from this point forward he will be telling his own stories. The characters reach the points from which they are capable of telling and confident enough to tell their own stories, both verbally and visually. Jolene moves from painting elders to painting herself and praying confidently. Ray retains the rights to telling his own story. These depictions of characters' telling their own stories and painting their own portraits reach outside the film as well. Shane Belcourt too is telling his own story visually, and the film thereby takes on a very self-reflexive quality. Photographs, taped recordings, written stories, paintings, film, all of these various media suggest that in the film *Tkaronto* Indigenous people represent themselves. They no longer need rely on outsiders, non-Indians to portray them. They are no longer compromised by others' depictions of them.

In this sense, Belcourt's film parallels a film like *Imagining Indians*, in which the Indian woman scratches out the lens as the Catlin portraits pixelate and dissolve. It is like *The Exiles* in which the Curtis photographs are displaced and replaced by photographs of the actors. *Tkaronto* replaces any non-Indian depictions with the story and self-portraits of Indigenous people. A Métis man tells and keeps the rights to his own story, and an Ojibwa woman takes control of her own image. They take control of their own images, their own history, their own destiny.

THIRTEEN

People Come Around in Circles

Harjo's *Four Sheets to the Wind*

People come around in circles. Never ending circles, but you're never
that far away from home. You always come back.

—*Four Sheets to the Wind*

Four Sheets to the Wind, writer-director Sterlin Harjo's first feature-length
film, tells the story of two young adult siblings in the days and weeks just
after the death of their father. The opening scene depicts the son, Cufe Smallhill (Cody Lightning), as he drags his dead father into a pond, where he lays
him to rest. Following this internment, Cufe, his mother (Jeri Arredondo),
and his cousin Jim (Jon Proudstar) improvise a funeral complete with a coffin
and singing, but without the father's body. After the funeral Cufe travels to
Tulsa to visit his sister, Miri (Tamara Podemski), and there he meets and goes
out with his sister's neighbor Francie (Laura Bailey) before returning home.
Meanwhile, after a failed suicide attempt, Miri herself comes home. In the
final sequence, Cufe leaves the house on his way to travel with his new friend
Francie, and the film comes full circle in that he stops to revisit the pond
where he placed his father in the opening sequence. Interspersed throughout
the film are several voice-overs that the viewer ultimately discovers are spoken
by the dead father himself, Frankie (Richard Ray Whitman).

   This brief plot summary indicates that *Four Sheets to the Wind*, like several other American Indian films discussed in previous chapters, prizes how
an Indian man's importance and influence remain well after his death. Much
like *Smoke Signals*, *The Business of Fancydancing*, *Skins*, and other recent
American Indian films, *Four Sheets to the Wind* portrays and contextualizes
the death of a significant character and insists upon the subsequent lives of
those who survive that death. The dead father maintains an influence, as we
have seen, well after his literal death, and in a figurative sense, he does not die
at all; he certainly does not vanish. Indeed, the film insists on the centrality
of the Indian man who dies, and it thus lends itself to an argument about an
Indigenous film's need to talk back to and refute Hollywood's insistence on
the vanishing Indian. This chapter argues specifically that Harjo makes central the legacy of the deceased American Indian father. The film moves well

beyond a depiction of the individual's death and a mere refutation of Holly-wood, however. Harjo's film ultimately points toward the future by focusing on the subsequent lives of that man's children.

At the same time it shares with several other Indigenous North American films the portrayal of the death of an Indian man, Harjo's film indicates how far American Indian film evolved in the nearly ten years between the re-lease of Chris Eyre's first feature, *Smoke Signals*, in 1998, and the release of Harjo's first feature in 2007. In the earlier film, the actor Cody Lightning plays the twelve-year-old Victor, whereas in the later film, the same actor plays the young adult Cufe Smallhill. Tamara Podemski (who plays Miri Smallhill) performed roles as the teenaged character Little Margaret in *Dance Me Outside* (1994) and as Rox in *Johnny Greyeyes* (2000). Jeri Arredondo, who plays Hunter's mother in *The Doe Boy*, takes the role of the widowed mother, Cora Smallhill in *Four Sheets to the Wind*. In this sense, the members of the cast of young leads and supporting actors in Harjo's film have grown up with, and come of age with, American Indian film as a very present reality. The director, Sterlin Harjo, is of the same generation as many in his cast. To-gether they constitute a young generation of Indigenous artists involved in film and filmmaking. In this context the title of a review essay about the ten-year anniversary of Chris Eyre's film—"Gone with the Wind: A Decade after *Smoke Signals*, Success Remains Elusive for Native American Filmmakers" (see Fleischer)—misrepresents the achievements of several recent Indigenous filmmakers, Sterlin Harjo among them. One can quibble about what consti-tutes success, especially if one limits a concept of success to the box office, but clearly Indigenous North American film developed significantly in those particular ten years.

Take for example the film's title: *Four Sheets to the Wind*. The title and the dead father's name play on a slang expression for being drunk: "three sheets to the wind" or "three sheets in the wind." Cora Smallhill tells her son Cufe the story of the name and of her first meeting Frankie, the man who becomes her husband and father to Cufe and Miri. She recalls getting up her nerve to approach him and ask him his name: "He looked at me out of the corner of his eye, said in that quiet voice of his, he said, 'Four Sheets to the Wind.' I said, 'What?' He said, 'That's my name.' Those were his first words to me" (*Four*).

Some disagreement exists about the specific etymology of the phrase, but there is consensus that its origins are nautical. Sheets refer to the ropes used to control the sails, and each sail typically has two sheets, a lee-side sheet and a weather sheet. One suggestion for the origin of the expression is thus that even with three sheets (control ropes) a drunken person could not manage the sails, and the ship would thus toss about like a person under the influ-ence. Another possibility is that if there were three sheets rather than two, when it came time to tack, the sails would flap in the wind and the ship would stagger. The phrase seems to have originally been "sheets in the wind" rather than "to the wind" (Beavis and McCloskey). Given the use of the phrase for both the title and for the dead father's name, the film immediately evokes thoughts about drinking and thus about the stereotype of Indian alcoholism. As it does so, however, it calls the stereotype into question, that is, by presenting a character named Four Sheets to the Wind who does not seem to drink much, certainly not to excess. The film also presents fully developed Native characters who happen also to drink, but not necessarily overly much. The one exception is Miri, as noted below. In this way, the film challenges any easy reduction. The title itself suggests a complexity in that it is a variation on the actual expression.

Additionally, the relationship between the character's name and the film's title can be seen as an ironic reference to two of the biggest blockbuster "Indian" Westerns in Hollywood history. In both *Little Big Man* and *Dances with Wolves* the non-Indian title characters, Dustin Hoffman and Kevin Costner respectively, have "Indian" names that also serve as the respective films' titles, names the Indian characters have given them as a form of acknowledgment and acceptance. Hence this low-budget, contemporary Indian "Indian" film, this David, references and at the same time subverts and rivals these two Goliaths. In Harjo's film the Indian man takes a common English language usage and apparently names himself. Within the fiction of the film there is humor here, especially in that the man may have gotten the expression wrong to start with, using four sheets rather than three. But intertextually, by naming himself, the implication is that this Indian man takes control of his own identity and defies both Hollywood and a long tradition of American Indians being forced to take common English-language given names as was done commonly in Indian boarding schools as a means of killing the Indian to save the man.

In addition to the ironic and intertextual import of the father's naming, the title also suggests that the dead father hovers over the film's entire present action, but not as a drunk. The father, whose given name the viewer eventually finds out is Frankie, evidently commits suicide by overdosing on prescription drugs. He is referred to as quiet, eerily silent in fact, sometimes a difficult man to get along with according to Cora, a good father according to Cufe, and hardly a drunk. Despite the title, that is, there is little filmic evidence that the title character is a heavy drinker. The one exception is when Jim tells a lighthearted story about Frankie's having had a few drinks at the approach of a tornado. It is not the father in *Four Sheets to the Wind* who has a drinking problem; it is the daughter, Miri. Miri gets drunk every day, as the film makes clear, and Miri mirrors her father in that she attempts suicide. She differs significantly, however, in that unlike him, and unlike a character such as Arnold in *Smoke Signals* or Mogie in *Skins*, she survives the end of the film.

This idea of survival is critical in that it constitutes a challenge to mainstream conceptions of filmic Indians, both the conception that they die and that they are necessarily male. Like *Naturally Native* and *Tkaronto*, *Four Sheets to the Wind* features a female lead.

If the film does not depict the title character as a drunk, one is tempted to ask what else the title might suggest about the film. If the title does not necessarily have to refer exclusively to drinking, it could also refer to the four members of the family itself. In this reading, Harjo can be seen to make a move that allows him to very subtly adopt and pervert a mainstream expression and coopt it by applying it in his own unique way. Such a move can certainly be seen to suit his needs at the same time it achieves an ironic reversal of Indian characters' naming white men in the films mentioned above. One can see *Four Sheets to the Wind* in this sense as a coming of age story for both of the dead father's children, of course, but also as a coming-to-awareness story for both the children's mother, Cora, and for the dead father himself. One could argue, that is, the title also emphasizes and reinforces the argument that although dead, the father is still somehow an active, participating member of the family, that he is one of the four. Such a reading is clearly suggested in that it is the father who speaks as a voice-over narrator from the film's very beginning. His participation is also suggested filmically when during the funeral scene there is a brief crosscut to a shot of the pond where Cufe interred the father in the film's opening sequence. The effect of that cut is to let the viewer know that although not actually present, not actually in the casket in front of the mourners during the funeral ceremony, the father does somehow maintain a presence, almost as if he is listening to the funeral oration from his watery grave.

The absent father in *Four Sheets to the Wind* retains his presence, as does a character like Arnold in *Smoke Signals* after he leaves his family. Both films emphasize in different ways the continuing power and influence of the absent and/or dead father. Frankie's death and the fake funeral in *Four Sheets* motivate the plot and are related, as cause and effect, to the reunion of the rest of the family, the reconciliation between mother and daughter, for example, as well as the coming of age of the son. Each of the family members left behind by his death speaks of him at various moments throughout the film, but the most forceful indication of his continued presence is made evident through his voice-over narrations, especially during the film's opening and closing sequences. The father assumes the role of storyteller and even moralizer, and he thus maintains control of the narrative; he has the first and last words. As storyteller he is the oral historian and can thus shape and control the narrative. The dead father becomes omniscient, seeing and speaking from beyond his literal death. This garrulousness comes across as somewhat ironic in that in life he is reputed to have been a man of few words. Cora relates that he could go weeks without talking to her, and Cufe tells his new friend Francie that he and his father could spend the day fishing, that they could exchange as few as four words, but it would seem to him as if they had "been talking all day" (*Four*). Further ironic in the context of the father, Frankie, as narrator is that he claims to be the great listener, yet from the grave he is the one doing the speaking, and there is no indication that he listens from there or had ever been much of a listener when alive.

The film embodies an obvious humor in the fake funeral sequence, but Harjo's directorial playfulness is evident more subtly as well. That is, although the father is speaking from the grave and could thus be thought omniscient, he is not necessarily a reliable narrator, and the viewer can justifiably doubt his reliability in that he seems more than once simply to get the facts wrong. He offers an interpretation of his daughter Miri's independence, for example, but the film suggests a personality quite different from the characterization he offers: "Once when Miri was young, she came to her mother with a problem. Her mother said to go ask her father. So she went to her father for help, and he just sat there not saying anything. She never asked for help again" (*Four*). Is the father making a confession here? Is he submitting an explanation? Or is he offering an excuse? Rationalizing? Apologizing? Whatever his motivation, the statement is misleading, even incorrect and ironic, in that Miri actually asks for help throughout the entire film, both literally and figuratively. She asks her neighbor Francie for help when her car fails to start before the funeral, and much more significantly, several times throughout the film she asks for help from her family in subtle and sometimes not-so-subtle ways. Her pleas culminate in her attempted suicide. The father claims to be a listener, but he does not seem—as his representation of Miri suggests—to have heard much or well while he was alive.

Cufe's friend Francie, in contrast to the father, is a good listener, and Cufe is able in turn to talk freely to her. Reiterating the importance of listening is Cora's question about this new friend of her son's: "Is she someone you can talk to?" she asks (*Four*). She is, Cufe insists. She is such a good listener that the viewer knows very little about her, other than that she works and has traveled to Rockaway Beach (whether Oregon, New York, California, or somewhere else is not clear however). Francie does ask questions, and she does listen. The viewer knows about her beach trip only because she has a framed photograph on her dresser. She also has several frames without photographs, and this piques Cufe's curiosity:

CUFE: Why don't these have any pictures in them?
FRANCIE: 'Cause I don't have any to go in them yet. (*Four*)

Francie takes a Polaroid of Cufe at that moment, and thus she has a photograph to go into one of the frames. The existence of empty frames may evoke echoes of invisible or vanished Indians, but concurrently those frames suggest potential and future promise, especially in that near the end of the film the viewer actually sees her put the photo of Cufe into one of them. Her act points clearly toward a future for the two characters beyond the end of the film, and it thereby denies the notion of anyone's vanishing. They are never far from home.

The on-location filming, done completely in a particular region in Oklahoma, indicates in yet another way the distance American Indian film traveled in the ten-year period between the respective releases of *Smoke Signals* and *Four Sheets to the Wind*. The main characters in *Smoke Signals*, we remember, travel from their reservation home in Idaho in the north to Phoenix, Arizona, and back. The characters in Harjo's film, in contrast, require no such epic journey; the film is set and filmed entirely in and around Tulsa, Oklahoma. Stressing the importance of place in American Indian art, Craig Womack writes that the "land is at the center of everything, not only the legal realm of federal Indian law but the imaginative world of contemporary Native fiction, drama, and poetry as well. Acts of the imagination can and should serve to define, protect, preserve, and renew tribal relationships to the landscapes of the respective sovereign nations of tribal writers" ("Alexander Posey" 53–54). If there is validity in Womack's contention that land is at the center of Native art and literature, it is of course no less true for Native film, and Harjo's commitment to setting his films in central Oklahoma suggests as much. "Simply put," continues Womack, "to write effectively as a Native writer, at least to write toward the end of contributing to an intellectual discourse within one's own tribe, means knowing something about home. The most accomplished Native creative work has come from those authors writing tribally-specific work" (51). In *Indigenous Aesthetics*, Steven Leuthold makes a similar point, arguing that "film and video give us a sense of context that can be achieved only through a visual familiarity with the artist's native environment." Such a film, he continues, "fosters an appreciation for the importance of place in all Native American artistic expression" (153). Harjo insists on the importance of place through both the filming and the setting of *Four Sheets to the Wind*, and further still through the filmic stress on specific locales throughout the film.

Aside from Francie's snapshots, the film does not make much use otherwise of photographs and photography per se, but early in the film Harjo does use long takes, shots long enough (about six seconds each) to suggest photographic stills, and these "stills" inevitably emphasize and call attention to the importance of place. The shots are especially prevalent in the film's opening sequence. Francie's picture of Rockaway Beach suggests something far away and thus relatively generic as a place somewhere else; she even suggests it "looks like a postcard" (*Four*). The establishing long takes, in contrast, serve to ground the film and insist on its occurring very close to home. The long takes offer the viewer somewhat intimate glimpses of Cufe's community as opposed to the generic views a postcard might offer. There is, for example, a shot of the town with a railroad crossing and light signal, another of several abandoned oil well pumps, and yet another of a leaning street sign with an outdoor basketball backboard in the background. One shot is of a junked car parked beside a fire hydrant. A shot of a church shows the sidewalk in front to be littered with a beat-up trash dumpster, rusty oil drums, and an old sofa.

This implicit emphasis on the importance of and everydayness of locale is contrasted throughout the film with Cufe's wanting to get away from his hometown. His desire to get away is further contrasted with other characters' being content to stay put. At one point he asks his cousin Jim whether he ever feels like getting away, and Jim replies, "Yeah, but where would I go? I mean this is home." Later in the film, Cufe tells his mother he wants to travel with Francie because in part he just wants to get a way for a while. His mother responds: "Don't know why you'd wanna go anyway" (Four). Although Cufe does talk about traveling and getting away from home, within the action of the film, other than a brief trip to Tulsa, he never does so. Another element of the plot concerns the return home of Cufe's sister Miri. In this sense, place retains the centrality suggested by the establishing shots of the community. This is the place the characters come home to.

One of the establishing shots pauses on a one-story storefront church, and gives the viewer plenty of time to read the sign emblazoned across the facing board of the roof. The sign, without question mark punctuation, reads: "WHAT HAVE YOU DONE FOR THE LORD TODAY" (Four). A cross hangs on the exterior wall beside the door. There is never any explicit mention of religion in the film, but shots that include crosses abound, including the one placed with flowers on the father's gravesite, though the viewer remembers the father will not actually occupy that plot of ground beneath that cross. Cufe does indeed, ironically enough, do something for the Lord that day: he inters his father according to the dead man's wishes. Cufe's act has to be seen as contrary to what the established church might stipulate, however. The son is carrying out his father's wishes even though by so doing, he defies the mainstream with its religious conventions and legal restrictions. In doing something for the Lord, in this sense, he actually defies the mainstream and thereby adds an ironic twist to the church's interrogative.

The film suggests that the viewer may consider the father's burial and funeral ceremony, at least in part, as a trickster act. According to Creek storytelling tradition, in any case, one version of Trickster is called Choffee, or the Rabbit, and as Craig Womack writes, Choffee is "the famous southeastern miscreant Rabbit" (Art 100). As such, he (the character is most commonly male) "embodies comedy and mischief" (Womack, "Alexander Posey" 55). The lead in Harjo's film shares Trickster's name (it was his grandfather's name, he tells Miri's friend at one point). Miri explains that *cufe* means *rabbit*, and her explanation evokes the Rabbit-Trickster tale that Frankie tells in voice-over in the opening moments of the film. Frankie narrates in Creek (with English subtitles): "I was once told by my grandmother a long time ago, Rabbit ate Bear whole. She said, that Rabbit told Bear that he had a belly full of honey. This made Bear curious so he went into Rabbit's mouth and down his throat into his belly. This made Rabbit full for years to come" (*Four*). Cufe's name alone evokes notions of Trickster, but the young man's acts of dragging his father to the pond and his then orchestrating the fake funeral declare emphatically that Cufe himself shares with Trickster the characteristic of mischievousness. That mischievousness results in some lighthearted comedy, especially evident in the painting of a smiley face on a watermelon used as ballast in the casket.

Cufe may well be taking the trickster role from his own father. The viewer gets a sense of the father as a trickster by his account of his name when he meets his future wife, certainly, and another indication is when Cufe's cousin Jim recalls his childhood in an account of how Cufe's father stopped a tornado from coming. This is the film's only reference to the father as a drinker. Cufe's dad, Jim begins,

> was a funny guy. I remember this one time he had been drinking all afternoon, and there was this tornado warning, and I was freaking out, crying and shit, and he came over to me and told me not to worry, that he knew a dance that was going to protect us from the tornado, and he went out into the front yard, started dancing and singing and shit, and that tornado, it never came. When I was older your mom told me he was watching the weather channel. . . . He knew that tornado was never coming. (*Four*)

Whatever the degree to which Cufe takes on the role of Trickster, his carrying out his father's burial wishes sets the tone for the film and motivates much of its plot.

The preparation of the body for the funeral itself is supposed to be strictly a family issue, with only family and close friends involved. In a sense, this exclusiveness suggests a kind of sovereignty, but it is also rich with humor. Because there is no body to prepare, Jim, an undertaker by trade anyway, must pretend that the ceremonial preparing of the body has to be kept strictly within the family. His coworker, however, is not convinced:

> JIM: Seminole culture says that if the family wishes it, only a family member, such
> as myself, can see and/or prepare the body.
> LARRY: I never heard of that. Sounds like horseshit to me. (*Four*)

The visual focus throughout the bogus ceremony is on Miri's late arrival and her finally joining and sitting with her mother and brother in the chair

Frankie's funeral. *Four Sheets to the Wind*. Screen Capture. Indion Entertainment Group.

they have saved for her. Her car has stalled, coincidently, just at the head of the path that leads to the pond where unbeknownst to her the father is interred. The focus of the audio, in contrast to the visual that follows Miri, is on the singing of the group of mourners standing beside the casket. The viewer hears the music and the words the mourners are singing and only then sees them as they sing. In the midst of the singing, Miri arrives, having walked from the stalled car, and takes her place between mother and brother. With the funeral sequence, this film echoes or even recalls several such sequences: *House Made of Dawn*, *Skins*, and *The Business of Fancydancing*, for example, which also depict an actual ceremony for the dead Indian man. Of these, however, only that depicted in *Four Sheets to the Wind* is rife with distraction and humor.

The somberness of the moment is most obviously undercut in that the viewer—along with the dead man's wife, son, and nephew but no one else—knows that inside the brightly and somewhat ludicrously painted coffin are watermelons, one of which wears a hand-drawn smiley face. Part of the joke is on Sonny (Mike Randleman) because he has donated the coffin with the exclamation that "it would mean the world to me if you'd bury Frankie in it." When Cora agrees to accept his offer, he tears up and explains himself by saying, "it just makes me feel so good to think that Frankie's gonna make his final journey in a coffin I made, or fixed up." The film pokes fun at Sonny too when he claims to have one-eighth Cherokee ancestry, saying that he feels that "art comes natural to our people" (*Four*). At the moment of his assertion the film cuts to a shot of the painted coffin. It is sky blue with two hand prints painted on opposites ends of one side, one red, one white, which are reaching or leaning slightly toward each other but are separated by two vertical lightning bolts, also one red, one white.

Aesthetics aside, the artwork can be seen to symbolize on some level a distinction between Native and mainstream America, and the humor of the funeral sequence can be seen to further emphasize the divide. The settler culture proscribes one sort of burial that Cufe and his mother subvert. As Cufe relates it, his father made his wishes clear. He told Cufe that "funerals ain't nothing but a big circus. He told me to put him in the pond where the lady lives. That's what he said." Cora counters with a nod to cultural norms: "It's expected to have a funeral," she says. "Body and all." Cufe responds: "Well let's fake it" (*Four*). In this exchange and throughout the entire funeral sequence, the film subverts and even ridicules mainstream cultural practices. Meanwhile the choices Cufe makes as he respects his father's wishes indicate an agency independent from mainstream cultural restrictions and customs. Cufe's behavior thus constitutes at once both a trickster and a sovereign act. The humor bordering on the absurd in this sequence establishes Cufe as something of a trickster character, but it contrasts sharply with the more serious mien of the rest of the film. The turn from the strictly humorous to the more serious is not necessarily uncommon with tricksters, however. Trickster is a character whose actions and impulses often lead to something other than what he intends, and this irony is made manifest when Cufe's act of burying the father in the pond ultimately causes the complications involved in faking a funeral.

It becomes clear in the course of the film just how the father's initial story about Rabbit and Bear might apply to the son Cufe. The idea of Rabbit eating Bear and thus being full for years to come certainly foreshadows an ultimately affirmative outcome. The film suggests affirmation in that it comes full circle, ending where it begins: with Cufe at the pond at dawn accompanied by the voice-over. As a result of the final narration, again in Creek with subtitles in English, the viewer comes to know with certainty that it is and has been Cufe's father's voice doing the narrating all along, though this is hinted at before being fully revealed. The speaker seems to know things, for example, that maybe only a family member would know, and through the narration he certainly reveals am intimacy with and a caring for the family, even though, as mentioned above, he does not always get his facts right.

The final sequence reviews the whole past action of the film, and it simultaneously looks to the future. In an effort to reflect the scene cuts throughout the sequence, the following discussion divides the voice-over narration into sections to reflect the ways in which the visual is broken but at the same time contiguous. Throughout its entirety is the interpolation of nondiegetic music. The final sequence begins with Miri's return home and Cora's giving money to her son for his planned trip with Francie, and the voice-over begins at the moment Cufe discovers that money. As he lies down on his bed in the dark, the viewer hears the narrator, again in Creek with English subtitles: "That night . . . Cufe fell into a deep sleep. He had visions of life . . . and of love, and of traveling. Then he had visions of his sister and his mother . . . and even a few of his ole father" (*Four*, ellipsis in the original subtitle). A cut to a shot of the trees against the sky outside the house indicates that night is passing. The next shot shows Cufe up before dawn. He walks into the room where his sister is sleeping and in an endearing gesture pulls the blanket over her. He then looks in on his sleeping mother. Meanwhile, uninterrupted, the voice-over narrator pretends to know Cufe's long-standing habits: "Cufe never gets up early. When he was a child he would fall asleep in the shower before school" (*Four*). This assertion by the dead father echoes his earlier comment about Miri, in that once again a statement he makes suggests that he does not know his children as well as he thinks he does. Earlier he makes evident that he doesn't know that Miri has indeed asked for help, and at this moment he indicates an ignorance of his son's habits. As far as the viewer knows, that is, Cufe *always* rises early; he is always up before anyone else. He is up early to drag his father to the pond; he is up early while Francie sleeps; he is up early to find his sister sitting on the couch in her apartment; and he is up early on that final morning to leave for Tulsa to meet Francie. The disjuncture between what the film leads the viewer to know or seem to know and what the dead father thinks he knows but does not suggests once again his unreliability as a narrator. His misunderstandings, or misrememberings, add an element of humor. The viewer listens to the voice-over but at the same time sees Cufe is up early. Conversely, in a sense, the comment can of course suggest the importance of the moment for Cufe, at least through his father's (dead) eyes. If he never gets up early, his being up early on this morning marks it as special. And as the father's voice-over insists, something special is underfoot on this morning. For one thing, Cufe has made a friend in Tulsa, and he wants to travel with her. Francie is someone he can talk to because she is someone who listens extremely well. But perhaps more important to the father than Cufe's immanent departure is the reunion of his family. Also special, from the dead father's point of view, might be that Cufe, though he does not even know it himself yet, is about to return to the pond.

After the comment about Cufe's sleeping habits, there is a cut to Cufe's mother and sister, both still sleeping. The narrator recollects a line from the beginning of the film: "Once in a while something great happens in Oklahoma, not that often, but once in a while. For Cufe Smallhill, on this day, something did happen." Neither the specific day nor the specific happening is clear in this early moment of the film, but it certainly foreshadows the reuniting of the family members at the end of the film: "But the house was different that day. The whole family had slept under one roof" (*Four*). With these two sentences of voice-over, there is a cut to a shot of Cufe's mother sleeping, sunlight on the bed covers.

During a break in the narration, Cufe leaves the house. He pauses on the front porch to put on his cap and his jacket; he then walks to the truck and starts it up. There is a cut to Cora, who, with the sound of what seems to be the truck's squeaky water pump in the background, gets up and looks out the window to see her son drive off. In one of the film's most poignant scenes, Cora walks into the room where her daughter, Miri, is still sleeping and climbs onto the bed with her. In her sleep, Miri turns toward her mother, and in the midst of this shot, the voice-over resumes: "I know something wonderful happened that day in Oklahoma. It was a silence that everyone shared . . . and I know . . . it resembled something like love" (*Four*, ellipses in the original subtitles). At this point, the film again recalls those beginning shots of the town and community, again suggesting the circularity of the film's action. This time around, however, the community is peopled. A cut to Sonny's flower shop, for example, depicts him at work. He is the man who donated the coffin and who has gone out with Cora a couple of times since her husband's death, but this shot suggests that he will find a girlfriend other than Cora. The viewer sees a customer approach him with the flowers she is buying, the accompanying voice-over offers this hint: "People come around in circles." There is immediately another cut, this one to Cufe's cousin Jim buffing the wax on his hearse, accompanied by the line, "Never ending circles." The line is mimicked in the action of Jim's rubbing his car with a rag, in circular motion. Midsentence there is a cut to a low-angle shot back to Cufe driving his father's truck: "but you're never that far away from home" (*Four*).

In the context of home, there is a cut to a shot of Francie in her Tulsa apartment, placing one of the snapshots she took of Cufe into one of her empty frames. The narration continues right through this action: "You always come back." One can interpret the cut to Francie at this moment in at least one of two ways. In the sense that Cufe has told his mother he will come back, it can be seen to refer to him and his family and the certainty of his eventual return to them, especially now that his sister has come home. But in that the cut in this instance is to Francie, the line also suggests that Cufe will come back to her. "You better come back," she has told him earlier (*Four*). The film of course cues the viewer to assume that he is indeed on his way to see Francie. He has the money for their planned trip; he is driving away from home; and the viewer has just seen Francie slip one of the photos she took of him into one of her frames, something she doesn't typically do as she has indicated earlier in the film.

During this final sequence Cufe arrives at the head of the path he took to the pond when dragging his father into the woods at the beginning of the film. Here, a small herd of cattle block the road, preventing him from simply driving past. At first Cufe honks the horn as if he is in a hurry, but he then notices the "No Trespassing" sign and seems at that moment to recognize and remember that this is the very path along which he dragged his dead father. He climbs out of the truck and walks into the woods toward the pond. There is a hint that it is not pure coincidence that the cattle block the road at just this place at just this moment. It is as if Cufe's father wills his son to visit the pond. The hint is embedded in the voice-over narration, spoken while Cufe walks through the woods toward the pond: "My grandmother used to always tease me about her stories. She'd say, 'You better learn how to exaggerate and tell stories'" (*Four*).

In the context of exaggerating and of telling stories, there is just the slightest hint of a trickster at work here, the slightest hint that the trickster father has blocked the road at this exact place on purpose. Of course, the viewer still does not necessarily know for certain at this point in the film that the voice-over narrator is Cufe's father. There have been hints throughout, but the speaker's identity has not yet been made explicit. Once Cufe reaches the pond, however, it becomes obvious: the grandmother refers to the narrator's children and the narrator himself refers to them by name. The narrator quotes the grandmother: "'How do you expect your children to learn anything?'" Just as the film cuts to a close-up of Cufe at the pond's edge, the narrator, as if responding to his grandmother's question, acknowledges for the first time explicitly that he is the children's father: "I don't know if I taught Cufe and Miri much" (*Four*). This revelation is accompanied by a close-up of Cufe with his eyes watering a little as he wipes his nose with his jacket sleeve. At the very least, it seems, the father can take some credit for having taught Cufe to respect the wishes of a dying father and to honor him once dead.

At this point Cufe finds a fishhook in the dirt at his feet. The moment of course recalls an earlier story in which Cufe informs Francie about fishing with his father: "I can't even bait a fishhook without him, you know. He used to always do that. [That was] his job." The symbolism of the fishhook is rich, and it can certainly be seen to suggest that the father is passing on a heritage to his son. The film suggests this legacy, as noted above, when Cufe assumes the role of a trickster, but the importance of such a legacy is also evident in the film's final moments. The father survives through this legacy, and such a legacy clearly indicates that his importance continues. In some very important ways, the father, the dead Indian man, survives the end of the film. After an extreme close-up on the fishhook Cufe holds between his fingers, there is an over-the-shoulder shot, suggesting that Cufe is looking beyond the hook and out over the pond. The reflection of a cloud with the early morning sunlight on it predominates. The shot is accompanied by the film's and the father's final words: "People all my life have said, 'You never talk.' I just like listening, I guess" (*Four*).

The film circles back to end where it begins: in the Oklahoma countryside, beside the pond at dawn. The difference between the beginning and the ending, or what has been accomplished since the beginning of the film, since the father's death, however, is that the rest of the family has circled back together home. The last shot the viewer gets of Cora and Miri demonstrates emphatically the reunion. Equally important is that Cufe has come of age, in a sense. The shot of Cufe holding the fishhook suggests, metaphorically of course, that the young man is now in some way to be responsible for baiting his own hook. There is also a figurative suggestion that the father, his family, and his home have hooked him. Certainly the film's denouement suggests that beyond the father's death, the son's life will go on. He and Francie will travel together, but just as likely a part of that future is that he will return. The film hints of life beyond its ending and demonstrates that Cufe is very centered and is still at home.

American Indian film does indeed travel a great distance in the decade between *Smoke Signals* and *Four Sheets to the Wind*. The latter film suggests or makes manifest a different confidence in self-representation. Take two examples of differences in representation. First, as noted above, there is no epic journey in *Four Sheets to the Wind*. The importance of home and the land is evident in the plot, in the setting, and in the on-location filming. The actual exact location of the father's burial specifically is made paramount through repeated crosscuts to shots of the pond. Second, there are no overt references to Hollywood in Harjo's film. Whereas Victor and Thomas in *Smoke Signals* talk about the Hollywood film *Dances with Wolves* and later see and comment on a Western on television, Harjo's film implies that such an overt reference is unnecessary. The emphasis on the death of Frankie and the insistence on his continued importance throughout the film are implication enough. The film suggests, if only implicitly, Indians have roles in films beyond that of dying. In these ways *Four Sheets to the Wind* is able to subtly counter mainstream discourses concerning filmic representation of Indigenous peoples without overt reference to Hollywood.

As Native North American film comes of age, as it were, through self-representation, and as it begins to define its own parameters and invent its own plot structures and themes, it enables itself both to evoke and at the same time to ignore Hollywood. In its use of Creek language, history, and story; in its use of Indigenous actors who have grown up with Native American film as an alternative to Hollywood cinema; in its concern with a particular homeland, with land, and with landscape; and in its inherent sense of the characters' own worth and lived experiences, *Four Sheets to the Wind* marks an important moment in Native self-representation and in the cinema of sovereignty as it insists emphatically on the future of its Indigenous protagonists.

Barking Water and Beyond

Yeah. Anyway, it's going to be chief. —Cvpon in *Barking Water*

Sterlin Harjo's second feature film, *Barking Water* (2009), like *Four Sheets to the Wind,* is very situated and centered in Oklahoma. The earlier film is set and filmed in Holdenville and Tulsa, Oklahoma, and as one reviewer points out "almost the entire cast and many of the crew members are American Indians" (John Anderson). *Barking Water* too is set and filmed entirely on location in Oklahoma, and it is in every way local. From the opening shot of an Oklahoma river onward, the film is replete with shots of rural Oklahoma. The actors too are from the land. Richard Ray Whitman (who plays Frankie, different character, same name as the dead father in *Four Sheets to the Wind*) is Muscogee Creek, born in Claremore, Oklahoma. Casey Camp Horinek (who plays Irene) is Oklahoma Ponca, a tribal activist, and a delegate in the Indigenous Environmental Network. The connection between place, person, and character reaches outside the fiction of the film in that within the film the character Irene wears the actor Casey's T-shirt from the Indigenous Environmental Network. Even the soundtrack is in large measure Oklahoman. When the non-Indian hitchhiker Wendy (Laura Spencer) says she has a compilation tape of some local artists, the viewer can take her at her word. Samantha Crain, who contributes to the soundtrack, for example, is Choctaw from Shawnee, Oklahoma. Fiawna Forte, who also contributes to the soundtrack, grew up in Tulsa; and the Sand Creek Eufala Baptist Church choir from Seminole, Oklahoma, contributes to the soundtrack as well. The film thus does much to preserve and renew tribal relationships to the landscape and the people.

Both complementing and contrasting with the film's local setting and filming, *Barking Water* borrows from the epic road-movie genre. The terminally ill man Frankie escapes the hospital bed with the help of his on-again-off-again lover, Irene, and together they drive through the state, fulfilling Frankie's wish to see the land and several friends and relatives. His ultimate goal is to visit and reconcile with his daughter, who lives with her baby daughter in the town of Wewoka (Barking Water). Frankie and Irene are in some ways quite typical of generic road-movie travel companions. They have very different personalities, and as former lovers they have animosities toward each other that must be reconciled in the course of the journey. The film uses flashback to inform the viewer of their checkered past, and yet the journey points always to the future. One of the film's tensions, of course, is the stress of their relationship; another is the suspense surrounding the question of whether or not they will make it to Barking Water before the death of Frankie, who gets ever sicker as they travel.

Despite the geographical proximity of the friends and family members along the Oklahoma highways, the film investigates emotional and psychic distances. As Frankie looks at photographs of his children, for example, he laments the distance that exists between himself and those children: "I can tell you by looking at these pictures, where my kids were. They should have been with me, but they weren't. I don't even know if they want to see me anymore. They've got no reason to" (*Barking*). Like *Four Sheets to the Wind*, the film *Barking Water* is in large measure about an absent father, but in this film that absent father is filmically completely present: it is his story; he is, in fact, in every scene. Only from his daughter's perspective has Frankie, her father, been absent, a circumstance that makes for a very neat ironic twist as the film wends its way toward this daughter's home. Harjo borrows from and embraces some road-movie tropes, and as is typical of the genre, the two travelers come to a closer understanding of each other as a result of their journeying together. This is the case even though Irene insists throughout that they are no longer a couple. The film makes clear, however, that they still love each other, Irene's protestations notwithstanding. Like *Medicine River* and *The Business of Fancydancing*, this film also tells a coming-home story, but in this film that homecoming is painfully ironic in that Frankie does not quite make it home, not alive at any rate, or at least not literally alive.

Frankie's death presents the film with a challenge similar to the challenges several other films in this study have taken on. The film must overcome the association of Frankie's death with the deaths of so many Native characters throughout the history of Indians in film. In *Four Sheets to the Wind* the issue of the absent father hardly need arise because despite the father's presence from beyond the grave, or from beyond the pond, the primary focus and energy of the film is on those who survive, especially the dead man's children, Cufe and Miri. In *Barking Water*, in contrast, the dying Frankie is very much at the center of the film throughout. The film repudiates Hollywood perhaps most pointedly, though implicitly, in its final moments. Irene keeps her promise to Frankie: she kisses his grandchild. The circle is not broken. In the final shot Irene stands in the doorway of the daughter's house; she is framed right and left by Frankie's daughter and grandchild respectively. Frankie and the infant have an identical hand gesture, and the infant looks toward the camera. Credits roll. In Gerald Vizenor's terms, "the eyes that meet in the aperture are an obscure assurance of narratives and an ironic presence" ("Intermage"

Tidings. *Barking Water*. Screen Capture. Indion Entertainment Group.

235). Harjo both circumvents and refutes the stereotype of Native actors cast as expendable characters, extras created only to die, in part, by pointing throughout toward the future.

Harjo also manages an ironic refutation of Hollywood on a different level altogether. In one particular scene he seems to have great fun with some of the most prevalent Hollywood stereotypes: he draws them out and actually caricatures them, but then he deletes that scene altogether. It remains available only as part of the bonus materials on the *Barking Water* DVD (2009), not as a part of the final cut. The deleted material would have been part of a sequence in which Frankie and Irene meet two young relatives for lunch. The scene as it does exist in the final cut is already ironic in that the elders have invited two "cousins" to buy them lunch at a diner as they are passing through town. They are trying to get Frankie back to his daughter before he dies, but they are broke and hungry, so they stop to be fed, as it were. During that lunch, in the cut material, the character Cvpon (Quese iMC) describes a film that he and his friend are making, a film rife with some of the very stereotypes Harjo himself seeks to challenge and refute in *Barking Water*:

> CVPON: We're doing this crazy video, where we're warriors, like old time warriors, and when the video starts there's this sound of a flute and a eagle calling up above and then we look up from our horses at the eagle and Blaah! . . . Our hip-hop gig comes on. . . . That's when the beat comes in. That's when this fool, he starts dancing on the prairie with the breechcloth,

buck underneath; he ain't got nothing underneath. And then I come in,
dancing like one of them monkey-style Indians, kind of like in the movie . . .
FRIEND: *The New World.*
CVPON: Yeah. Anyway, it's going to be chief. (*Barking*, DVD Bonus Material)

As cut material, the scene can be thought to be doing double duty: it demonstrates Harjo's awareness of prevalent filmic stereotypes, their ubiquity,
and of the impact those Hollywood stereotypes have on young contemporary Indian men. Harjo is able to ridicule many of the most prominent characteristics of such films by depicting the cousins' presentation of their own
film. At the same time, however, the fact that the scene is both deleted and
yet included as a scene in the bonus materials on the DVD suggests that it is
precisely such stereotypes that must be purged from American Indian film in
general. The scene the boys are filming, as described above, is clearly an allusion to a film like *Dances with Wolves* with its dancing on the prairie, its
horses, its eagles screeching. It also actually references the non-Indian Indian
film *The New World*, and calls attention to one of early scenes in which the
Native actors do indeed seem to do a sort of monkey dance as they watch the
approach of European ships.

The deleted scene can be seen to spoof some current American Indian films
as well. *Naturally Native*, for example, is chock-full of background nondiegetic flute music. Several films, such as in the final scene of *The Doe Boy*,
also include the call of an eagle (typically a hawk's cry is used but meant to
be an eagle's). And there is the nonchalant glossing over the fact of these old-
time warriors are always riding horseback, a reference that in a sense echoes
Marvin Clifford's account in *Imagining Indians* recalling his experiences as
an extra on the movie set for *Dances with Wolves:* "I had quite an experience on that one, riding bareback all day with just a G-string on. I tell you,
I earned my forty-five dollars on that set. I really, really worked off every bit
of that forty-five dollars. Still sore from it as a matter of fact" (*Imagining*).
Harjo's cut scene is quite rich, yet the director makes the decision to exclude
even any reference to it in the final cut. Thus the scene *does* and yet *does not*
exist. The suggestion is that Harjo felt the need to comment on such tropes
that continue to haunt American Indians in film and in American Indian film
itself, but at the same time had the desire *and the power* to annihilate such
tropes in one stroke. Not only are such Hollywood tropes spoofed in this
scene, they are disappeared by being deleted from the final cut altogether.
They vanish under Harjo's splicing knife, and that splicing is a sovereign act.

If we consider the innovations evident Harjo's films and look beyond *Barking Water* to the future of American Indian film, we might do well to consider briefly another Midwestern filmmaker, one who also works on location,

one who also has a relatively small budget, and one who also uses local, Indigenous talent. Rodrick Pocowatchit offers the viewer films that include references to Hollywood and that quickly subvert or convert those references into works that are very much his own. He offers local counternarratives to the grandiosity of Hollywood, and his films repeatedly circle around family, culture, and home, and offer the viewer a sense of geographical as well as cultural place.

Sleepdancer (2006), Pocowatchit's first feature, tells the story of an Indian man, Tommy (played by writer and director Pocowatchit himself), whose father dies immediately before the film's present action. That death motivates the plot. Derek (Mark Wells), the county coroner, befriends the bereaved man, who refuses to speak a single word, and through this official's investigation the viewer discovers Tommy's past: his own son has died in a car crash some years earlier. Meanwhile, Tommy's brother Ben Running Scout (played by the actor's actual brother, Guy Ray Pocowatchit), locates him and attempts to bring him home. Ben appears indifferent to the news of his father's death, saying, "Doesn't matter; he's been dead to me for a long time" (*Sleepdancer*). A father's death clearly, once again, initiates and motivates a plot, and that elder, though never actually on screen, has presence from beyond the grave throughout the film. The motif of the absent father is doubled in this film in that the coroner Derek has grown up without knowing his own father or even having ever met him. This commonality of their pasts brings the two men closer, but it is the brother Ben who first discovers that Tommy is sleepdancing. Each dawn he gets out of bed and walks to a grassy field to perform a grass dance. In his dream-state he envisions himself in full regalia, and he dances with his dead son. It is the brother who brings the entire family to help cure Tommy of his muteness and despondency. The film thus has much in common with several other American Indian films, and like them the ending insists that the survivors will indeed live beyond the final credits.

In his second feature, *Dancing on the Moon*, Pocowatchit makes overt reference to the Hollywood classic *The Wizard of Oz* (1939), but subverts that film's emphasis on Dorothy's getting home by abandoning the non-Native Dorothy character midway and focusing thereafter exclusively on the three Indian companions. Further undermining this studio-filmed Hollywood classic, the final credits make clear that *Dancing on the Moon*, despite the title, is "shot entirely on location in Council Grove, Mayetta and Wichita, Kansas." In addition to the overt evocation of a Hollywood classic, Pocowatchit's film is self-reflexive, calling attention to itself as film. Joey, the character Pocowatchit plays, refers to himself *outside* the film. That is, Joey the character, played by director Rodrick Pocowatchit, alludes to himself as the director. As a character he wears what in the opening scene he calls a director's cap, for example: "It's my director's hat. I'm a director." The idea of Joey as both character and director is further embedded in that the character Joey actually directs or controls the action of the plot: he gets the car stolen, he finds the car, he wins gas money, and ultimately he orchestrates the trick that gets Dean to dance again. He fakes jumping off a bridge to inspire his brother to dance by making him promise: "You gotta dance again Dean. Everything will be okay if you dance again, I know it. . . . Promise me." In the final moments, the film again takes on a metafilmic feel when Dean reminds the viewer in a voice-over that this is indeed a film: "Joey said, our adventure would make a great movie" (*Dancing*).

Within the fiction of the film that adventure is to some degree inspired by the death of Dean's mother before the present action, and her death does motivate the plot insofar as the three men are on their way to a powwow even though the former competitive dancer Dean (Guy Ray Pocowatchit) has been refusing to dance. One reason for their going is to offer the mother's shawl for an honor song.

The very title of Pocowatchit's third feature, *The Dead Can't Dance*, indicates the importance of death and dying in Pocowatchit's comic zombie movie. In this film Pocowatchit again casts himself and his brother, and again they are brothers in the fiction of the film. Dax (Rodrick Pocowatchit) and Ray (Guy Ray Pocowatchit) are driving Ray's son, Eddie (T. J. Williams), to college, and en route the three Indian men confront an airborne toxic event, an epidemic that is apparently fatal to everyone but Native Americans. In a wonderful ironic twist, what makes American Indians susceptible to diabetes and alcoholism, concludes some scientists within the fiction of the film and as a radio journalist reports it, also makes them immune to whatever is causing the non-Natives to turn into zombies. The three men hunker down in a school building, avoiding death and enduring attacks by the zombies. As they attempt to figure out how to survive the attacks of the white zombies, the film is not without other ironies. The radio announcer reports that "vaccines are being developed, thanks to the help of Native American leaders and tribal doctors with the donation of Native people's blood" (*Dead Can't*). In what has become a Pocowatchit trademark, the calamity brings the characters to overcome their differences and gain newfound respect for one another. This film, like the others in this director's opus, presents death as a way to emphasize the survival of Indigenous peoples, and thus despite its somewhat trite and humorous zombie-film-genre premise, the film makes an important statement about indigeneity and Indigenous self-representation. Uncle Dax does not succumb to the disease, but he does die at the end of the film. In saving his nephew by distracting the hoard of zombies, he falls on a length of rebar he has been carrying as protection. As he is dying, he confesses to his brother, who has been a somewhat negligent father, that he hopes that he did a good job of caring for his nephew: "I did good didn't I. I mean, I tried to" (*Dead*

Can't). The film makes clear throughout that he has indeed done well by his nephew, including motivating him to go to college. In this way, the legacy of Dax Wildhorse is guaranteed to live on even though the individual dies. Dax does not die until just before the final sequence, however, and so the film has almost its entirety to develop the uncle's character. He is certainly more than a mere extra cast simply to die.

All three of Pocowatchit's films share common themes that can be summarized, somewhat reductively perhaps, but effectively, by noting that the death of an elder or a family member influences the actions and ultimately works an ameliorative effect on the surviving characters, characters whose survival and continuance beyond the end of the film becomes an important aspect of the film. This is brought home emphatically in *The Dead Can't Dance* when Ray and Eddy literally walk into the rendezvous point past a large sign on which is painted the word, hyphenated thus:

SURV-
IVORS.

They are both literally and figuratively survivors. In Gerald Vizenor's terms, "The fugitive poses of the *postindian* and the poses that come after the discoveries and inventions of the *indian* and the portraiture of dominance are the simulations of survivance that undermine ethnographic evidence and manifest manners ("Interimage" 233). *The Dead Can't Dance* makes clear that the characters who arrive at the rendezvous point are indeed survivors. A final scene shows the nephew and his father, reconnected through the uncle's death, leaving a hospital after Eddie has been cured. Alive and well, having told their story, they walk together into their future. In Vizenor's terms, "Native American Indians are the originary storiers of this continent, and native stories are the arcane creations of a real existence that arise in a customary modernity. Native stories of totemic associations, visionary, imagic moments, or those tacit images of an ontic sense of presence, and survivance, are the actual turns of native modernity" ("Ontic" 161).

Chris Eyre is also interested in telling a story and privileging survivance, as one sees in the conclusion of his documentary *Trail of Tears*, the third of the five-part PBS We Shall Remain series. Eyre emphasizes that the Cherokee people ultimately rebound and in fact thrive in their new homeland in Indian Territory despite the horrors of removal and the startling executions of Elias Boudinot, John Ridge, and Major Ridge. According to the documentary, their businesses flourished, they organized and ran the "finest system of public education in all American for men and women" and their ancient traditions and customs continued to be honored and practiced. The film's voice-over narrator comments that "the Cherokees had reestablished themselves as a strong and sovereign nation, deeply connected to the land upon which they lived" (*Trail*). Eyre's film represents the Cherokee tribe, of course, but his argument is perhaps no less applicable to other removed or displaced tribes whose members find themselves in their new homeland, whether the literal or a figurative Indian Territory. Also thriving in the arts one can argue are members of the Muskogee Creek and the Pottawatomie Nations, for example. It should come as no surprise that many new contemporary Indigenous artists and filmmakers tell their own stories, make manifest Indigenous agency, counter and even subvert the mainstream versions of their history.

To take just one example of the importance of continuing to challenge and offer alternatives to mainstream Hollywood representations of American Indians: in remaking the 1969 film *True Grit* (2010), Joel and Ethan Coen added an opening sequence in which three men are to be executed. The directors include an unnamed condemned Indian man (acted by Jonathan Joss) to suggest the racism of the times. This man, in contrast to the others, is not allowed any final words. He is merely hanged. This man is the only adult Native character in a film that takes place almost entirely and exclusively on Indian land. His only role in the film is to die, and this limited role in 2010 echoes over a hundred years of Hollywood and its thousands of films. His death is gratuitous in that he has no other purpose in the film: he has otherwise nothing to do with the plot or the film's themes, he has no influence, no descendants, no past, and of course no future.

If Hollywood is to continue with and insist on such (mis)representations, it is of utmost importance that Indigenous filmmakers such as Chris Eyre, Randy Redroad, Sterlin Harjo, Rodrick Pocowatchit, Valerie Red-Horse, Shane Belcourt, and many others accept the responsibility and take on the challenge of offering counternarratives. They have the right, of course, and they have the responsibility to create and control their own representation of Indigenous peoples. They have the obligation to continue to counter majority or mainstream culture, and they must continue to film against the grain. They must, in the words of New Zealand's Maori filmmaker Barry Barclay, continue to take their cameras ashore: "The First Cinema Camera sits firmly on the deck of the ship. It sits there by definition. The Camera Ashore, the Fourth Cinema Camera, is the one held by the people for whom 'ashore' is their ancestral home" (Barclay 10). As these Indigenous North American filmmakers represent the yearning, the love, and the compassion evident in contemporary urbane Indian life and as they tell their own stories in these films, they create a cinema of sovereignty and by so doing make manifest their own survival. They take control of the past and thereby of the future. They refute Hollywood by insisting that despite the deaths of particular individual characters, particular named and fully humanized individuals, there is a future. They insist that the children and grandchildren survive, and their films so often and so forcefully conclude with such an insistence.

This is precisely what is happening throughout Indigenous North
American film. Chris Eyre, perhaps the most prolific contemporary Native
filmmaker, continues to be productive as director and producer. He directed
three episodes of the PBS We Shall Remain series and directed *A Thousand
Roads* (2005), a centerpiece of the Smithsonian's National Museum of the
American Indian. He is producer for *Imprint* (2007), a film in which a Native
American attorney returns to her reservation to visit her dying father. The accomplished Cherokee actor Wes Studi is executive producer of and an actor
in *The Only Good Indian* (2009), a film that looks back to revise the history
of the boarding school era. Meanwhile, new and young Indigenous directors
and actors continue to step forward.

Although digital technology changes the mechanics and radically reduces
the cost of filmmaking, in *Film Nation: Hollywood Looks at U.S. History*,
published in 1997, Robert Burgoyne writes that "Native Americans have yet
to gain access to the resources to tell their own stories in feature length films"
(39). This difficulty in acquiring funding seems to have remained true another
several years. In his 2003 essay in *Illusions*, "Celebrating Fourth Cinema,"
Barry Barclay counts only a total of five Indigenous films completed in New
Zealand "and six completed abroad. . . . So far then, we are looking at a
very slim body of work. In fact we will always be looking at a relatively small
body of work" (7). A mere five years later, however, in *Native Features* (2008),
Houston Wood counts significantly more Indigenous films: "Beginning with
a pioneering handful in the 1980s, now fifty or so Indigenous features have
appeared. Within another decade, there will likely be hundreds more" (2). Of
those, Sterlin Harjo has already contributed two. Rodrick Pocowatchit, three.
Certainly there is more Indigenous cinema to come. There is a future.

And whatever is still to come, in the words of the character Cvpon in *Barking Water*, "Yeah. Anyway, it's going to be chief."

Filmography

The Appaloosa. 1966. Universal. Dir. Sidney J. Furie.

Atanarjuat (The Fast Runner). 2001. Sony Pictures. Dir. Zacharias Kunuk.

Avatar. 2009. 20th Century Fox. Dir. James Cameron.

Barking Water. 2009. Indion Entertainment Group and Dolphin Bay Film. Dir. Sterlin Harjo.

The Battle at Elderbush Gulch. 1913. General Film Company. Dir. D. W. Griffith.

Broken Arrow. 1950. 20th Century Fox. Dir. John Woo.

The Business of Fancydancing. 2002. A FallsApart Production. Dir. Sherman Alexie.

Captain John Smith and Pocahontas. 1953. United Artists. Dir. Lew Landers.

Cheyenne Autumn. 1964. Warner Bros. Dir. John Ford.

Clearcut. 1991. Northern Arts. Dir. Richard Burgajski.

Dance Me Outside. 1995. Shadows Shows Distribution. Dir. Bruce McDonald.

Dances with Wolves. 1990. Orion. Dir. Kevin Costner.

Dancing on the Moon. 2003. Harmy Films. Dir. Rodrick Pocowatchit.

The Dead Can't Dance. 2011. Harmy Films. Dir. Rodrick Pocowatchit.

Dead Man. 1995. Miramax. Dir. Jim Jarmusch.

Death Wish V. 1994. Paramount. Dir. Allen A. Goldstein.

The Doe Boy. 2001. Wellspring. Dir. Randy Redroad.

The Exiles. 1961. Milestone Films. Dir. Kent Mackenzie.

Flags of Our Fathers. 2006. DreamWorks. Dir. Clint Eastwood.

Fort Apache. 1948. Argosy Pictures. RKO. Dir. John Ford.

Four Sheets to the Wind. 2007. Indion Entertainment Group. Dir. Sterlin Harjo.

Grand Avenue. 1996. HBO. Dir. Daniel Sackheim.

Harold of Orange. 1984. Film in the Cities. Dir. Richard Weiss.

House Made of Dawn. 1972. Firebird Productions. Dir. Richardson Morse.

Imagining Indians. 1992. Documentary Educational Resources. Dir. Victor Masayesva Jr.

I'm Not the Indian You Had in Mind. 2007. Big Soul Productions. Dir. Thomas King.

Imprint. 2007. Linn Productions. Dir. Michael Linn.

In a World Created by a Drunken God. 2008. Independent. Dir. John Hazlett.

Incident at Oglala. 1992. Miramax. Dir. Michael Apted.

The Iron Sheriff. 1957. United Artists. Dir. Sidney Salkow.

Joe Kidd. 1972. Universal. Dir. John Sturges.

Johnny Greyeyes. 2000. Nepantla Films. Dir. Jorge Manuel Manzano.

The Last Hunt. 1955. Metro-Goldwyn-Meyer. Dir. Richard Brooks.

The Last of His Tribe. 1992. HBO Pictures. Dir. Harry Hook.

Last of the Comanches. 1953. Columbia Pictures. Dir. André De Toth.

Last of the Dogmen. 1995. Savoy Pictures. Dir. Tab Murphy.

The Last of the Mohicans. 1992. 20th Century Fox. Dir. Michael Mann.

The Last of the Redmen. 1947. Columbia Pictures. Dir. George Sherman.

Laughing Boy. 1934. Metro-Goldwyn-Mayer. Dir. W. S. Van Dyke.

Little Big Man. 1970. National General. Dir. Arthur Penn.

The Lone Ranger. 2013. Disney. Dir. Gore Verbinski.

A Man Called Horse. 1970. National General Pictures. Dir. Elliot Silverstein.

Medicine River. 1994. Canadian Broadcasting Company. Dir. Stuart Margolin.

Naturally Native. 1998. Red-Horse Native Productions. Dirs. Jennifer Wynne Farmer and Valerie Red-Horse.

The New World. 2005. New Line Cinema. Dir. Terrence Malick.

North by Northwest. 1959. Metro-Goldwyn-Mayer. Dir. Alfred Hitchcock.

Northwest Passage. 1940. Metro-Goldwyn-Mayer. Dir. King Vidor.

The Only Good Indian. 2009. TLC Productions. Dir. Kevin Willmott.

The Outlaw Josey Wales. 1976. Malpaso/Warner Bros. Dir. Clint Eastwood.

The Plainsman. 1936. Paramount. Dir. Cecil B. DeMille.

Pocahontas. 1995. Disney. Dir. Mike Gabriel and Eric Goldberg.

Powwow Highway. 1989. Handmade Films. Dir. Jonathan Wacks.

Reel Injun. 2009. Rezolution Pictures International and National Film Board of Canada. Dir. Neil Diamond, et al.

The Searchers. 1956. Warner Bros. Dir. John Ford.

She Wore a Yellow Ribbon. 1949. RKO. Dir. John Ford.

Skins. 2002. First Look Media. Dir. Chris Eyre.

Sleepdancer. 2006. Harmy Films. Dir. Rodrick Pocowatchit.

Smoke Signals. 1998. Miramax. Dir. Chris Eyre.

Soldier Blue. 1970. Avco Embassy. Dir. Ralph Nelson.

Stagecoach. 1939. Walter Wanger Productions and United Artists. Dir. John Ford.

Taza, Son of Cochise. 1954. Universal. Dir. Douglas Sirk.

Thelma and Louise. 1991. Metro-Goldwyn-Mayer. Dir. Ridley Scott.

A Thief of Time. 2004. Granada Film Productions. Dir. Chris Eyre.

A Thousand Roads. 2005. Mandalay Entertainment. Dir. Chris Eyre.

Thunderheart. 1992. Tristar. Dir. Michael Apted.

Tkaronto. 2007. Breath Films. Dir. Shane Belcourt.

True Grit. 2010. Paramount. Dirs. Ethan Coen and Joel Coen.
Trail of Tears. 2008. PBS, We Shall Remain series. Dir. Chris Eyre.
Tushka. 1996. Barcid Productions. Dir. Ian Skorodin.
Ulzana's Raid. 1972. Universal. Dir. Robert Aldrich.
The Vanishing American. 1925. Paramount. Dir. George B. Seitz.
Windtalkers. 2002. Metro-Goldwyn-Meyer. Dir. John Woo.

Works Cited

Adams, John Quincy. "Oration at Plymouth Delivered at Plymouth Massachusetts in Commemoration of the Landing of the Pilgrims." *The Daily Republican*, 22 Dec. 1802. Web. 23 July 2012. http://www.dailyrepublican.com/plymouth-orate.html.

Aleiss, Angela. *Making the White Man's Indian: Native Americans and Hollywood Movies*. Westport, Conn.: Praeger, 2005.

Alexie, Sherman. *The Business of Fancydancing: Stories and Poems*. New York: Hanging Loose Press, 1992.

———. *The Business of Fancydancing: The Screenplay*. New York: Hanging Loose Press, 2003.

———. *First Indian on the Moon*. New York: Hanging Loose Press, 1993.

———. *The Lone Ranger and Tonto Fist Fight in Heaven*. 1993. New York: Harper-Perennial, 1994.

———. *Smoke Signals: A Screenplay*. New York: Miramax Books, 1998.

———. *The Summer of Black Widows*. New York: Hanging Loose Press, 1996.

Allen, Richard. *Projecting Illusion: Film Spectatorship and the Impression of Reality*. Cambridge: Cambridge University Press, 1995.

al-Solaylee, Kamal. "Tales of Loss That Find a Purpose." *Globe and Mail*, 15 Aug. 2008.

Anderson, Eric Gary. "Driving the Red Road: *Powwow Highway*." *Hollywood's Indian: The Portrayal of the Native American in Film*. Ed. Peter C. Rollins and John E. O'Connor. Expanded ed. Lexington: University Press of Kentucky, 2003. 137–52.

Anderson, Jason. "Pressed for Time, Director Shane Belcourt Found His Voice with Tkaronto." Movie Review. *Eye Weekly*, 14 Aug. 2008. Web. 23 Aug. 2012. http://www.tkaronto.net/news/press_EYEreview_Aug08.html.

Anderson, John. "This Time, the Indians Tell Their Own Story." *New York Times*, 27 Aug. 2006: Arts and Leisure, 19.

Andrew, J. Dudley. *The Major Film Theorists: An Introduction*. New York: Oxford University Press, 1976.

Arnold, Ellen L. "Reframing the Hollywood Indian: A Feminist Re-reading of *Pow-wow Highway* and *Thunderheart*." *American Indian Studies: An Interdisciplinary Approach to Contemporary Issues*. Ed. Dane Anthony Morrison. New York: Peter Lang, 1997. 347–62.

Ashcroft, Bill, Gareth Griffiths, and Helen Tiffin. *The Empire Writes Back: Theory and Practice in Post-Colonial Literatures*. New York: Routledge, 1989.

Athearn, Robert G. *William Tecumseh Sherman and the Settlement of the West*. Norman: University of Oklahoma Press, 1995.

Barclay, Barry. "Celebrating Fourth Cinema." *Illusions* 35 (Winter 2003): 7–11.

Baringer, Sandra. "'Captive Woman?': The Re-writing of Pocahontas in Three Contemporary Native American Novels." *Studies in American Indian Literatures* 11.3 (1999): 42–63.

Barthes, Roland. *Camera Lucida*. New York: Hill and Wang, 1981.

Bastian, Jon. "The Doe Boy (2001)." *Filmmonthly*, 30 May 2001. Web. 23 Aug. 2012. http://www.filmmonthly.com/Video/Articles/DoeBoy/DoeBoy.html.

Bataille, Gretchen. "Interview with N. Scott Momaday." *Conversations with N. Scott Momaday*. Ed. Matthias Schubnell. Jackson: University Press of Mississippi, 1997. 64–66.

Bataille, Gretchen, and Charles L. P. Silet, eds. *The Pretend Indians: Images of Native Americans in the Movies*. Ames: Iowa State University Press, 1980.

Bazin, André. "Adapation." *Film Adaptation*. Ed. James Naremore. New Brunswick: Rutgers University Press, 2000. 19–27.

———. "The Ontology of the Photographic Image." *What Is Cinema?* Vol. 1. Trans. Hugh Gray. Berkeley: University of California Press, 1971. 9–16.

———. *What Is Cinema?* 2 vols. Trans. Hugh Gray. Berkeley: University of California Press, 1971.

Beavis, Bill, and Richard G. McCloskey. *Salty Dog Talk: The Nautical Origins of Everyday Expressions*. 1983. Dobbs Ferry, N.Y.: Sheridan House, 1995.

Belcourt, Shane. "Takaronto." 2007. Web. 5 Feb. 2010. http://www.tkaronto.net/the_film/con_sab_identity.html.

Bennett, Kirsty. "Fourth Cinema and the Politics of Staring." *Illusions* 38 (Winter 2006): 19–23.

Bisagni, Melissa. Opening Remarks. Film Indians Now! Film Series. National Gallery of Art. Washington, D.C. 28 Nov. 2008.

Blaeser, Kimberly. "The New 'Frontier' of Native American Literature: Dis-Arming History with Tribal Humor." *Native American Perspectives on Literature and History*. Ed. Alan R. Velie. Norman: University of Oklahoma Press, 1994. 37–50.

———. "Trickster: A Compendium." *Buried Roots and Indestructible Seeds: The Survival of American Indian Life in Story, History, and Spirit*. Ed. Martin Zanger and Mark A. Lindquist. Madison: University of Wisconsin Press, 1994. 47–66.

Blair, Elizabeth. "Text as Trickster: Postmodern Language Games in Gerald Vizenor's *Bearheart*." *MELUS* 20.4 (1995): 75–90.

Bowers, Neal, and Charles Silet. "An Interview with Gerald Vizenor." *MELUS* 8.1 (1981): 41–49.

Boye, Alan. *Holding Stone Hands: On the Trail of the Cheyenne Exodus*. Lincoln: University of Nebraska Press, 1999.

Buhler, James, David Neumeyer, and Rob Deemer, eds. *Hearing the Movies: Music and Sound in Film History*. New York: Oxford University Press, 2010.

Burgoyne, Robert. *Film Nation: Hollywood Looks at U.S. History*. Minneapolis: University of Minnesota Press, 1997.

Burt, Larry W. "Roots of the Native American Urban Experience: Relocation Policy in the 1950s." *American Indian Quarterly* 10.2 (1986): 85–99.

Buscombe, Edward. *"Injuns!" Native Americans in the Movies*. Bodmin: Reaktion Books, 2006.

Carmichael, Deborah. *The Landscape of Hollywood Westerns: Ecocriticism in an American Film Genre*. Salt Lake City: University of Utah Press, 2006.

Carroll, Noël. "Kracauer's Theory of Film." *Defining Cinema*. Ed. Peter Lehman. New Brunswick: Rutgers University Press, 1997. 111–31.

Casetti, Francesco. "Adaptation and Mis-adaptations: Film Literature and Social Discourses." *A Companion to Literature and Film*. Ed. Robert Stam and Alessandra Raengo. Malden, Mass.: Blackwell, 2004. 81–91.

Charles, Jim. "Contemporary American Indian Life in *The Owl's Song* and *Smoke Signals*." *English Journal* 90.3 (2001): 54–59.

Chaw, Walter. "Skins Game, An Interview with Chris Eyre." Film Freak Central, 2 Oct. 2002. Web. 14 Jan. 2011. *http://filmfreakcentral.net/notes/ceyreinterview.htm*.

Christie, Stuart. "Time-Out: (Slam)Dunking Photographic Realism in Thomas King's *Medicine River*." *Studies in American Indian Literatures* 11.2 (1999): 51–65.

Churchill, Ward. "Smoke Signals in Context: An Historical Overview." *Z Magazine*. Nov. 1998. Web. 23 Sept. 2012. http://www.zcommunications.org/smoke-signals-in-context-by-ward-churchill.

Columpar, Corinn. *Unsettling Sights: The Fourth World on Film*. Carbondale: Southern Illinois University Press, 2010.

Cooper, James Fenimore. *The Last of the Mohicans: A Narrative of 1757*. 1826. Albany: State University of New York Press, 1983.

Corrigan, Timothy, and Patricia White. *The Film Experience: An Introduction*. 2nd ed. Boston: Bedford/St. Martin's, 2009.

Currie, Gregory. "Film, Reality, Illusion." *Post-Theory: Reconstructing Film Studies*. Ed. David Bordwell and Noël Carroll. Madison: University of Wisconsin Press, 1996. 325–44.

Curtis, Edward S. *The North American Indian*. 20 vols. 1907–1930. New York: Johnson Reprint Corp., 1970.

Deloria, Philip J. *Indians in Unexpected Places*. Lawrence: University Press of Kansas, 2004.

Dix, Douglas, Wolfgang Hochbruck, Kirstie McAlpine, Dallas Miller, and Mary Tynett. "Textual Interstices: Mirrored Shadows in Gerald Vizenor's Dead Voices." *Loosening the Seams: Interpretations of Gerald Vizenor*. Ed. A. Robert Lee. Bowling Green: Bowling Green State University Popular Press, 2000. 178–91.

Ebert, Roger. "Skins." *Chicago Sun Times* 18 Oct. 2002. Web. 23 July 2012. http://rogerebert.suntimes.com/apps/pbcs.dll/article?AID=2002210180310.

Erdrich, Louise. *Love Medicine*. 1984. Expanded ed. New York: HarperPerennial, 1993.

Estrada, Gabriel S. "Two-Spirit Film Criticism: *Fancydancing* with Imitates Dog, Desjarlais and Alexie." *Post Script: Essays in Film and the Humanities* 29.3 (2010): 106–18.

Eyre, Chris. Address. Film Indians Now! Film Series. National Gallery of Art. Washington, D.C. 28 Nov. 2008.

Fleischer, Matthew. "Gone with the Wind: A Decade after Smoke Signals, Success Remains Elusive for Native American Filmmakers." *Native Review* 11 Apr. 2007. Web. 28 Oct. 2009. http://www.nativevue.org/blog/?p=513.

Fox, David. "Box Office Hasn't Seen the Last of 'Mohicans.'" *Los Angeles Times* 6 Oct. 1992. Web. 7 Oct. 2012. http://articles.latimes.com/1992-10-06/entertainment/ca-599_1_box-office.

Freedberg, David. *The Power of Images: Studies in the History and Theory of Response*. Chicago: University of Chicago Press, 1989.

Friar, Ralph E., and Natasha A. Friar. *The Only Good Indian . . . : The Hollywood Gospel*. New York: Drama Book Specialists/Publishers, 1972.

Gilroy, Jhon Warren. "Another Fine Example of the Oral Tradition? Identification and Subversion in Sherman Alexie's *Smoke Signals*." *Studies in American Indian Literatures* 13.1 (2001): 23–42.

———. "A Conversation with Evan Adams, 6/1/00." *Studies in American Indian Literatures* 13.1 (2001): 43–56.

Goldsmith, Leo. Review of *The Exiles*. "Not Coming to a Theater Near You." Posted 18 Nov. 2009. Web. 19 Sept. 2012. http://notcoming.com/reviews/theexiles/.

Grant, Barry Keith. "Bringing It All Back Home: The Films of Peter Jackson." *New Zealand Filmmakers*. Ed. Ian Conrich and Stuart Murray. Detroit: Wayne State University Press, 2007. 320–35.

Grinnell, George. *The Fighting Cheyennes*. 1915. Norman: University of Oklahoma Press, 1956.

Hafsteinsson, Sigurjón Baldur, and Marian Bredin, eds. *Indigenous Screen Cultures in Canada*. Winnipeg: University of Manitoba Press, 2010.

Hall, Stuart. "Cultural Identity and Cinematic Representation." *Film and Theory: An Anthology*. Ed. Robert Stam and Toby Miller. Oxford: Blackwell Publishers, 2000. 704–14.

Hausman, Blake. "Alexie's Nutshell: Mousetraps and Interpenetrations of *The Business of Fancydancing* and *Hamlet*." *Studies in American Indian Literatures* 22.1 (2010): 76–112.

Hearne, Joanna. "John Wayne's Teeth: Speech, Sound, and Representation in *Smoke Signals* and *Imagining Indians*." *Western Folklore* 64.3–4 (2005): 189–205.

———. "Larry Littlebird Interview." 4 and 25 Sep. 2003. Native Networks. Smithsonian Museum of the American Indian. Nov. 2005. Web. 23 July 2012. http://www.nativenetworks.si.edu/eng/rose/littlebird_1_interview.htm.

———. "N. Scott Momaday Interview." 11 Mar. 2003. Native Networks. Smithsonian Museum of the American Indian. Nov. 2005. Web. 23 July 2012. http://www.nativenetworks.si.edu/eng/rose/momaday_n_interview.htm.

———. "Richardson Morse Interview." 28 Jan. 2004. Native Networks. Smithsonian Museum of the American Indian. Nov. 2005. Web. 23 July 2012. http://www.nativenetworks.si.edu/eng/rose/morse_r_interview.htm.

Heil, Douglas. "Conventionalism as a Virtue: A Study of *Powwow Highway*." *American Indian Culture and Research Journal* 33.2 (2009): 23–44.

Hilger, Michael. *The American Indian in Film*. Metuchen: Scarecrow Press, 1986.

———. *From Savage to Nobleman: Images of Native Americans in Film*. Lanham, Md.: Scarecrow Press, 1995.

Hoberman, J. "Cheyenne Autumn." *Village Voice* 34 (28 Mar. 1989): 57+.

Huhndorf, Shari. *Going Native: Indians in the Cultural Imagination*. Ithaca: Cornell University Press, 2001.

Hutcheon, Linda. *A Theory of Adaptation*. New York: Routledge, 2006.

Isaacs, Bruce. *Toward a New Film Aesthetic*. New York: Continuum, 2008.

Jackson, Andrew. "Second Annual Message to Congress." *Messages and Papers of the Presidents*, vol. 2 of *Native American Voices: A History and Anthology*. Ed. Steven Mintz. St. James, N.Y.: Brandywine Press, 1995. 115–16.

Jacobs, Karen. "Optic/Haptic/Abject: Revisioning Indigenous Media in Victor Masayesva, Jr. and Leslie Marmon Silko." *Journal of Visual Culture* 3.3 (2004): 291–316.

Jojola, Ted. "Absurd Reality II: Hollywood Goes to the Indians." *Hollywood's Indian: The Portrayal of the Native American in Film*. Ed. Peter C. Rollins and John E. O'Connor. Expanded ed. Lexington: University Press of Kentucky, 2003. 12–26.

Josephy, Alvin M., Jr., Joan Nagel, and Troy Johnson. *Red Power: The American Indians Fight for Freedom*. Lincoln: University of Nebraska Press, 1999.

Kilpatrick, Jacquelyn. *Celluloid Indians: Native Americans and Film*. Lincoln: University of Nebraska Press, 1999.

King, Thomas. *Medicine River*. Toronto: Penguin Canada, 1989.

Knopf, Kerstin. *Decolonizing the Lens of Power: Indigenous Films in North America*. New York: Rodopi, 2008.

Kracauer, Siegfried. *Theory of Film: The Redemption of Physical Reality*. New York: Oxford University Press, 1960.

Kuhn, Annette. *Women's Pictures: Feminism and Cinema*. London: Routledge and Kegan Paul, 1982.

Langen, Toby, and Kathryn Shanley. "Culture Isn't Buckskin Shoes: A Conversation around Powwow Highway." *Studies in American Indian Literatures* 3.3 (1991): 23–29.

Lawson, Angelica. "Native Sensibility and the Significance of Women in Smoke Signals." *Sherman Alexie: A Collection of Critical Essays*. Ed. Jeff Berglund and Jan Roush. Salt Lake City: University of Utah Press, 2010. 95–106.

Leuthold, Steven. *Indigenous Aesthetics: Native Art, Media, and Identity*. Austin: University of Texas Press, 1998.

———. "Native American Responses to the Western." *American Indian Culture and Research Journal* 19.1 (1995): 153–89.

Lewis, Randolph. *Alanis Obomsawin: The Vision of a Native Filmmaker*. Lincoln: University of Nebraska Press, 2006.

Lincoln, Kenneth. *Native American Renaissance*. Berkeley: University of California Press, 1983.

Louis, Adrian. *Skins*. 1995. Granite Falls, Minn.: Ellis Press, 2002.

Loving v. Virginia. 388. U.S. 1. U.S. Supreme Court. 1967.

Martinez, A. "Interview Series Soap Opera Stars" 1986–87. Web. 10 June 2008. http://www.imagine92009.net/Interviews/8687SOStarsInterviewSeries.htm. (Cite no longer available as of June 2012.)

Marubbio, Elise. "Introduction." *Post Script: Essays in Film and the Humanities* 29.3 (2010): 3–12.

————. *Killing the Indian Maiden: Images of Native American Women in Film*. Lexington: University Press of Kentucky, 2006.

Masayesva, Victor, Jr. "Kwikwilyaqu: Hopi Photography." *Hopi Photography/Hopi Images*. Comp. Victor Masayesva Jr. and Erin Younger. Tucson: Sun Tracks and University of Arizona Press, 1983. 10–12.

Maslin, Janet. "Review/Film: A Cheyenne Mystic Who Transmutes Bitterness." *New York Times*, 3 Apr. 1989: C11.

McDonald, Thomas. "A Cinema Saga of the 'Vanishing American.'" *New York Times*, 12 Mar. 1961: X7.

Metz, Christian. "'Identification, Mirror' and 'The Passion for Perceiving.'" *Defining Cinema*. Ed. Peter Lehman. New Brunswick: Rutgers University Press, 1997. 171–187.

Mihelich, Hohn. "Smoke or Signals: American Popular Culture and the Challenge to Hegemonic Images of American Indians in Native American Film." *Wicazo Sa Review* 16.2 (2001): 129–37.

Mitchell, W. J. T. *Picture Theory: Essays on Verbal and Visual Representation*. Chicago: University of Chicago Press, 1994.

Momaday, N. Scott. *House Made of Dawn*. 1968. Perennial Classics, 1999.

Morgan, William T., Jr. "Landscapes: N. Scott Momaday." 1975. *Conversations with N. Scott Momaday*. Ed. Matthias Schubnell. Jackson: University Press of Mississippi, 1997. 45–56.

Morse, Jedediah. "A Report to the Secretary of War of the United States on Indian Affairs." *Quarterly Review* (1840): 384–419.

Murray, Duane. Personal interview. Film Indians Now! Film Series. National Gallery of Art. Washington, D.C. 1 Nov. 2008.

Murray, Stuart. *Images of Dignity: Barry Barclay and Fourth Cinema*. Wellington: Huia Publishers, 2008.

Nichols, Bill. *Representing Reality: Issues and Concepts in Documentary*. Bloomington: Indiana University Press, 1991.

Nolley, Ken. "John Ford and the Hollywood Indian." *Film History* 23.1–4 (1993): 44–56.

O'Connor, John E. "The White Man's Indian: An Institutional Approach." *Hollywood's Indian: The Portrayal of the Native American in Film*. Ed. Peter C. Rollins and John E. O'Conner. 1998. Expanded ed. Louisville: University Press of Kentucky, 2003. 27–38.

Owens, Louis. *Other Destinies: Understanding the American Indian Novel*. Norman: University of Oklahoma Press, 1992.

Palmer, R. Barton. *Twentieth-Century American Fiction on Screen.* Cambridge: Cambridge University Press, 2007.

Perkins, V. F. *"Cheyenne Autumn."* 1964. *The Pretend Indians: Images of Native Americans in the Movies.* Ed. Gretchen M. Bataille and Charles L. P. Silet. Ames: Iowa State University Press, 1980. 152–55.

Pewewardy, Cornel. "Recapturing Stolen Media Images: Indians Are *Not* Mascots or Logos." *American Indian Stereotypes in the World of Children: A Reader and Bibliography.* Ed. Arlene Hirschfelder, Paulette Fairbanks Molin, and Yvonne Wakimet. 2nd ed. Lanham, Md.: Scarecrow Press, Inc., 1999. 189–92.

Phelman, Sarah. "Giving Hollywood the 'Business.'" *Metro Santa Cruz,* 8 May 2002. Web. 23 July 2012. http://www.metroactive.com/papers/cruz/05.08.02/fancy dancing-0219.html.

Plantinga, Carl. *Moving Viewers: American Film and the Spectator's Experience.* Berkeley: University of California Press, 2009.

Pulitano, Elvira. *Toward a Native American Critical Theory.* Lincoln: University of Nebraska Press, 2003.

Punter, Jennie. "'I Didn't Have Time to Filter.'" *Globe and Mail,* 14 Aug. 2008.

Purdy, John. *Writing Indian, Native Conversations.* Lincoln: University of Nebraska Press, 2009.

Raheja, Michelle. "Reading Nanook's Smile: Visual Sovereignty, Indigenous Revisions of Ethnography, and *Atanarjuat (The Fast Runner)." American Quarterly* 59.4 (2007): 1159–85.

Rich, Adrienne. "When We Dead Awaken: Writing as Re-Vision." *American Poets in 1976.* Ed. William Heyen. Indianapolis: Bobbs-Merrill, 1976. 278–92.

Robotech. Syndicated (for television). 1985–88.

Rollins, Peter C., and John E. O'Connor, eds. *Hollywood's Indian: The Portrayal of the Native American in Film.* Lexington: University Press of Kentucky, 1998.

Rony, Fatimah Tobing. "Victor Masayesva, Jr., and the Politics of 'Imagining Indians.'" *Film Quarterly* 48.2 (1994–95): 20–33.

Rosen, Steven. *"The Exiles* Exiled No More." *Sonic Boomers.* 29 Nov. 2009. Web. 4 Dec. 2009. http://www.sonicboomers.com/onthecorner/exiles-exiled-no-more.

Ruoff, LaVonne. *American Indian Literatures: An Introduction, Bibliographic Review, and Selected Bibliography.* New York: Modern Language Association, 1990.

———. "Gerald Vizenor: Compassionate Trickster." 1985. *Studies in American Indian Literatures* 2nd ser. 5.2 (1993): 39–45.

Ruppert, James. "'Imagination Is the Only Reality. All the Rest Is Bad Television': *Harold of Orange* and Indexical Representation." *Loosening the Seams: Interpretations of Gerald Vizenor.* Ed. A. Robert Lee. Bowling Green: Bowling Green State University Popular Press, 2000. 225–32.

———. *Mediation in Contemporary Native American Fiction.* Norman: University of Oklahoma Press, 1995.

Sanders, Julie. *Adaptation and Appropriation.* New York: Routledge, 2006.

Sandoz, Mari. *Cheyenne Autumn.* 1953. Lincoln: University of Nebraska Press, 2005.

Santa Fe Reporter, 14 Mar. 1990: 11. Web. 29 Sept. 2012. http://newspaperarchive .com/santa-fe-reporter/1990-03-14/page-11/.

Sasano, Mari. "Metis Mishmash: Tkaronto Explores Cultural, Personal Identity Loss." *Ottawa Citizen*, 8 Aug. 2008. Web. 29 Sept. 2012. http://www.canada.com /ottawacitizen/news/arts/story.html?id=211921a8-fbad-4fe6-8e9c-2191d7370bac.

Schiwy, Freya. *Indianizing Film: Decolonization, the Andes, and the Question of Technology*. New Brunswick: Rutgers University Press, 2009.

Schmidt, Nancy J. "Ethnographic Films about American Indians." *Council on Anthropology and Education Quarterly* 6.1 (1975): 34–36.

Seals, David. *The Powwow Highway*. 1979. New York: Plume, 1990.

Silberman, Robert. "Gerald Vizenor and *Harold of Orange*: From Word Cinemas to Real Cinema." *American Indian Quarterly* 9.1 (1985): 4–21.

Simard, Rodney. "Easin' on Down the *Powwow Highway*(s)." *Studies in American Indian Literatures* 3.3 (1991): 19–23.

Simon, John Y. *The Papers of Ulysses S. Grant*. Vol. 16, 1866. Carbondale: Southern Illinois University Press, 1988.

Singer, Beverly R. *Wiping the War Paint off the Lens: Native American Film and Video*. Minneapolis: University of Minnesota Press, 2001.

Slethaug, Gordon E. "Hurricanes and Fires: Chaotics in Sherman Alexie's *Smoke Signals* and *The Lone Ranger and Tonto Fistfight in Heaven*." *Literature Film Quarterly* 31.2 (2003): 130–40.

Smith, Linda Tuhiwai. *Decolonizing Methodologies: Research and Indigenous Peoples*. Dunedin: University of Otago Press, 1999.

Sontag, Susan. *On Photography*. New York: Farrar, Straus and Giroux, 1977.

Stam, Robert. "Introduction: The Theory and Practice of Adaptation." *Literature and Film: A Guide to the Theory and Practice of Film Adaptation*. Ed. Robert Stam and Alessandra Raengo. Oxford: Blackwell Publishing, 2005. 1–52.

———. *Reflexivity in Film and Literature: From Don Quixote to Jean-Luc Godard*. Ann Arbor: UMI Research Press, 1985.

Stromberg, Ernest. "Out of the Cupboard and Up with the *Smoke Signals*: Cinematic Representations of American Indians in the Nineties." *Studies in Popular Culture* 24.1 (2001): 33–46.

Svenson, Michelle. "Randy Redroad Interview." Native Networks. Smithsonian, Museum of the American Indian. Apr. 2001. Web. 22 Feb. 2011. http://www.native networks.si.edu/eng/rose/redroad_r_interview.htm#open.

Tatonetti, Lisa. "Visible Sexualities or Invisible Nations: Forced to Choose in *Big Eden, Johnny Greyeyes*, and *The Business of Fancydancing*." *GLQ: A Journal of Lesbian and Gay Studies* 16.1–2 (2010): 157–81.

Toman, Marshall, and Carole Gerster. "*Powwow Highway* in an Ethnic Film and Literature Course." *Studies in American Indian Literatures* 3.3 (1991): 29–38.

Tompkins, Jane. *West of Everything: The Inner Life of Westerns*. New York: Oxford University Press, 1992.

Trahant, Mark. "Explaining Sovereignty through the Media." *Shoot the Indian: Media, Misperception and Native Truth*. Ed. Kara Briggs, Ronald D. Smith, and José Barreiro. Buffalo: American Indian Policy and Media Initiative, 2007. 27–30.

Utley, Robert Marshall. *The Indian Frontier of the American West, 1846–1890*. Albuquerque: University of New Mexico Press, 1984.

Velie, Alan. "The Trickster Novel." *Narrative Chance: Postmodern Discourse on Native American Indian Literatures*. Ed. Gerald Vizenor. Albuquerque: University of New Mexico Press, 1989. 121–39.

Vizenor, Gerald. *An American Monkey King in China*. Minneapolis: University of Minnesota Press, 1987.

———. "Anishinaabe Pictomyths." *Native Liberty: Natural Reason and Cultural Survivance*. Lincoln: University of Nebraska, 2009. 171–90.

———. *Darkness in Saint Louis Bearheart*. St. Paul: Truck Press, 1978.

———. *Dead Voices*. Norman: University of Oklahoma Press, 1992.

———. *Earthdivers: Tribal Narratives on Mixed Descent*. Minneapolis: University of Minnesota Press, 1981.

———. "Edward Curtis." *Native Liberty: Natural Reason and Cultural Survivance*. Lincoln: University of Nebraska Press, 2009. 191–206.

———. *Harold of Orange* [screenplay]. *Shadow Distance: A Gerald Vizenor Reader*. Hanover, N.H.: Wesleyan University Press, 1983. 297–333.

———. *Heirs of Columbus*. Hanover, N.H.: Wesleyan University Press, 1991.

———. "Interimage Simulations." *Multiculturalism in Contemporary Society: Perspectives on Difference and Transdifference*. Ed. Helmbrecht Breinig, Jürgen Gebhardt, and Klaus Lösch. Erlangen: Erlanger Forschungen, 2002. 229–47.

———. *Landfill Meditation: Crossblood Stories*. Hanover, N.H.: Wesleyan University Press, University Press of New England, 1991.

———. "Ontic Images." *Native Liberty: Natural Reason and Cultural Survivance*. Lincoln: University of Nebraska Press, 2009. 159–78.

———. "Trickster Discourse." *American Indian Quarterly* 14 (Summer 1990): 284.

———. "Trickster Discourse: Comic and Tragic Themes in Native American Literature." *The Survival of American Indian Life in Story, History, and Spirit*. Ed. Mark A. Lindquist and Martin Zanger. Madison: University of Wisconsin Press, 1994. 67–81.

———. *The Trickster of Liberty: Tribal Heirs to a Wild Baronage*. Minneapolis: University of Minnesota Press, 1988.

Weatherford, Elizabeth, and Victor Masayesva Jr. "To End and Begin Again: The Work of Victor Masayesva, Jr." *Art Journal* 54.4 (1995): 48–52.

West, Dennis, and Joan West. "Sending Cinematic Smoke Signals: An Interview with Sherman Alexie." *Cineaste* 23.4 (1998): 28–31, 37.

Whitt, Laurie Anne. "Cultural Imperialism and the Marketing of Native America." *Natives and Academics: Researching and Writing about American Indians*. Ed. Devon A. Mihesuah. Lincoln: University of Nebraska Press, 1998. 139–71.

Womack, Craig S. "Alexander Posey's Nature Journals: A Further Argument for Tribally-Specific Aesthetics. *Studies in American Indian Literatures* 13.2–3 (2001): 49–66.

———. *Art as Performance, Story as Criticism: Reflections on Native Literary Aesthetics*. Norman: University of Oklahoma Press, 2009.

―――. *Red on Red: Native American Literary Separatism*. Minneapolis: University of Minnesota Press, 1999.

Wood, Houston. *Native Features: Indigenous Films from around the World*. New York: Continuum, 2008.

Youngberg, Quentin. "Interpenetrations: Re-encoding the Queer Indian in Sherman Alexie's *The Business of Fancydancing*." *Studies in American Indian Literatures* 20.1 (2008): 55–75.

Index

absent father, as motif, 123, 205, 217, 220
Adams, Evan, 8, 128
Adams, John Quincy, 23–24
adaptation, 9–10, 17, 77–78; and *The Doe Boy*, 173; and *Harold of Orange*, 73, 77–78, 82; and *House Made of Dawn*, 53, 56–59; and *Medicine River*, 92–93; and *Powwow Highway*, 96; and *Skins*, 164–65; theory of, 56; and visual representation, 70–71
alcoholism, 46, 114, 157, 162–66; and Pine Ridge Reservation, 160; representations of, 150; as stereotype, 185–86, 204
Alexie, Sherman, 113, 165; "How to Write the Great American Indian Novel," 138–39; "Memorial Day 1972," 134; *Smoke Signals* (screenplay), 118–19, 123, 124–25; *The Summer of Black Widows*, 138. See also *Business of Fancydancing, The*
"Amazing Grace" (song), 141
American Horse, 160, 166–67, 169–70; mentioned, 168
American Indian Film Festival (San Francisco), 174
American Indian Religious Freedom Act, 59–60
Anderson, Kevin, 177

anti-Westerns, 33, 53, 59, 146
Appaloosa, The (Furie film), 54
Apted, Michael, 5. See also *Thunderheart*
Arcand, Nathaniel, 172, 178
Archuletta, Beulah, 146
Arredondo, Jeri, 148, 177, 202, 203
artifice of film, 15, 25, 31, 143; and *The Business of Fancydancing*, 129–30, 132–33, 135; and *Medicine River*, 95, 97
Atanarjuat (*The Fast Runner*; Kunuk film), 3
auteur theory, 5–6
Avatar (Cameron film), 106

Bahktin, Makhail, 79
Bailey, Laura, 202
Baker, Carroll, 101
Baker, Simon, 120
Bancroft, George, 121
Barclay, Barry, 55, 132, 168–69
Barking Water (Harjo film), 216–19; and absent-father motif, 217–18; as coming-home story, 217; location shooting of, 216; and photographs, 217; plot of, 216–17; and repudiation of Hollywood, 217–19; as road movie, 216–17

239

Dix, Richard, 108
documentary, 13–14; and authenticity,
    133, 161–63, 164; and *The Business
    of Fancydancing*, 129, 132, 135; and
    The Exiles, 39–40; and genre, 21–23,
    40, 41, 133, 135, 195; and *Imagining
    Indians*, 16–17, 21, 35; use of, in
    Skins, 158–60, 161–63, 164, 172; use
    of, in *Tkaronto*, 19, 188–89, 195–96
Doe Boy, The (Redroad film), 8, 9, 19,
    173–87, 219; budget of, 174; and
    The Last of the Mohicans, 173–77,
    181; opening sequence of, 173–77;
    reversals in, 184–87; role of women
    in, 147–48; and *Skins*, 161
dream catcher, defined, 149–50
drinking. *See* alcoholism
Dull Knife, 103–4
Duval, James, 183

Eaglebear singers, 120–21
Eccles, Amy, 146
ethnographic photography. *See*
    photography
Exiles, The (Mackenzie film), 17, 36–50,
    87; budget of, 41; plot of, 36–37; use
    of photographs in, 142, 168, 201
Eyre, Chris, 113, 168, 170–71, 224;
    A Thief of Time, 5; *A Thousand
    Roads*, 224; *Trail of Tears*, 6, 9, 222–
    23. *See also Skins* (Eyre film); *Smoke
    Signals* (Eyre film)

Farmer, Gary, 8, 98–99, 118–19
Ferchland, Andrew J., 8, 183
First cinema, 4, 12, 223. *See also*
    Hollywood film
Flags of Our Fathers (Eastwood film), 5
Ford, John, 101, 104–5; *Cheyenne
    Autumn*, 98, 100–105, 107, 111; *Fort
    Apache*, 121; *The Searchers*, 43, 100–
    105, 109, 121, 146; *She Wore a Yellow
    Ribbon*, 121; *Stagecoach*, 16, 121
"Forgiving Our Fathers" (Lourie poem),
    127

Fort Apache (Ford film), 121
Forte, Fiawna, 216
Fort Robinson, 100, 102
Four Sheets to the Wind (Harjo film),
    19, 202–15, 216–17; and Hollywood,
    202–3, 215; humor in, 206, 210–11,
    212; importance of land in, 208;
    and location shooting, 207, 215; and
    photography, 206–8; plot of, 202;
    and role of women, 204–5; title of,
    significance of, 203–4
Fourth cinema, 4–5, 15, 193, 223

"Garry Owen" (song), 120
Gascon, Jean, 146
Geary, Cynthia, 129
genres: and *The Business of
    Fancydancing*, 132; in film, 13, 33;
    hybrids of, 40–41; and *Powwow
    Highway*, 99–100. *See also Skins*
    (Eyre film)
George, Chief Dan, 146
Ghost Dance, as filmed, 32–33
Grand Avenue (Sackheim film), 148
Greene, Graham, 147, 158
Guerrero, Kimberly Norris, 8, 143
Guthrie, Robert A., 178

Hamlet (Shakespeare play), 130, 131,
    137
handheld camera, 129–35 passim, 173
Harjo, Sterlin, 148, 202–3, 216. *See also
    Barking Water; Four Sheets to the
    Wind*
Harold of Orange (Vizenor screenplay),
    69, 74–76
Harold of Orange (Weiss film), 17,
    68–82, 94; and adaptation, 10, 70–71;
    and dialogue with Hollywood, 11;
    distribution of, 83; role of women in,
    147; and trickster figure, 69–70
Harris, Richard, 146, 185
Hart, William S., 107, 111
Hazlett, John, 145
Heirs of Columbus (Vizenor novel), 86

naming, importance of, 81, 119–20
Naturally Native (V. Red-Horse film),
8–9, 18, 142–57, 219; and depictions
of alcoholism, 165; happy ending of,
171; and pedagogical moments, 14,
149–52, 192; plot of, 143; and *Skins*,
158; use of photography in, 142, 143,
157; and women's space, 155–56
Nelson, Dillon, 161
New World, The (Malick film), 219
Nish, Homer, 45–48
North by Northwest (Hitchcock film), 160
Northwest Passage (Vidor film), 76

Obomsawin, Alanis, 4
O'Connor, Jordan, 196
One Star, Canku, 161
Only Good Indian, The (Willmott film),
224
"Oration at Plymouth" (J. Q. Adams),
23–24
Outlaw Josey Wales, The (Eastwood
film), 53

Padgett, Debra, 43
Peltier, Leonard, 5, 167, 168
Pettibone, Yellow Pony, 167
peyote ceremony, depiction of, 52, 59–
62, 63, 164
"Peyote Healing" (Robertson
composition) 161, 181
Phillip, Kevin, 135
photography: and ethnographic
tradition, 84–85; and
politics/censorship, 85; and
portraiture, 89–90; and realism,
71–73; as self-conscious, 83–84; still
versus motion pictures, 86–87, 207–8;
as stolen, 89; and story, 85, 96–97
picture postcards, role of, 32, 94, 207–8
Pine Ridge, 159–60; and alcohol abuse,
164
Plainsman, The (DeMille film), 28–31
Pocahontas (Gabriel and Goldberg film),
6, 8–9

Pocahontas, representations of, 152, 153
Pocowatchit, Guy Ray, 220, 221
Pocowatchit, Rodrick: *Dancing on the
Moon*, 220–21; *The Dead Can't
Dance*, 221–22; *Sleepdancer*, 220
Podemski, Tamara, 202, 203
police, depictions of, 49, 59, 65–66
"Positively Lost Me" (Podrasky song),
178–79
Powwow Highway (Wacks film), 8, 18,
98–112, 117–18; and adaptation,
10; and humor, 98, plot of, 99; and
politics, 171; role of women in, 147;
and *Skins*, 158
Powwow Highway, The (Seals novel),
98, 101–2, 103, 111
Proudstar, Jon, 202

Randleman, Mike, 210
Raven, Lowell, 150
Red Cloud, 166–67
Red Dog, 167
Red-Horse, Valerie, 8, 143. See also
Naturally Native
Red-Horse Mohl, Courtney, 143
Redroad, Randy, 8, 9, 19, 175, 176, 183,
185; and undercutting Hollywood,
186. See also *The Doe Boy*
Red Shirt, 166–67
Reel Injun (Diamond film), 21–22
religion, 57, 60; and Christianity, 61,
149, 151, 208; and ritual, 52; and the
sacred, 31–32
religious freedom, 150; and peyote
ceremony, 59–60
relocation, 17, 50, 68; Urban Indian
Relocation Project, 41, 43, 57–59
Removal Act (1830), 24
reversals, 88, 89. *See also* Hollywood
film
Reynolds, Tommy, 48–49
Richards, Clement "Sonny," 31–33
Ridge, John, 222
Ridge, Major, 222
Riel, Louis, 194

ritual: depictions of, 52, 61–62, 137, 154–
55, 161, 181, 186. *See also* ceremony;
peyote ceremony, depiction of
Rivas, Geoffrey, 111
Robertson, Robbie, 161, 181
Robinson, Fort, 100, 102
Robotech (TV show), 106–7
Rocha, Glauber, 13
Roland, Gilbert, 105
Rossini, Gioachino, 79
Running Wolf, Myrton, 162
Rushmore, Mount, 159, 160, 162, 166–
67, 171–72

Sackheim, Daniel, 148
Sand Creek Eufala Baptist Church choir,
216
Sandoz, Mari, 101, 104
Sarris, Greg, 148
Saxon, John, 8, 17, 54–55
Schweig, Eric, 158, 173, 181
Seals, David, 98; *The Powwow
Highway*, 101–2, 103, 111
Searchers, The (Ford film), 43, 100–105,
109, 121; role of women in, 146
self-determination, 2, 3, 11, 13, 176
self-representation, 12, 55–56,
114, 201, 204, 215, 221; and *The
Business of Fancydancing*, 114;
as form of resistance, 3–4, 14–15,
98; importance of, 3, 95–97; and
reflexivity, 129–30, 131; and women,
148–49
sexual politics, 148, 154–55
Shenandoah, Joanne, 152
Sherman, William Tecumseh, 23–24
She Wore a Yellow Ribbon (Ford film), 121
simulation, 3
Skerritt, Tom, 121
Skins (Eyre film), 18, 158–72; and
authenticating, 162–63; budget of,
12; and death of main character,
158–59, 162, 166, 171–72; and
depictions of alcoholism, 165–66;
and documentary, 14, 158–72 passim;

and *The Doe Boy*, 161; and educating
viewer, 162–63; final scene of, 171–
72; and *Naturally Native*, 158; plot
of, 158–59; and ritual, 181; role of
history in, 163, 166; role of women
in, 147; and *Smoke Signals*, 158; and
use of photography, 166–69
Skins (Louis novel), 158, 162, 169, 170–
71; and adaptation, 164–65
Skinwalkers, 31
Sleepdancer (Pocowatchit film), 220
Smith, James, Jr., 189
Smoke Signals (Alexie screenplay), 118–
19, 123, 124–25
Smoke Signals (Eyre film), 8, 18, 113–
27, 130, 176; and adaptation, 10;
budget of, 12–13, 113; depiction of
alcoholism in, 165; distribution of,
113; and Hollywood, 136, 215; humor
in, 170, 171; male orientation in, 144–
45, promise of, 203; release of, 113; as
road movie, 207; scholarly attention
to, 113–14; and *Skins*, 158; survival
of Arnold in, 205; and vanishing
Indians, 30–31, 114–15, 127
Soldier Blue (R. Nelson film), 53
Sooktis, Charles, 28–31
sovereignty, 3, 111–12, 209, 219; cinema
of, 2–4, 186–87, 215, 223–24;
understandings of, 3, 4. *See also*
visual sovereignty
Spencer, Laura, 216
Stagecoach (Ford film), 16, 121
"Star Spangled Banner, The" (song), 140
stereotypes, 3, 6, 189–90; challenging of,
3, 11–12, 14, 39, 53, 84, 100, 186; and
drinking, 69, 114, 150, 165, 204; and
ethnography, 87–88; and Hollywood,
38, 61, 104, 107, 112, 166, 172,
218; and identity, 189–90, 219; and
noble savage, 176, 185; in *Powwow
Highway*, 117; and sports mascots,
150–51; and vanishing, 30, 61; and
women, 18, 147, 149, 151
St. John, Michelle, 131, 145

storytelling, 3, 34, 115, 123, 208; control of, 133, 176–77; significance of, 2, 4, 12, 205–6, 214
Studi, Wes, 9, 224
Summer of Black Widows, The (Alexie book), 138
Sundance Film Festival, 174
survival, themes of, 2, 4, 223

Tagabon, Gene, 128
talking back, 10–14, 137, 186; and intertextuality, 14, 175–76; through photography, 83, 132, 142, 143–44; in *Powwow Highway*, 98; and survival, 11, 115, 129
Taylor, Drew Hayden, 145
Taza, Son of Cochise (Sirk film), 25, 33
"Ten Little Indians" (music composition), 140
terminology, in reference to American Indians, 19–20
Thelma and Louise (Scott film), 118
Thief of Time, A (Eyre film), 5
Third cinema, 4
Thousand Roads, A (Eyre film), 224
Thunderheart (Apted film), 32–33, 60; and depictions of the sacred, 164; role of women in, 147
Tkaronto (S. Belcourt film), 19, 188–201; definition of, 190; and documentary genre, 188–201 passim; and educational moments, 14, 190–94; plot of, 188; and portraiture, 200–201; role of women in, 148, 188, 201
Tootoosis, Gordon, 176
Tousey, Sheila, 147, 148
Trail of Tears (Eyre film), 6, 9, 222–23
treaties, and loss of land, 28
trickster figure, 70, 91, 208–9; as community in *Medicine River*, 89–94; as filmic embodiment, 73–76, 78; and humor, 86, 88–89; and shape shifting, 81–82
True Grit (E. and J. Coen film), 223
Tsopei, Corinna, 109

Tupou, Manu, 146
Tushka (Skorodin film), 144

Ulzana's Raid (Aldrich film), 7, 53
Urban Indian Relocation Project, 41, 43, 57–59. *See also* relocation

Vanishing American, The (Seitz film), 108
vanishing of Indians, 4, 15, 22, 30, 129–30; and anthropology, 38, 39, 71, 76; and *The Business of Fancydancing*, 129, 138, 141; countered in Indigenous film, 31, 40, 57, 61–62, 93–94, 119–20, 202, 207, 219; and *The Doe Boy*, 175; as Hollywood motif, 16, 53–54, 56, 61, 98, 144; in *Smoke Signals*, 114–15, 127
Varela, Jay, 55
Vietnam War, 53, 57–58, 122, 158, 177–78, 179–80; and anti-Westerns, 18, 59
visual sovereignty, 1, 11, 22, 111–12, 133, 143, 168–69, 176; in *The Doe Boy*, 176, 187; in *Medicine River*, 87, 97. *See also* sovereignty: cinema of
Vizenor, Gerald, 69–70, 190; *Dead Voices*, 77–78, 81–82; *Harold of Orange* (screenplay), 69, 74–76; *Heirs of Columbus*, 86

Wacks, Jonathan, 98, 117. See also *Powwow Highway* (Wacks film)
Warhol, Andy, 71
Watts, Noah, 159
Wayne, John, 109, 118, 120, 121
Weiss, Richard, 68. See also *Harold of Orange* (Weiss film)
Wells, Mark, 220
Westerns, 10, 11, 121, 136, 190; as blockbusters, 6–7, 204; casting of, 7, 11, 17, 22, 26, 99; and common tropes, 15, 16, 79, 100, 109, 112, 138; popularity of, 43, 44. *See also* women's roles
Whiteclay, Neb, 160–61